Vexed with Devils

WITHDRAWN

VEXED WITH DEVILS

Manhood and Witchcraft in Old and New England

ERIKA GASSER

New York University Press

NEW YORK

NEW YORK UNIVERSITY PRESS
New York
www.nyupress.org

ISBN: 978-1-4798-3179-1

For Library of Congress Cataloging-in-Publication data, please contact
the Library of Congress

A version of chapter 2 was published as "Witchcraft, Possession, and the Unmaking of
Women and Men: A Late Sixteenth-Century English Case Study," in *Magic, Ritual &
Witchcraft* 11, no. 2 (Winter 2016): 151–75; copyright 2016, University of Pennsylvania
Press; reprinted by permission.

A version of chapter 3 was published as "Samuel Harsnett, John Darrell, and the Use
of Gender as an English Possession Propaganda Strategy," in *The Devil in Society in
Premodern Europe*, ed. Richard Raiswell and Peter Dendle, 257–82 (Toronto: Centre for
Reformation and Renaissance Studies, University of Toronto, 2012).

References to Internet Web sites (URLs) were accurate at the time of writing. Neither the
author nor New York University Press is responsible for URLs that may have expired or
changed since the manuscript was prepared.

New York University Press books are printed on acid-free paper, and their binding
materials are chosen for strength and durability. We strive to use environmentally
responsible suppliers and materials to the greatest extent possible in publishing our
books.

Manufactured in the United States of America
10 9 8 7 6 5 4 3 2 1

Also available as an ebook

To my parents
Gary and Nancy Gasser

Contents

Acknowledgments   xi

Introduction: Possession, Gender, and Power   1

1   Discerning Demonic Possession and Witchcraft-Possession
    in Early Modern England   13

2   Engendering English Witchcraft-Possession:
    The Samuel Family in Warboys   37

3   Disputing Possession in England: Samuel Harsnett
    versus John Darrell   67

4   Engendering New England Witchcraft-Possession:
    George Burroughs in Salem   94

5   Disputing Possession in New England: Robert Calef
    versus Cotton Mather   133

    Epilogue: Continuity and Patriarchy at the Turn
    of the Eighteenth Century   169

    Notes   177

    Index   215

    About the Author   225

Acknowledgments

In the many years since I first began this work, I have had the good fortune to receive considerable help and encouragement. At the University of Michigan I received support from the Horace H. Rackham School of Graduate Studies, the Department of History, the Department of Women's Studies, and the Institute for Research on Women and Gender. The University of Michigan also provided resources and people without whom this book would never have gotten off the ground. I owe a great deal to all of the students, office staff, and professors with whom I worked, and particularly to Carol Karlsen, Sue Juster, Michael Mac-Donald, and Scotti Parrish for their engagement, encouragement, and generosity.

While in Ann Arbor, I received valuable comments and suggestions from two writing groups. The first was made up of welcoming European historians: Erik Huneke, Mia Lee, Kathrin Levitan, Marti Lybeck, Mary O'Reilly, Roberta Pergher, Natalie Rothman, Jessica Thurlow, and especially Tara Zahra—who was and is a model historian and friend. I would never have survived without her humor, encouragement, and suitcases of protein. The second group was made up of welcoming American Culture "Girl Turtles," whose insight and support meant a great deal to me: Jennifer Beckham, Laura Halperin, Kathy Jurado, Shani Mott, Nikki Stanton, Carla Vecchiola, and Grace Wang. I am grateful to many people who made both work and life in Michigan better, including Chandra Bhimull, Rebecca Brannon, Tamar Carroll, Shaun Lopez, Jen Manion, Jennifer Palmer, Rebekah Pite, and Chris Talbot. Andrea Dottolo had better be on her way to pick me up for dinner. Nick Syrett and Holly Dugan taught me that white w(h)ine and country music, in combination with hilarity and steadfast friendship, make up more than the sum of their parts. I am so grateful for their wit and camaraderie after all these years. I know that Mary Harris O'Reilly would suggest we celebrate the completion of this project with a sundae, so I will have one in her memory and in honor of her brilliance, which so many of us miss dearly.

I am very grateful for the financial and scholarly assistance I received from archives and institutes, and the kind aid of archivists and staff at the American Antiquarian Society (particularly Caroline Sloat), the British Library, the Clements Library, the Danvers Archival Center, and the Massachusetts Historical Society. I was fortunate to have opportunities to present parts of this project at several conferences and workshops, and to have received especially helpful feedback from Richard Godbeer, Ann Little, Mark Peterson, the participants in the Ohio Seminar in Early American History and Culture, and the Women's, Gender, and Sexuality History Workshop at Ohio State University. At New York University Press I have been fortunate to work with Clara Platter, Constance Grady, Amy Klopfenstein, and the two anonymous readers who offered constructive feedback that has left the book better than when they found it. I also owe thanks to Brian Halley and the two reviewers he commissioned to read the manuscript, whose comments also considerably shaped the book's final form.

I want to thank my colleagues, friends, and students in the History Department at Sacramento State for four wonderful years, and the professors, teachers, and students I met in Teaching American History Grant programs through the Placer County Office of Education and the History Project at UC Davis. I thank Mimi Coughlin and Valerie Becker for being such inspiring teachers and friends. Kim and Dana Moore made our time in California a delight, with such epic dinners and porch time that I choose to believe they are still living right next door.

At the University of Cincinnati I have benefited from the support of the History Department, the University Research Council, research assistance (all too briefly!) from Emily Filinger-Huggins, and especially the Charles Phelps Taft Research Center. I was grateful for having received a Taft Center Fellowship and appreciate those who helped make it both enjoyable and worthwhile, particularly Erynn Masi de Casanova, Angela Potochnik, and Kate Sorrels. I owe thanks to all of my colleagues who have given feedback on chapters of the book, shared teaching ideas, and provided encouragement and advice. I especially thank Wendy Kline for giving us the best possible welcome to Cincinnati, and Holly McGee for rallying the troops to help me get through a difficult winter. I have also greatly enjoyed teaching our students, who inspire and teach me in turn.

I owe special thanks and unending gratitude to those who have discussed and/or read significant parts of the manuscript over the years: Tobin Anderson, Zvi Biener, Andrea Dottolo, Kate Sorrels, Nick Syrett, and Tara Zahra. Clay Howard and Brianna Leavitt-Alcántara were especially generous readers whose good sense helped guide my revisions. Kate Sorrels deserves additional thanks for her willingness to share the process of writing and revising with me, and for agreeing that thinking can be accompanied by drinking. Lastly, I can only begin to thank my parents for their generous support over the years and for their kindness. The only flaw I am aware of in my sisters is that they and their families live too far away from me; our reunions remind me how fortunate I am to have sisters who are my favorite people. Finally and above all I owe thanks to Jonathan Barber, who by now understands (more than he should have to) what Cotton Mather meant when he referred to a woman "craz'd in her Intellectuals." I am so lucky to have him as my partner in our adventures.

Vexed with Devils

Introduction: Possession, Gender, and Power

In 1596, thirteen-year-old Thomas Darling, in Burton, England, became dramatically unwell in a way that defied diagnosis. His convulsive fits and vomiting suggested illness, but when he pointed out apparitions of angels and a green cat, bystanders knew that his was more than a natural distemper. Darling later lost the use of his legs and alternated between ardent prayer and violent contortions. He also suffered when he strove to read from the Bible, and writhed and groaned as he conducted one-sided conversations with the devil that tempted him to turn away from God. Some suspected he might be bewitched, and witnesses closely questioned and tested the woman he named as a suspect. In time, after Darling spoke in the strange voices of his invading devils, Puritan ministers managed to deliver the boy who rapturously recommitted himself to a godly life. The accused witch made a partial confession but died before she could be tried.[1] Witchcraft-possession cases like Thomas Darling's, by which I mean cases in which those who suffered the spectral torments associated with demonic possession also named a witch as the cause, were strongly grounded in specific conditions of the homes, congregations, and courts where they originated. At the same time, however, they depended upon shared cultural scripts in order to have reliable meaning. This book tells a transatlantic story of some of the people in early modern England and colonial New England who acted as if they were possessed, and the ways that demoniacs—as people purportedly possessed by devils were called—were handled within and beyond their communities. When published possession accounts documented their subjects' symptoms, they reinforced customary notions of possession and expanded the precedents that shaped officials' new judgments. Thus these sources became conceptual primers both for those who needed to discern a true possession and for those who needed to perform one. Ultimately, the fate of demoniacs and accused witches appears to have depended as much on the cultural and discursive realm as on particular interactions with neighbors, ministers, and magistrates.

After the English Reformation, when acts by King Henry VIII and Parliament brought about a separation of English rule and law from Rome in the 1530s, the Church of England grew distinctly Protestant. While the extent of this transformation fluctuated, Protestantism was firmly entrenched—if nonetheless hotly and continuously debated—by Elizabeth I's ascension to the throne in 1558. Yet even as England developed a singular brand of Protestant rule, both common folk and elites continued to draw upon traditional cultural views of the preternatural realm.[2] By the mid-sixteenth century concerns about witchcraft as a threat to church and state had increased, and England's first secular statute against witchcraft was passed in 1542. While the statute did not articulate a vision of witchcraft as a pact with the Devil, it named practices such as conjuring, divination, and the use of magic and malefic—or harmful—witchcraft as punishable by death. The act was repealed as early as 1547, however, and no new statute addressed witchcraft as a crime until 1563. That new statute continued to define witchcraft as a crime primarily in terms of the harm it caused, and set out levels of punishment based upon the severity of the damages; only those who had allegedly killed by witchcraft were to be hanged for that felony crime. A subsequent statute, passed in 1604, extended the death penalty to those convicted of having harmed people, goods, or animals as a first offense, and to any form of witchcraft upon a second offense.[3] Fewer witches were accused and executed in England than in western Europe, in part because England's accusatorial legal system prevented the kinds of inquisitorial trials that configured witchcraft as heresy. Nonetheless, widespread religious, economic, and political upheavals contributed to the kind of social instabilities that led both England and its Continental counterparts to experience an increase in prosecutions during the turbulent decades before and after 1600.

Demonic possession cases, which centered on individuals who appeared to suffer from stylized fits, convulsions, and torments brought on by preternatural malice, shared to a certain extent a related trajectory in law and custom. In the aftermath of the English Reformation, as the Church of England displaced Catholics and sought to centralize its authority, the Anglican leadership struggled to maintain control of the style and substance of religion. By removing the Catholic ritual of exorcism from the second edition of the Edwardian prayer book in 1552, the established church left Protestant England without the official means to cast out devils.[4] Possessions continued to occur, nonetheless, and a church that could offer no viable response appeared at a competitive disadvantage. Protestants had rejected ritual exorcism in part because it maintained that individuals could adjure the Devil to depart from a person's body. Over time Puritans, the "hotter" sort of godly Protestants who were determined to purge from the Church of England what they saw as the vestiges of popish extravagances,[5] nonetheless developed a strategy to *dispossess* those suffering from demonic assaults. Dispossession, they noted, relied only upon the methods used in Scripture: prayer and fasting. Ministers could petition God's mercy, but not command devils to depart in His name.[6] In the 1580s, when tensions about a potential Catholic threat ran high, some Puritan ministers sparked controversies with the Anglican establishment by putting these premises into action. Ultimately, both possession and witchcraft were difficult for authorities to discern because they involved humans actuated, whether willingly or helplessly, by demonic power. Throughout early modern England, most people wholeheartedly accepted the prospect of authentic possession and witchcraft cases while also subjecting instances of both phenomena to testing and debate.

This book analyzes published cases of demonic possession and witchcraft-possession in England and New England from 1564, when the first English possession narrative was published, through the period when godly Puritans on both sides of the Atlantic stood their best chance of substantively directing the rhetoric surrounding witchcraft-possession cases, until around 1700.[7] Possession and witchcraft overlapped considerably, and given that approximately 80–90 percent of Anglo-American accused witches were female,[8] the book explores what new perspectives on power can be offered by analysis of the varied implications of gender for men. Specifically, it examines the role of gender in published accounts about men and women who performed the symptoms of possession and analyzes particular cases of men who were accused of witchcraft by possessed accusers or who published possession propaganda. Despite the overwhelming association of witchcraft with women, I argue that manhood was a crucial factor in the articulation of judgment upon both the women and men who were implicated in these incidents. For possession and witchcraft to work, participants had to rely upon customary scripts in which images of honorable and degraded womanhood and manhood operated intricately alongside other concerns. Anglo-American possession cases thus provide a lens through which to see how people—powerful and lowly, godly and worldly—invoked gendered power, both explicitly and implicitly, to do the cultural work necessary to compete and survive in early modern society.

A second component of the argument aims to differentiate this work from existing scholarship by emphasizing transatlantic links, and continuity rather than change. Although many early modernists have turned their attention to a circum-Atlantic world and globalization, recent scholarship on European and American witchcraft has aimed to update long-standing generalizations by emphasizing geographic specificity.[9] This has resulted in some necessary corrections of past assumptions, but it also indirectly reinforces an analytical separation between witchcraft-possession in England and colonial New England. There were important differences between witchcraft-possession cases in the two regions over this period; most notable among these was the presence of Native Americans both in the physical realm of New England's colonial project and in colonists' imaginings of their wars with Indians as part of the war between godly and demonic forces. Nonetheless, English people on either side of the Atlantic in the seventeenth century, despite the differences between their communities and institutions, drew upon shared foundational beliefs about gender, power, and the preternatural even as they vigorously disputed them. In addition to the convention of viewing the regions separately, both scholarly and popular treatments of demonic and witchcraft-possession cases emphasize change over time and decline. That impulse is accurate; although belief in these phenomena persisted, and indeed persists, the likelihood that cases could gather the necessary momentum to goad magistrates to action unraveled in the first half of the eighteenth century. Nonetheless, focusing on differences and declension obscures the remarkable degree of continuity in meanings of manhood, possession, and witchcraft in the Anglo-Atlantic. Rather than understand the decline of official confidence in demonic and witchcraft-possession cases primarily as change, we can see it as an indication of continuity in patriarchy, that mechanism for the ordering of power—kings over subjects, and fathers over dependents—to which both early modern England and colonial New England remained committed.[10]

Possession and witchcraft-possession cases provided opportunities for participants to access an unprecedented degree of agency, as when the speech and actions of young maids and apprentices suddenly took on great significance, even to the extent that they could subvert power dynamics within families and communities. Confessed witches, similarly, crafted narratives to explain their capitulation to Satan in ways that blended customary beliefs with personal accounts that sometimes resisted the very sins they admitted. However, this agency was fleeting, profoundly ambivalent, and ultimately subsumed in the community's recommitment to customary patriarchal values. Even though individual possession cases failed to endanger patriarchal authority as a system, the resulting controversies were sufficiently destructive to community order to become distasteful to those in power and to result in the suppression of both published possession and witchcraft narratives.[11] As men in power found their interests better met by avoiding the controversies inherent in these preternatural matters, this trend cemented authority in the hands of certain men while excluding others. The gendered language of published possession narratives reveals some of the myriad ways patriarchy sustained itself, by prompting authors to assert their right to wield power in ways that were otherwise obscured. As disruptive and fearful as these episodes were, and however grave the consequences for accused witches or ministers who risked sanction for treating demoniacs, the system of patriarchal authority within which they operated remained fundamentally unchallenged across the long seventeenth century (confined here to approximately 1560–1700) and the Atlantic.

Given the Protestant repudiation of exorcism, it was impossible for writers in early modern England to describe an apparent case of demonic possession or witchcraft-possession without simultaneously staking religious and political claims. Catholic exorcisms, though suppressed, retained their power as tools of conversion, and it became clear over the course of this period that views of how properly to respond to preternatural interference were more fluid than orthodox. This climate, and demonological disagreements about how to define even the central terms, meant that an author's choice of words held thorny implications. There was considerable slippage between possession and bewitchment, both because the symptoms of possession were sometimes attributed to a witch's malice and also because demoniacs who performed too convincingly could come to resemble those they accused of harming them. One central theological question centered on how to differentiate possession from obsession; the former involved a foreign spirit that took control over the afflicted individual from within—a condition some suggested required the individual's consent—whereas the latter involved an assault upon an innocent subject from without.[12] Some writers maintained the distinction carefully; others allowed that the terms blurred intricately into one another.[13] This was particularly true when a propaganda war broke out in response to high-profile possession cases. Historian Brian P. Levack acknowledges that "the two categories have often been confused, possibly because *obsessio* was sometimes used to identify both external and internal attacks by the Devil," but he omits from his analysis of possession instances in which, as in Salem, Massachusetts, the afflicted parties did not perform some of the distinctive features of demonic possession.[14] I refer to a broad spectrum of cases in which subjects performed symptoms of demonic interference as "possession," not to discount the theological distinction between possession and obsession but to acknowledge the fluidity of the terms as they were invoked in published sources and as early modern people used them.[15]

New England writers invoked possession when describing preternatural afflictions in the outbreak at Salem and Essex County, even if they should not have done so,[16] and their use of the term tapped into long-standing transatlantic debates about the implications of witchcraft-possession in ways that belied any simple attribution of culpability.[17] Since it was not always clear what to conclude about the guilt of those deemed possessed, they usually survived these episodes to reintegrate, if uneasily, with their communities.[18] Would-be demoniacs frequently invoked witchcraft in part because the externalization of blame bolstered their claims of innocence. But like those who accused witches of harming them, people who attempted to perform direct demonic possessions also had to tread carefully lest they end up being perceived as devilish anti-Christians themselves. Whatever words they used, a variety of observers and writers appeared to take a view compatible with the one expressed in Joseph Glanvill's *Saducismus triumphatus* (1681), that "they that are bewitched are not themselves, and being possessed are actuated in the parts of their body, and their mind driven by that ugly inmate in them, to what he will."[19] As a godly English minister, Glanvill represented a particular religious and political view, but even his opponents would have recognized this slippage between bewitchment, obsession, and possession as interrelated phenomena. Because this book is more concerned with the politics and language of disputation than with pinpointing stable diagnoses for early modern demoniacs, it takes the broadest possible view of published accounts of these phenomena as they appeared during a period of especially strong contention among Puritans, Anglicans, and Catholics.

Scholars have analyzed these struggles over worldly and spiritual authority—which culminated in and persisted after the English Civil War (1642–51)—from myriad angles, but the part most pertinent to this study is the way that witchcraft-possession cases provided infrequent but disproportionately influential opportunities to interpret the preternatural realm in ways that forwarded partisan religious and political claims. To navigate these issues, men who wrote about possession in early modern England and colonial New England had to defend the reliability of their sources and assert their authority to define what had taken place. And because the languages of authority, religion, and politics shared a cultural legacy that—like gender—was based on binary conceptions of order and disorder, they frequently invoked gender in explicit and implicit ways. For example, when the eminent New England Puritan minister Increase Mather wrote about how to discern between angelic and demonic spirits in 1696, he advocated consideration of the sex of the visionary: "If these White Angels appear to Females only, who are the weaker Sex, and more easy to be imposed on, that renders the case yet the more suspicious. . . . If ever an Age for Angelical Apparitions shall come, no question but men, and not women only, will be honoured with their Visits."[20] Mather reminded his readers that men were the undisputed arbiters of such matters, however closely visions, witchcraft, and possession might be associated with women. Similarly, when early modern people acted like demoniacs or claimed to be bewitched, observers struggled to determine the vital truth of these provocative events. Because the great majority of accused witches in England and New England were female, and because preternatural phenomena were culturally, though not exclusively, associated with women, an implicit ambivalence about the extent to which men *as men* suited the roles of demoniac and witch lay behind more explicit concerns. When navigating witchcraft-possession cases, though, both men and women used gendered language to persuade others to see them not as liars or fools—or worse, as agents of evil—but as victims who deserved concern and pity rather than censure.

One of the challenges of a cultural approach to possession phenomena is to account for the blurriness of the boundary between demonic possession and witchcraft on the one hand, and the stark binary conceptions that pervaded early modern European writing on the other. Men and women represented one of these fundamental binaries, and their bodies' physical and humoral formation was believed to explain the sexes' different capacities for intellect, reason, and the moderation of passions; these capacities were believed to be both the cause of and justification for patriarchal rule.[21] Women, with their leaky and permeable bodies, their loose tongues, and ambitious discontent, were believed to be more susceptible to spectral interference and more likely to seek power to harm others.[22] Because not all men could access patriarchal authority in the same ways, and because women as well as men internalized their culture's patriarchal values, women's active role in witchcraft prosecution serves as a palpable reminder that gender in early modern England and New England resists simplistic explanations of agency or misogyny.[23] Historians of manhood have uncovered the costs and opportunities of patriarchy for both sexes, and the ways that a man's honor and relations with other men factored for his reputation, but most ground their work in more representative social contexts than those of witchcraft and possession.[24] Studies that do explicitly address manhood in possession and witchcraft primarily focus on Europe or investigate male witchcraft's associations with elite magic such as astrology or alchemy.[25] Many witchcraft scholars have profitably analyzed the social, psychological, and political factors that contributed to witchcraft trials, but in this book I attempt to move away from the consideration of causes and toward the interpretation of gendered cultural meanings of possession and witchcraft.[26] It is possible that the cultural turn's emphasis on meaning over causation indicates the alienation of feminist scholarship from history,[27] but the role of patriarchal power in lived and rhetorical cases of witchcraft-possession suggests that the preternatural realm has a good deal to offer early modern gender historians outside of a stable view of the processes of transition. And for witchcraft scholars, the book's deliberate emphasis on gender as a central category of analysis argues that feminist scholarship and witchcraft history, despite their rocky past relationship,[28] can work together profitably.

In addition, this book builds upon Alexandra Shepard's argument that although "men were often better placed to benefit from them, patriarchal imperatives nonetheless constituted attempts to discipline and order men as well as women. Men, like women, might have experienced such imperatives in one or more of three ways: as beneficiaries; as subordinates; and as opponents. . . . [P]atriarchal ideology itself was muddled, contradictory, and selectively invoked rather than a monolithic system which simply received adherence or rejection."[29] Invoking a monolithic or transhistorical patriarchy creates problems for social histories that aim to account for the complex realities of early modern lives, and scholars have been right to question models that reduce men to victims anxiously competing to maintain their positions, or that extrapolate from witchcraft trials a rigidly dichotomous view of gender relations.[30] But in this period, at the cultural level, patriarchy was the overarching model for household and social relations. That not all men fell within all of its categories, and that men invoked it inconsistently and not always successfully, did not diminish patriarchy's viability; this remained the case even as changing social and economic factors affected many men's ability to invoke its claims to power.[31] There was continuity in patriarchal language and authority across this period, not in spite of patriarchy's many limitations and exceptions but because of them. Its malleability, and the gaps between the aforementioned literatures, leaves room for a transatlantic analysis of gender for men and women involved with possession and witchcraft, such as the one undertaken here.

Chapter 1 begins the book's cultural history of possession narratives by exploring the evolving story of Margaret Cooper, whose possession inspired three purportedly unrelated publications in 1584, 1614, and 1641. The chapter then analyzes the possession script itself, noting the symptoms that helped observers determine the origin of these afflictions, and the implicit gendered references that guided readers' judgment toward the authors' desired conclusions. The possession performance and the narrative about it were mutually constituted and continually evolving; those who attempted to determine the outcome had to defend their authority to discipline unruly bodies into reliable meaning. Ideally, the resolution of a possession case would entail a restoration of proper authority, as demonstrated by the subjects' return to comportment that suited their sex, age, and sort.

The next two chapters provide case studies that illustrate the workings of gender, both explicitly and implicitly, in English witchcraft-possession and propaganda. Chapter 2 examines the particularly influential witchcraft-possession case that took place in Warboys from 1589 to 1593, when the daughters of one Robert Throckmorton accused the neighboring Samuel family of bewitching them. A few authors sympathetic to the accusers compiled a lengthy narrative, entitled *The most strange and admirable discoverie of the three Witches of Warboys*, which reveals how questions of power, patriarchy, and claims to legitimate authority operated through the prosecution of witches of both sexes. Compared to his wife and daughter, John Samuel was able to claim a degree of authority, which resulted in conflict with Throckmorton over which man would direct the proceedings and command the deference of the female Samuels. Even in a phenomenon so overwhelmingly associated with womanhood, people invoked manhood in their attempts to assert control over the rituals intended to determine the meaning of preternatural suffering.

Chapter 3 turns to the men who debated the significance of possession cases for the English religious and political order. A particularly important propaganda war took place between 1599 and 1603, when Anglican chaplain Samuel Harsnett and Puritan minister John Darrell matched wits and words over the legitimacy of the witchcraft-possession cases Darrell had overseen. As much as their struggle over the meaning of possession centered on religion and politics, both men relied extensively upon gendered strategies to bolster their attacks upon their opponents. Their writings also highlighted the ways that manhood—constituted by credit, legitimate authority, and the ability to marshal reputable supporters to one's side—was inextricable from debates about the implications of these controversial preternatural episodes.

After addressing the continuity in transatlantic possession phenomena that appeared intermittently over the course of the seventeenth century, the next two chapters place New England witchcraft-possession into a transatlantic context, from its initial colonization to the turn of the eighteenth century. Changing political conditions in the seventeenth century made their mark on possession narratives, particularly in the authors' growing awareness of the need to anticipate critique, but on the whole the arguments for credulity and for skepticism in these matters were much the same as they had been a century earlier. In New England the challenges of the Indian wars, and political and religious struggles over the fate of the colony's charter and leadership, shaped witchcraft-possession phenomena. But these particularities were expressed within a larger transatlantic continuity, marked by godly ministers' determination to use possessions and other "remarkable providences" to combat indifference and atheism. The case studies in chapters 4 and 5 investigate gender's role in Puritan New England's episodes of witchcraft-possession,[32] focusing in particular on the outbreak in Salem and Essex County in 1692, when hundreds of people were accused and twenty were put to death. Although Salem's story is well-trodden ground, it was the episode that inspired the greatest number of published accounts and was most intimately linked to the intellectual and political elites whose viability was implicated in its resolution. The writings of Increase Mather and his son, Cotton Mather, who were caught in their own shifting relationships to power, particularly reveal a reliance upon patriarchal authority to weather the sudden reversals that made the Salem outbreak so alarming.

Chapter 4 centers on the Reverend George Burroughs, who was accused of witchcraft in Salem and executed in August 1692. In many respects, the testimony against Burroughs—both from afflicted and nonafflicted accusers—centered on the proper limits of manly power and his failures both of lack and excess. His subsequent conviction and execution demonstrated that despite the overwhelming cultural association of women with witchcraft, accusers did not need to feminize the men they named as witches.[33] Instead of being made more like a woman, Burroughs was unmade as a man whose faults were excesses as well as deficiencies in manly qualities. Ultimately, Burroughs's access to power and authority as a man and minister made him resemble the kind of inverted seducer who might lead witches in praising the Devil rather than Christians in praising God.

Chapter 5 focuses on the case of Margaret Rule, a seventeen-year-old from Cotton Mather's congregation, whose possession symptoms appeared nearly a year after the end of the Salem trials and confirmed his belief that New England remained under siege by witches and devils. In his manuscript about the case, Mather relied upon customary gendered language to shore up Rule's reputation as a believable demoniac and used the episode to advocate on behalf of his own view of what constituted proper patriarchal order for New England. Unfortunately for Mather, a copy of his manuscript fell into the hands of skeptic Robert Calef, who subsequently embarked upon a long and bitter campaign to engage Mather in debates about witchcraft-possession and the legitimacy of the Puritan leadership, all of which culminated in a book attacking Mather in 1700. Mather feared the power that witches had to harm the colony, but he and his peers also clearly realized that its survival depended upon the triumph of patriarchal hierarchy over upstarts who sought greater authority for themselves in turbulent times.

The conclusion of witchcraft-possession trials at Salem in New England did not mean the end of these phenomena or popular belief in them, though it became riskier to pursue such cases officially. At the turn of the eighteenth century, people in the Anglo-Atlantic continued to explain witchcraft-possession phenomena by drawing upon many of the same cultural scripts used at the end of the sixteenth. Furthermore, in the course of determining what made a demoniac or a witch, early modern people still grappled with what made a proper woman and man. Gender's malleability, and its tendency to vacillate between explicit and implicit references, can make it difficult to follow, but it was this flexibility that encouraged its use by various parties in contradictory ways. Ultimately, authors on both sides of the Atlantic used gendered language in ways that tracked the vicissitudes of power.

Even given the amount of scholarly attention that witchcraft has received, scholars remain vexed with devils, or at least vexed by them, because they prompted conflicts that resist stable interpretation. Episodes of possession and witchcraft were unusual, but if they provide less in the way of representative conditions, they reveal the telling possibilities that emerged in times of crisis. These cases' complexities oblige us to resist monocausal explanations and bring to studies of preternatural phenomena the flexibility we allow for broader histories. We need to attend to the full implications of gender in extreme circumstances, even or especially where we do not expect to see manhood, because it is there that we see the inconsistent but powerful ways that gender fed the languages of power and authority. The inherent malleability of manhood and womanhood, and of the figures of the demoniac and the witch, marks them as unstable categories of meaning that nonetheless saw considerable stability over the course of the seventeenth century. Even the decline in the willingness of officials to take possession cases seriously reflected a continued investment in patriarchal control over these events and their religious and political implications. Ultimately, while the discourse and propaganda under investigation here may appear removed from the lived realities of the early modern people caught up in witchcraft-possession, their stories and voices emerge from the records in ways that continue to fascinate and unsettle us. However disinterested scholars must be when attempting to describe such episodes, in the end the reason to scrutinize their fates is to come closer to understanding the many complicated ways that their world produced and perceived them. As the continuing prosecution of suspected witches around the world demonstrates, there is no shortage of lessons to be gleaned from these intricate human predicaments.[34]

1 / Discerning Demonic Possession and Witchcraft-Possession in Early Modern England

In 1584, an anonymous pamphlet entitled *A true and most Dreadful discourse of a woman possessed with the Devil* described the trials of one Margaret Cooper, who had recently suffered at the hands of the Devil in the shape of a headless bear. Her troubles first presented themselves as idle talk, for which her husband, Stephen Cooper, reproved her and prayed on her behalf. Soon she grew restless and called for her wedding ring and a coin her son had found, prompting her husband to pray "that it would please God to send her a more quiet spirit, and . . . that faith might speedily vanquish such vanity in her."[1] Instead, Margaret grew increasingly reckless, and began to suffer from fits during which she foamed at the mouth and shook so violently that the bedchamber rattled as her husband and sister sought to restrain her. As her husband and others prayed, she relayed her vision of the headless bear, and another of a snail-like creature. In time the witnesses also saw these spirits and, after Margaret was rolled around and nearly tossed from a window, saw the flames that filled the room with a terrible stench. Finally, her husband and his brother "did charge the Devil . . . to depart from her and to trouble her no more: then they laid hands on her and cried to the Lord to help them." Subsequently, Margaret recovered herself and first she and then the company "espied a thing like unto a little child with a very bright shining countenance, casting a great light in the Chamber." After the child vanished, Margaret asked forgiveness of God and acknowledged that her own sins had brought the evil spirits to her. The narrator reported in the end that she remained in "some reasonable order" from that time forward.[2]

Whatever "really happened" at Margaret Cooper's bedside, the published narrative contains a wealth of suggestive information about her preternatural affliction. Demonologists might have considered Cooper obsessed rather than possessed because her symptoms were largely external assaults, but her range of symptoms and the title of the piece demonstrate that her suffering fell within the realm of possession phenomena. Possessions attracted converts and, many believed, presaged the impending day of reckoning, which helps to explain why these cases sparked fundamental disagreements among Protestants and Catholics.[3] Despite their relative rarity, printed possession cases reveal the ways authors mobilized discourses, both explicitly and implicitly, to tell stories, sell pamphlets, and aid broader agendas. The Cooper narrative's emphasis on sin as an overture from the Devil, and on prayer as the proper response, follows the "script" of the sort of godly Protestant possession narratives that viewed possession phenomena with great seriousness. While commanding the Devil to depart may have smacked of the Catholic ritual of exorcism, its emphasis on prayer and reliance upon God's power channeled through a godly community demonstrates that the piece intended to provide moral instruction for Protestant readers.[4] Even on its own, therefore, this account of Margaret Cooper's ordeal is a rich source of early modern perceptions of possession phenomena.

Attempts to determine the meaning of Margaret Cooper's story are complicated by the fact that it reemerged in 1614, in a pamphlet called *A Miracle, of Miracles: As fearful as ever was seen or heard of in the memory of man*. The new text retained the vast majority of the original, changing only "the ninth day of May last past *Anno. 1584*" to "the ninth day of *September* last past."[5] The subject matter stayed the same, but the erasure of the thirty intervening years helped to retain a sense of urgency. Another innovation was that the publisher appended other wonders to the Cooper story, including the story of "a poor country maid" who apparently died for twenty-four hours, revived, and then spent five days weeping and prophesying until she died a second time. This, plus news of a recent flood that had submerged several villages, marked the 1614 version of Margaret Cooper's possession as part of a broader genre of literature devoted to the sensational presentation of miraculous wonders.[6]

Further complicating attempts to pinpoint the meaning of Margaret Cooper's possession is her appearance a third time, in 1641, as Margaret

Hooper. This pamphlet's new title altered the protagonist's identity and location, claiming to provide *Most Fearful and strange News from the Bishopric of Durham, Being a true Relation of one Margaret Hooper*. In its first sentence the author established that the events had taken place "Upon the 15 day of November now last past 1641," and in Durham, where Stephen "Hooper" was the same "yeoman of good and honest reputation" despite his new name.[7] The three lives of Margaret Cooper's possession narrative, which spanned 1584, 1614, and 1641, demonstrate the staying power of the genre.[8] The third iteration also accompanied a broader increase during the turbulent 1640s and 1650s in the number of published pamphlets about witchcraft and related wonders.[9] The story persisted because it continued to offer something to readers; it was saleable because it was sensational, and both provocative and permissible because it exhorted the reader to godliness while avoiding some of the more controversial aspects of contested witchcraft-possession cases. These aspects of the Margaret Cooper narrative help to explain how it managed to be many things at once: a sincere godly account of an apparent possession, a snapshot of beliefs about the Devil and the unknown, a tract baldly recycled for profit, and a text that made use of symbols—such as the headless bear—with which modern readers are largely unfamiliar.[10] Taken together, the Cooper narratives illustrate that the language of possession was powerful enough to captivate and flexible enough to serve the occasionally contradictory motives of various authors and narrators.

To encounter one version of Margaret Cooper's narrative invites reflection upon what the source reveals about possession phenomena in early modern England, whereas to encounter all three versions necessarily destabilizes a historian's sense of what truths they hold. But however circumspect the reader must be when considering such narratives' objective meaning, the fact that they functioned as propaganda does not mean that the authors did not believe in the reality of what they described. In fact their sincerity frequently merged with strategy because, as Stuart Clark has explained, "it was intrinsic to the very notions of possession and exorcism that a contest for power should take place. . . . Propaganda was in this sense not extraneous to possession but one of its very presuppositions."[11] This fusion of possession, propaganda, and power recommends the reading of possession narratives as cultural texts. Given how many possession events were never published or were published but lost, any study of this sort provides less of a complete record than snapshots of early modern mentalities. Taken together, the Margaret

Cooper narratives may destabilize our certainty about what happened at the bedsides of those who acted as if they were possessed, but they also highlight the ways possession cases reflected discourses of good and evil, revealed contests over social legitimacy, and posed critical questions about who had authority to pronounce judgment upon their meaning.

Possession Symptoms and Scripts

By the time Margaret Cooper's narrative first appeared in 1584, there was already a long history of publications that described strange and wondrous occurrences. Published possession cases, whether they invoked witchcraft or not, played an important role in shaping the cultural conversation about the nature of wonders and miracles—both by spreading popular conceptions of the preternatural realm and by affecting the reception such cases received from ministers and magistrates. Demonic possession cases, and those that blurred the boundaries between demonic possession, witchcraft-possession, and obsession, shared a broad set of symptoms that reflected long-held beliefs about the malice of the Devil and his desire to seduce souls away from God. These symptoms evolved over time into cultural scripts that were disseminated in published narratives, so that observers accepted or rejected demoniacs' behavior based upon their understanding of the proper parameters of spectral interference. It was possession's communal and performative nature that explains both its power and limitations as published propaganda.[12] Possessions were communal because, despite the immediate and primary focus upon the demoniac, a possession only became a possession as a result of observation and interpretation. The same strategies that helped authors make their case—paradoxically, describing extraordinary wonders and yet adhering to a familiar script—opened possession narratives to criticism from those who mistrusted the case's political and religious implications. Because possessions were mutually constituted by demoniacs and observers, participants struggled over the power to fix the meaning of what had taken place.

To perform a recognizable possession, demoniacs drew upon a set of symptoms based upon scriptural and European precedents but that reflected evolving English and Protestant particularities. While some of these symptoms might initially seem like little more than antics, phenomena such as embodied sensation, perception, and movement played essential roles in the cultural recognition of possession. As Stuart Clark notes, the need to transform movement into meaning was "an especially vital matter in an area like possession where so much that was constitutive both of the experience of being possessed and of the ability to interpret that experience was obviously gestural."[13] Among these symptoms, the most common were painful convulsive fits and contortions. When Alexander Nyndge became possessed in 1573, for example, his brother Edward described the convulsions of Alexander's face and body, and the incredible ways that his chest swelled, his eyes stared, and his back bent inward toward his belly.[14] The minister George More, who described the symptoms exhibited by the seven Starkie children in the 1590s, explained that the spirits "did rent, and tear the possessed, insomuch that they were sorer vexed and tormented" by pinching and pricking.[15] At other times what should have resulted in great pain did not, as when the young John Smith, whose witchcraft-possession took place in 1616, exhibited preternatural strength and violence by striking "himself such blows on his breast . . . that you might hear the sound of it the length of a long chamber . . . the least of them was able to strike down a strong man. And yet did to himself no hurt."[16] When acting as if they were possessed, demoniacs startled observers with a range of physical manifestations of their spiritual torment, frequently exhibiting such rapid transitions between contradictory behaviors that few could imagine how their affliction could be natural.

Demoniacs' convulsive fits frequently incorporated a range of related symptoms such as unusual strength, alternating rigidity and flexibility, and trances that authors consistently described as wholly beyond the power of the demoniac to fake. In 1574, seventeen-year-old Mildred Norrington was so strong when her spirit took hold of her that "four men could scarce keep her down."[17] Similarly, those who observed Joan Jorden's symptoms remarked that she had to be bound in a chair for restraint, but "she (or rather the Devil in her) struggled and strained so sore, that it broke in pieces. Being again bound in the chair, six strong men leaned with their whole strength thereon, each also setting one foot on the round of the chair to keep it down. But she, (though so bound) notwithstanding all their strength, removed the chair round about the house, a yard at a time, they hanging thereon."[18] In 1601, the twelve-year-old demoniac Thomas Harrison alternated between extreme weakness brought on by his debilitating fits and "extraordinary strength, that if he folded his hands together, no man could pull them asunder: if he rolled his head, or tossed his whole body . . . no man could stay, or restrain him."[19] Harrison sometimes lay "as if he had been stark dead," only to then leap up and skip with "such agility, as no tumbler could do the like.

And yet all this while his legs were grown up so close to his buttocks, so he could not use them." His contortions also affected his face, as when an observer reported, "Sometimes we saw his chin drawn up to his nose, that his mouth could scarce be seen: sometimes his chin and forehead were drawn almost together like a bended bow."[20] Because convulsive fits provided the backbone of the possession script, published sources emphasized these astonishing feats to convince readers of the cases' legitimacy.

If convulsive fits were the most common and widespread symptom of possession, broadly defined, then the one that most denoted demonic possession as opposed to obsession or bewitchment was the emission of strange voices from within. Frequently these were deep and guttural voices, like Alexander Nyndge's "base sounding or hollow voice," that differed enough from the subject's natural tone to convince observers of their preternatural origins.[21] Demoniacs also roared, hissed, and made noises like animals. At one point Mary Glover's voice sounded "loud, fearful, and very strange, proceeding from the throat (like an hoarse dog that barks)," and observers compared her utterances to "the hissing of a violent Squibbe . . . an Hen that hath the squacke: and . . . the loathsome noise that a Catt maketh forcing to cast her gorge."[22] Some demoniacs argued vehemently with the devil(s) who harmed them, modeling godly resistance to the forces of darkness and temptation. Mildred Norrington, while attempting to provide spectral corroboration for her accusation against a woman (possibly her own mother) for witchcraft, engaged in a long dialogue as the Devil. Using a strange deep voice, she provided myriad details of the sins of the accused, including the murder of three people, before she ultimately confessed to fraud.[23] Thomas Darling's possession also involved the emission of voices both "small" and "big and hollow." Darling performed an exhaustive show of resistance to the spirits, while pronouncing to observers that the prayer and fasting of faithful people was too strong for them to overcome.[24] As these cases demonstrate, demoniacs' dialogues with spirits made for effective propaganda because the practice allowed them to articulate doctrinal points that served Protestant or Catholic interests. Struggling against the utterances of the afflicting spirit, as well as struggling physically in convulsions, was a key part of the demoniac's crossing through painful trials toward redemption.

Another important component of the cultural possession script was the tendency of victims of demonic possession and witchcraft-possession to see apparitions. Common visions included the Devil, the witch whose malice instigated their suffering, or creatures that represented the Devil's servants and witch's familiars. Richard Galis's 1579 account made no explicit claims that he was possessed but neatly followed the witchcraft-possession script.[25] Galis's apparition took the form of a "Cat or the devil himself in a Cat's likeness" that would "haunt my Chamber hurring and buzzing about my bed, vexing and troubling me beyond all measure."[26] The "Seven of Lancashire," the group of demoniacs whom John Darrell and his associate George More treated in the late 1590s, helpfully reported the actions of their apparitions for the benefit of their audience: "They would say: look where Satan is: look where Beelzebub is: look where Lucifer is: look where a great black dog is, with a firebrand in his mouth: see how Satan runneth at me with a spear in his hand to stick me to the heart, but God will defend me."[27] Apparitions played an especially crucial role in witchcraft-possession cases because they directed observers' suspicions and provided the kind of spectral evidence that could prove decisive in trials. In 1612 Grace Sowerbutts reported seeing visions of the female relatives she accused of bewitching her, both in human form and in the shape of a black dog. Grace's narrative provided effective propaganda even after her eventual confession of fraud, because she accused a priest of orchestrating the false charges against her Protestant family members.[28]

Those suffering from possession symptoms frequently showed a strong aversion to prayer or the Bible and often lost their ability to hear or read Scripture. These aversions were sometimes accompanied by an avoidance of productive actions in favor of frivolous or blasphemous ones, as devils would seek to interrupt all that was wholesome or productive and to replace it with rebellion. At Warboys in the 1590s, the five possessed Throckmorton girls screeched and interrupted prayers with dramatic fits that ceased at the precise moment the prayers did, and Elizabeth Throckmorton had "merry fits" that resulted in the girls laughing "so heartily and excessively, as that if they had been awaked they would have been ashamed thereof." Elizabeth was "also full of trifling toys, & some merry jests of her own devising, whereat she would force both the standers by, and herself to laugh greatly."[29] This frivolity extended to Elizabeth's desire to play cards with her uncle, during which time her senses were restored and her fits ceased. When witnesses experimented with presenting her with a godly book, Elizabeth threw herself backward until it was removed and the card game resumed. At another point, the only way for the Throckmortons to escape their fits was for adults to bring them outside to a nearby pond, where Elizabeth "was left all day well, playing in the company of other children at bowls and other sport: (for the more foolish sport she useth, the more the spirit spareth her) but so soon as any motion was made of coming into the house, it presently took her, so that she was never out of her fit."[30]

Sometimes demoniacs' revulsion of prayer and the Bible enabled them to avoid religious instruction and services for years at a time. The possession of the seven young people in Lancashire followed a very similar pattern as that of the Throckmorton girls; they suffered brutal fits during prayer or reading of Scripture but fared very well at play (and at plays). According to George More, their suffering was so severe that for nearly two years "they never came to the church, only for fear to increase their torments."[31] They also "blasphemed God, and the Bible; they reviled the Preachers; railed upon such as feared God; scorned all holy prayers, & wholesome exhortations; which being offered and applied unto them, they ever became much worse."[32] The possessed children nimbly mocked what was most sacred. More reported that when observers called for the Bible, "they fell a laughing at it, and said, reach them the *Bibble bable, bibble babbell,* it went so round in their mouths from one to another, and continued with many other scornings and filthy speeches."[33] Though Protestants held that it was the Word and not the material Bible that held power, holy books frequently worked as charms to interrupt demoniacs' fits, or to demonstrate their preternatural aversion to holiness. For example, during Thomas Harrison's possession in 1601, if anyone approached him with a Bible, "though under his cloak and never so secret, he would run upon him, and use great violence to get it from him and when he could get any, he rent them in pieces."[34] Demoniacs' visions and violent fits set the scene for their claims of preternatural affliction, but their aversion to religion and embrace of sacrilege did a great deal to convince observers, and readers, that natural illness or melancholy could not explain what had taken place.

Another common category of symptoms entailed interruptions to the ability to eat or, alternatively, the vomiting of inedible items such as pins, nails, feathers, and hair. In 1564, Anne Mylner could not eat for five days following the onset of her symptoms, and "neither did eat during the time of her sickness, but once in each twenty-four hours, and then most commonly a little quantity of bread and cheese, which notwithstanding was done with wonderful snatching and rawness."[35] Abstaining from food demonstrated that the afflicted Anne had moved outside what was normal, and her greedy snatching up of what food she did eat signaled a loss of self-control that suggested her transition from a self-moderating young woman to one at the mercy of a malevolent force. As with fasting, the vomiting of foreign objects made a powerful statement about a demoniac's unnatural suffering, but readers knew that both could be faked. When feigning witchcraft-possession in 1574, Agnes Brigges cast from her mouth some of her own hair, a small piece of lace from her sleeve, a tenterhook, two nails pulled from her bed, and "many and sundry times she did caste out at her mouth crooked pins, which afore she had bowed, and put in her mouth, but to what number she doth not remember."[36] Anne Gunter, whose father coerced her to fake the symptoms of possession, appeared to fast for twelve days after which she vomited copiously and produced pins from her mouth, breasts, and fingers.[37] Such revelations of fraud neatly dismantled the standard defense of demoniacs' symptoms as defying natural explanation, but disordered consumption remained a central component of the range of behaviors that signified witchcraft-possession.

Some of those who acted as if they were possessed appeared to gain knowledge of secrets or things destined to take place in the future. Others appeared to speak beyond their natural capacity, either by delivering impassioned sermons or conversing in languages they were not expected to know. According to George More's account, the Seven of Lancashire exhibited this set of symptoms expertly. More described John Starkie's "very extraordinary knowledge" for one only twelve years old, as when in a trance he preached at length about the sins committed by all sorts of people and the fearful judgments of God that would surely follow. He went on to exhort his family and all present to repent, performing so admirably over the course of two hours that "they that heard it did admire it, & thought that a good preacher could very hardly have done the like. . . . All this was done in a trance, his eyes being closed up, & neither knew what he said nor did."[38] After this, John's father quizzed him on his ability to see despite having his eyes closed, which resulted in John's accurate listing of the room's eighteen or nineteen occupants even as some exited and returned. He increased their amazement by inviting a newcomer to take his hand and predicting this would bring him out of his fit; this came to pass, and he amazed them further by flatly denying that he had said anything at all. More recorded what an impression it made upon witnesses that the two youngest demoniacs, "though they were unlearned and never went to school, yet in their fits they were able to make answer to Latin questions propounded unto them, so truly and readily, as if they had soundly understood them."[39] Since the Devil was supposed to speak all tongues, some observers used such trials as a way to test for dissemblers. While Rachel Pindar struggled to maintain her possession performance, one of the observers "spake to her in Latin: she answered, that she would speak no Latin. And one there was that spake Dutch to her: and she answered, I will spreaken no Dutch."[40] While it might have been possible to feign this sort of new knowledge by invoking key phrases, it was much more difficult to maneuver around a suspicious learned audience.

Witnesses who attempted to test a demoniac's acquisition of foreign languages arrived at the scene with preconceptions—shaped by religion, politics, and education—that strongly colored their perception of what had taken place. Believers and skeptics alike mocked these biases as a symptom of their opponents' delusions. Abraham Hartwell, in his translation from the French of Martha Brossier's possession, demonstrates how the same demoniac could lead observers to divergent conclusions. A skeptic spoke to Martha in Latin, saying: "Thou wretched woman, how long wilt thou proceed to delude us? . . . Acknowledge thy fault, and crave pardon. For thy guiles are discovered: and unless thou do so, thou shalt shortly be delivered into the hands of the Judge, who by torture will wrest out the truth. She being demanded, whether she understood this or no, answered in good sooth, She did not." A few days later, a group of physicians gathered to test her languages for themselves: "One spoke certain Greek words unto her: and she answered in French. Another spake in English: she answered in French, but yet (as some say) somewhat to the purpose."[41] Authors of possession narratives were well aware that the performances of demoniacs like Martha Brossier appeared more or less convincing depending upon what observers already believed, so they strove to assure the reader of their orthodoxy in all critical matters. Despite their efforts, considerable ambivalence permeated most cases because the very nature of demonic possession, along with the proper methods of discernment and treatment, remained hotly contested throughout the period.

The aforementioned sets of possession symptoms drew upon long-standing cultural traditions that helped render strange wonders recognizable to witnesses and readers. The codification of these symptoms into a cultural script did not prevent individual demoniacs from innovating, however. In fact, it was the juxtaposition of familiar themes and shocking wonders that lent these episodes much of their social and ideological power. Still, authors of possession narratives, whether describing demonic possession or witchcraft-possession, relied upon the script to direct readers' interpretation of these frightening incidents. As in

Margaret Cooper's case, the aims of most published narratives fell on a spectrum between the not necessarily incompatible objectives of profit and propaganda. The possession script was flexible enough to survive across time and space, and through great religious and political discord, because it provided a powerful tool for explaining the human condition and exploring the implications of preternatural interference. Because possession cases were inherently strange *and* familiar, witnesses and authors used language strategically to engage readers' explicit understanding of possession and the implicit assumptions that guided their reception of the narrative. Read as texts, these narratives reveal the myriad ways that the language of possession invoked power and the authority to exert control over the meaning of mysterious and uncontrollable phenomena.

Gender, Power, and the Possession Script

Given the gendered nature of English witchcraft during this period, when approximately 80 to 90 percent of convicted witches were female, one might expect the possession script to reflect explicit expectations regarding the sex of demoniacs, but this was not the case. Sex and gender were not supposed to matter conclusively in either witchcraft or possession, as all people were vulnerable to the Devil's temptation and all could sin. Although women's bodies, minds, and temperament were believed to explain their particular susceptibility to preternatural interference, neither witchcraft nor possession was understood as exclusively female. For the most part, gendered analyses of early modern witchcraft have understandably focused on women and womanhood, but the comparatively subtler role of sex in possession—about 65 percent of the demoniacs in the published possession cases reviewed in this study were female[42]—demands an analysis that attends to womanhood, manhood, and power. This requires some reading between the lines, as the increasingly controversial climate for published possession cases compelled authors to focus on potentially divisive elements of their narratives to which sex and gender did not explicitly pertain. For example, they carefully documented the ways that observers discerned the nature and origins of demoniacs' symptoms and speculated upon the religious and political implications of the case for those who deemed it legitimate or fraudulent. But even while pursuing matters medical, psychological, religious, and political, possession narratives conveyed numerous implicit gendered assumptions and arguments that both directed readers' judgment and provided a powerful language of persuasion available to those on both sides of contested cases.

It is well known that demonologists, clerical officials, and everyday people overwhelmingly associated witchcraft with women, but those long-standing cultural beliefs bear revisiting because they demonstrate how profound that association was, and how it permeated the perennially blurry boundaries of witchcraft and possession. English authors who published on the subject in this period reiterated received classical and Continental sources while emphasizing a Protestant approach to key questions, such as the impossibility of miracles in the postapostolic age, the translation of key Scriptures, and how properly to dispossess a demoniac without succumbing to popish superstition.[43] Despite the need to distance English Protestant witchcraft texts from Catholic ones, authors relied upon learned European doctrine both for corroboration and for critique. Reginald Scot's early skeptical tract, *The Discoverie of Witchcraft* (1584), for example, did not wholly deny the possibility of witchcraft but cast doubt upon how suspects were prosecuted. In the course of making this argument, Scot drew upon European explanations for why women were more likely to be witches than men. On the one hand Scot believed that most accused witches were poor old women who were victimized by neighbors and magistrates, but he also replicated, if ambivalently, European accounts of women's immoderate "fury and concupiscence" that stemmed in part from the "venomous exhalations" and "pernicious excrements" they expelled.[44] An English translation of a French account included a chapter dedicated to proving "that women are more dedicated to Witchcraft then men are," which provided English readers with similar claims that women were predisposed to witchcraft because they were more fervent and obstinate in their evil. That tract affirmed that even if there were male witches, it was their female counterparts who did the bloodiest tasks; female witches strangled children and made ointment of their grease, the text explained, "but Sorcerers and men Witches do seldom or never dip their fingers in these bloody actions."[45]

English publications replicated many of these claims about why women were likely witches. Some drew the link almost unthinkingly, as suggested by the subtitle to a pamphlet that offered "a strange and most true trial how to know whether a woman be a Witch or not."[46] Others, like Alexander Roberts's *Treatise of Witchcraft* (1616), emphasized in terms that echoed Continental demonologists the weaknesses of body and mind that led women to seek unnatural power. He averred that more women "in a far different proportion prove Witches then men, by a hundred to one; therefore the Law of God noteth that Sex, as more subject to that sin." As in many witchcraft tracts, Roberts began with the "nature" of biological sex but quickly transitioned to gendered characteristics shaped by cultural expectations. He explained that women were more credulous and thus more easily deceived, more curious and therefore attracted to forbidden things, more easily impressed upon by the Devil, more likely to fall from grace, more desirous of revenge, and more "full of words" and slippery tongues that communicated their illicit knowledge to all they knew.[47] Other sources acknowledged the existence of male witches only to then reinforce the crime's association with women by reverting to the use of female pronouns. Echoing William Perkins's *A discourse of the damned art of witchcraft* (1608), Thomas Cooper's *The Mystery of Witchcraft* (1617) explained that "men as well as women may be subject to this Trade; seeing as both are subject to the State of damnation," but the work repeatedly used "she" and "her" in examples designed to demonstrate what "a witch" might do.[48]

In possession narratives, authors for the most part avoided the question of demoniacs' sex. Because believing authors wanted to demonstrate that malevolent forces had caused their subjects' symptoms, they initially depicted demoniacs as vessels—incidentally male or female—for the battle between holy and demonic forces. It was easier to do this when the protagonists were children, for although one could discount the antics of the very young, they were not so easily accused of the kind of gendered follies that characterized youths and adults. Such authors also invoked gender and age when attesting to the simplicity and innocence of those who acted as if they were possessed. If believing authors had relatively little to say about sex, they nonetheless contended with gendered cultural assumptions about rebellious young apprentices or foolish, and possibly lusty, maids. Both demoniacs' sex and gender became more legible as authors described the ways their behavior, speech, and comportment altered after the onset of their affliction. Since believing authors presented demoniacs as human sufferers in a cosmic struggle, they used gender to the extent that it elucidated the nature of their suffering and their transformation from recognizable subjects into something other.

Gender also proved to be a crucial tool for possession skeptics, whether they challenged the conditions under which witches were prosecuted or accused the advocates of high-profile possessions of perpetrating fraud. One of greatest critics of possession, Samuel Harsnett, emerged during a possession propaganda war at the end of the sixteenth century. As chaplain to the bishop of London, Harsnett could afford to be especially acerbic because he wrote as a defender of the Anglican establishment against what he saw as overzealous Puritans and scheming Catholics. Gendered language was one of many weapons Harsnett used against his enemies, as when he amplified the suspect nature of Catholic exorcisms by showing that foolish or devious women were the mainstay of their support. Catholic laity of the past and, he implied, in the present gave "the chief place to women . . . that sex (as it seemeth) having a general disposition, to like well of Exorcisms."[49] He invoked gendered weaknesses to draw a sharper and more recognizable portrait of how exorcists supposedly misled young people into feigning possession symptoms: "If they be boys . . . because they would remain from the school: if wenches, for that they would be idle, & both of them, that thereby they might be made much of, and dandled."[50] Harsnett found ways to join seamlessly gender, age, and social status in this critique, and he used similar strategies to discredit and ridicule both demoniacs and those who supported them: "For the most part such as are pretended to be possessed, are either men of the simpler sort, or women; . . . they say that the Devils do easier possess men and women of light brain, than those that be wise . . . and that they vex women & maids, rather than men."[51]

Authors of possession narratives did not intend to focus on sex or gender. Rather, they devoted the bulk of their explicit argumentation to controversial issues critical to the defense of their agenda. The paramount question was how to discern the origin and nature of the affliction. For the narrative to work as propaganda, authors had to clarify how a true possession differed from illness, insanity, melancholy, and fraud. To do this, authorities—physicians, clergy, and magistrates—had to assert control over the myriad competing elements of the script in order to transform the chaotic symptoms of the afflicted into legible phenomena. The main way they did this was by testing demoniacs for signs of disease or fraud, thereby laying the groundwork for possession and witchcraft's legal and theological implications. However much authorities invoked science and Scripture in pursuit of reliable discernment and diagnosis, however, it was inescapable that possession was an embodied experience over which men and women fought for control. And where people invoke power to assert control over bodies, in an attempt to discipline them into meaning, is gender.[52] Therefore it is necessary to attend to men and women, and manhood and womanhood, in order to appreciate the intricate ways that these cases tracked and replicated power within patriarchal contexts. Ultimately the outcome of these cases hinged upon the questions of who had legitimate authority to discipline unruly bodies in search of answers, and who was allowed to pronounce what bodies *meant*.

Because illness frequently preceded possession symptoms, and because hysteria and melancholy sometimes produced analogous symptoms, physicians played an important role at the beginning of many possession narratives.[53] Both supportive and skeptical accounts relied upon doctors to corroborate their interpretations of an affliction's origins in physical or mental illnesses and to comment on the boundary between natural versus preternatural causes. The 1574 narrative about Rachel Pindar's and Agnes Brigges's fraudulent possession even concluded with a "Commendation of Physicians" that exhorted readers to "Honor the Physician because of necessity. Honor thou him, for God hath created him. For of the highest commeth medicine. The Lord hath created medicine of the earth: and he that is wise will not abhor it."[54] The line between medicine and religion was not a clear one, and medical explanations for possession symptoms were unavoidably enmeshed with religious and political interests. A prime example was the eruption of controversy between the Church of England and Puritans over their dispossessions at the turn of the seventeenth century. Repercussions of Edward Jorden's treatment of Mary Glover—and his conclusion that her symptoms originated in hysteria, or the "suffocation of the mother," rather than the preternatural realm—resonated for more than a century because of the way it factored in battles between Anglicans and Puritans.[55]

Early modern science itself was gendered, notably in its attribution of characteristics to sexed bodies within a humoral system. In this system, bodies were constituted from four humors with qualities—hot, cold, wet, and dry—that in their fluctuations governed men and women's health, character, and different capacity for reason.[56] And because tests on a demoniac's body carried a good deal of explanatory power about the nature of a demoniac's affliction, their results particularly reveal possession's foundation in questions of gender and power. Demoniacs faced nowhere near as dire physical consequences as did suspected witches, for whom scratching, ducking, pin pricking, and swimming represented only the beginning of an ordeal that might end with their execution. But demoniacs were nevertheless seized by terribly painful contortions that bent, locked, and hyperextended their limbs. They lost control of their faces, tongues, and throats, and they swelled, burned, and raged. Many narratives described this suffering in horrified detail, and observers wept not only for fear of the powers of devils and witches but also for the demoniac's pain. At the same time, however, these same witnesses subjected demoniacs to brutal physical trials that used pain—a natural function of the body—to measure the extent to which preternatural forces governed their bodies. These tests were not only administered by skeptics, who might be expected to want to shock dissemblers back to their senses, but also by those who believed that demoniacs were innocent victims of devilish malice. Demoniacs faced tremendous pressure to react in ways that were appropriate to the script, whether to the touch of those they accused, to prayers or holy objects, or to examinations intended to verify their insensible trances.

One common approach, inherited from Continental concepts of demonic possession, was to try to drive out an invading devil by forcing the demoniac to inhale noxious and stinking fumes. In a 1564 dispossession account, John Fisher reported that bystanders had tried several times to bring eighteen-year-old Anne Mylner out of her trance by plying her with vinegar, to no avail. The minister John Lane asked them to bring him some again, "saying, that God might do that then, which he did not before, and so received vinegar, put it into his mouth & blew it into the Maid's nostrils, whereat she cryeth *a Lady, Lady.* He then willed her to call upon God, and the blood of Christ & in these doings she being astonished, he called again for more vinegar, Whereat she cried: *No, no, no more for God's sake.*"[57] Lane then instructed her to say the Lord's Prayer, which she did, and after "this her deliverance" she called upon God, dressed, ate, and continued well to the great surprise of those who had long attended her. In cases like this one, the experiments drew upon traditional notions of how to make the victim's body inhospitable to the invading spirit. Other attendants, though, might use the same tests with the intention of forcing a recalcitrant faker to give up the charade. Because physical trials served both credulity and skepticism, the investigators' intent and the observers' perception were frequently unclear despite the efforts of writers to make unambiguous claims for the trial's meaning.

This flexibility meant that physical tests on the bodies of demoniacs raised myriad questions about the nature of evidence that could scarcely be answered within the bounds of a published pamphlet, however many esteemed gentlemen swore to their disinterested certainty.[58] Abraham Hartwell's translation of Martha Brossier's case demonstrates how profoundly ambivalent possession narratives could be about what constituted a legitimate source of information. The epistle dedicatory reveals that Hartwell's explicit goal was to shore up the Church of England's critique of Puritan minister John Darrell's dispossession of

William Somers, by aligning Darrell's alleged trickery with other notorious examples. Marescot's text suited Hartwell's needs in the sense that it relayed the skeptical physicians' critique of the attending priests, but it was risky to reprint a possession account so squarely rooted in the Catholic tradition even if it did ultimately portray it as a convincing fraud. Hartwell's disdain for the priests fit in nicely with the tone of anti-Catholic writing of the period, but by allowing the physicians to be not only French, loyal Catholics and also *correct* created some dissonance.[59] The physicians' uneven reaction to the various tests performed on Brossier only increased this sense of dissonance by revealing how easily both skeptics and believers saw proof of their expectations in the results.

In Brossier's case, the doctors who believed that she was a fraud also found it impossible to provide any natural explanation for her performance during some physical ordeals. At one point Marescot, frustrated with the priests' gullibility and impatient with what he saw as Brossier's deception, "set his knee upon her knee, took her by the gorge [throat], and commanded her to be quiet. She being not able to stir her self, and seeing her cousinage [deceit] to be discovered, said, [the devil] *is gone: he hath left me.*"[60] When the priests attempted to use noxious smoke to drive out her devil, they set fire to "Perfume, and offered those villainous and stinking vapors to her Nose, she in the mean while being bound to a chair . . . and then began she to cry out, *Pardon me, I am choked, He is gone away.*"[61] Hartwell relished such moments because he agreed with Marescot that Brossier's capitulation illustrated her deception rather than her deliverance. But he also included the extraordinary ways that Brossier resisted other painful tests: "Notwithstanding touching the point of Counterfeiting, the insensibility of her body, during her ecstasies and furies, tried by the deep prickings of long pins, which were thrust into diverse parts of her hands and of her neck . . . without any show, that ever she made of feeling the same . . . took from us almost the suspicion of it."[62] Marescot's skepticism aided Hartwell's mission to liken Darrell to deluded priests, but other parts of the narrative suggested that Brossier's response to other tests were convincing enough "almost" to make convinced skeptics reevaluate their diagnosis. All of the pertinent details of the perfume test resembled those from the Mylner case in 1564, except that what had been taken as proof of deliverance in the first case signaled fraud in the second. Authors had to include testimony about bodily tests such as these because they touched on crucial and controversial questions, but their reliance upon observer testimony reinforced the fact that it was power—to control the meaning of demoniacs' unruly bodies—that mattered most.

Observers who believed in demoniacs' authenticity were not necessarily any gentler than the skeptics. In a text by an anonymous supporter of Darrell, published in 1599, the author described how Joan Jorden's dramatic symptoms prompted equally dramatic tests by those who attended her. To prove that her affliction did not have natural causes, the author relayed that during one of her trances her "teeth were so fast closed, that a man could not open them, though with all his strength he assayed it with his dagger and a key. And, (that which strange is,) a stiff dry Rush being put into her nostrils, so far, as it might touch her brains in the judgment of them that were present, yet she moved nothing thereat; neither at the violent bending of her fingers; nor yet at a great quantity of *Aquavitae*, which was poured into her mouth."[63] The results of such tests held great significance not only for demoniacs themselves, who would have to rejoin their communities in the wake of their affliction, but also for the legitimacy of those who had intervened in a climate with high religious and political stakes. Ministers who believed that demoniacs were genuinely possessed, obsessed, or bewitched pitied their charges but nonetheless evaluated their alternately convulsing and insensate bodies for ways to orchestrate their suffering. Believers and skeptics may have disagreed about how to interpret the results of these bodily tests, but both recognized the risks and opportunities they offered. Authors had to establish that they had both legitimate authority to be present and sufficient credit to be a trusted narrator, so that after laboring to wrest meaning from possessed bodies they could use the weight of the evidence to further reinforce that authority.

Restoration of Patriarchal Order

Gendered language and strategies permeated English demonic possession and witchcraft-possession narratives, whether the authors were believers or skeptics. For most participants, though, possessions were about the fearful power of devils and witches to trouble humans. Although they could not help but be aware of the controversial nature of these cases, especially when Protestants and Catholics disputed their implications, most participants did not view possession and witchcraft outbreaks as proxies for other conflicts or tensions. The suffering and harm done to bodies, families, and property demanded their complete attention. Modern readers, however, can view possessions as cultural episodes in which people competed for authority and legitimacy, which makes them particularly fruitful moments in which to gauge how the power to determine bodies' meanings provided a medium for battles over religious or political matters. For both believers and skeptics, the rightful end of a possession case was signified by the restoration of disorderly subjects to an orderly patriarchal authority, though not all cases ended so satisfactorily. Sometimes, when attending to demoniacs in intensely Calvinist environments, conditions converged in a way that produced a productive synergy between godly ministers and the demoniacs they sought to dispossess. Two examples of this were George More's relation of the demoniacs of Lancashire (1600) and John Swan's account of Mary Glover's possession (1603). In both cases the ministers had sufficient local support to buoy their conviction that they were engaged in a cosmic struggle against both the Devil and his worldly allies. Their narratives reveled in the shocking and unruly antics of the demoniacs, but only until the point that the subjects were transformed into orderly bodies that once again met expectations of sex, gender, age, and sort.

One of George More's subjects, fourteen-year-old Margaret Hurdman, was typical of many demoniacs in that she appeared to be driven to reject all that was good, right, and natural in exchange for the evil, illicit, and unnatural. And just as gender—in combination with age and social status—shaped cultural expectations about what was right and natural for children and young men and women, it also shaped expectations about the ways they embraced the opposite. For example, while demoniacs of both sexes expressed aversion to the Bible or prayer, their attraction to frivolous, worldly, or sinful things could manifest along gendered lines. When Margaret fell into one of her fits, she appeared to order a remarkable litany of luxurious clothes from a spirit she called her "lad." Margaret performed a breezy but precise monologue: "My lad, I will have a fine smock of silk, it shall be finer than thine. I will have a petticoat of silk, not of red, but of the best silk that is. . . . [I]t shall be laid on with gold lace; it shall have a French body, not of Whalebone, for that is not stiff enough, but of horn, for that will hold it. . . . [M]y lad, I will have a French farthingale, it shall be finer than thine."[64] This performance enabled Margaret both to express a fantasy and also to enact the kind of godly rejection of the fantasy required by her audience and her sense of self.

In the published narrative, George More reiterated what observers and readers would have immediately recognized as the cultural archetype of women's taste for frivolous vanities. He wrote that Margaret was "possessed at that time, as it seemed, with a spirit of pride," and that she "did most lively express both by words and gestures, the proud women of our times: who can not content themselves with any sober or modest attire, but are ever ready to follow every new and disguised fashion, and yet never think themselves fine enough." After calling for her lad to provide her with a suitable horse, saddle, and riding costume, Margaret presently "said, 'I defy thee Satan and thy pride, for this is thy illusion and deceit, I will none of it,' and then reverting [to her senses] said, 'Jesus bless me,' but remembered nothing that she had either said or done."[65] This performance was pedagogical in that it modeled the proper godly response to temptation, and it simultaneously corroborated the gathered clergy's sensibilities and allowed Margaret to shore up her role as an innocent sufferer. Margaret came to herself by regaining the beliefs and comportment suitable to a godly Protestant maiden, all of which amounted to her restoration to her proper place within the bounds of authority.

John Starkie, the twelve-year-old in Lancashire who so astonished witnesses with the quality of his preaching, also demonstrated a sophisticated understanding of his rightful place. He made one "most excellent prayer, first for the whole church, then for the Queen's Majesty for the subduing of her enemies, for the continuance of her life, and peaceable government, for the upholding of the Gospel, and for all the true Ministers of Christ, for those that have Authority, for his parents, and all the people of God."[66] Even if John produced these sentiments while in a fit, they helped send the right sort of message about the dispossession's deferential tone. Since Harsnett and other critics accused More and his compatriots of fraud and ambition, such speeches helped restore the reader's confidence that participants were fighting the Devil and not plotting against the monarch.[67] Upon the demoniacs' successful release from their affliction, More later wrote that "they all gave great thanks to God, for their deliverance, and that of themselves so freely and cheerfully in so excellent & heavenly manner, as that they could never do the like, neither before, nor since: they are also so changed in their conditions, and their manners so well reformed, that a man shall hear no evil come from them, nor any unseemly behavior: and now they can pray, and take delight in praising God. They go to church, to hear the word, and . . . are every way better than they were before."[68] More emphasized that these were decent and godly young people in order to undercut skeptics' typical characterization of demoniacs as lazy, manipulative, or fraudulent youths. The Starkie family's high status was a particular boon in More's mission and likely explains why the case received comparably little criticism.

John Swan's published account of fourteen-year-old Mary Glover's possession exhibited some of the same synergy found in More's account of the Seven of Lancashire. Glover had reacted very convincingly during the tests performed on her body and had startled the attending clergy by showing remarkable insensitivity to pain and by emitting a strange voice from her nose. For example:

> The Recorder called for a Candle, and a sheet of paper, which being lighted he held the flame to her hand till it blistered, the blister broke and water came out which dropt on the floor, the Maid lying senseless like a dead body, with the voice still coming out of her Nostrils saying, *hang her, hang her*. Then the Recorder called for a long pin which he held in the flame of the Candle till it was very hot, and thrust the head of it into her Nostrils to try if that would make her sneeze, wink, bend her brows, or stir her head, but nothing moved her lying still as dead.[69]

The tests by the recorder, John Croke, had been instigated at the insistence of Richard Bancroft, the bishop of London, who believed that Mary dissembled. But for the clergy who had become convinced of Glover's authenticity, her success at withstanding the tests revealed not her own fortitude but rather the power of her preternatural affliction. Indeed, some who came to her bedside as skeptics were so swayed by her performance that they utterly changed their minds. In Glover's case the stakes were extremely high, especially after her crowds attracted the critical attention of Samuel Harsnett, and one can only wonder at the physical and psychological conditions that contributed to her stoicism.

In Swan's text, Mary Glover provides an excellent example of a demoniac's eloquent restoration to proper patriarchal authority. Using language reminiscent of the influential possession case at Warboys, she modeled noble and godly forgiveness to the woman she accused of having caused her affliction. Glover promised to have mercy for the woman, saying: "I pray thee O Lord to forgive her, to give her grace to see her sin, and to repent, and to believe that so she may be saved. Satan was herein thy rod (O Lord) upon me, and she but the instrument, and as for the rod when thou hast done with it, it shall be cast into the fire. But the instrument that hath been (by that serpent) abused, O Lord have mercy upon her, and forgive her all her sins, even as I forgive her with all my heart." Having conveyed this magnanimity, Glover went on to exonerate herself for her own actions against the accused, which she elegantly linked to an account of herself as the martyred victim of those who questioned the legitimacy of her possession: "Thou knowest lord, that, that which hath been done against her, hath not been done of malice, or desire of revenge on my part, but that the truth might be known, and so thou to have the glory, and that I might be delivered from the slander of men."[70] Thus Glover absolved herself from what she had done while possessed and expressed a newly generous spirit to the woman she accused of bewitching her; she could afford to be particularly gracious since such comments generally had no bearing on what would happen to the accused should she be found guilty of witchcraft.[71]

But what made Mary Glover's restoration to order so masterful was her mingling of prayerful gratitude with a return to her proper place within her family and community. She managed to do this in a way that emphasized their long-standing reputation for godliness, which further reinforced her own, her family's, and John Swan's interests. After being ultimately dispossessed, she awoke and, glowing with holy certainty, looked upon the preachers and said, "The comforter is come, O Lord thou hast delivered me." As soon as her father heard this, he "also cried out and said (as well as his weeping would give him leave) this was the cry of her grandfather going to be burned." This reference to her grandfather's death as a Marian martyr had an electrifying effect on the Puritan audience. Immediately after her proclamation

> there was heard amongst us, a plain outcry or shouting, even like the victorious cry or shout of a conquering army, and yet the same was intermixed with [abundance] of most joyful tears: & even there withal the poor party (still crying *he is come*) did struggle and strive with all the strength she had, to be let loose which they that held her perceiving, yielded to see what she would do, and then she presently and suddenly, did slide down out of the chair, and very speedily recovering her self on her knees, with a countenance . . . exceedingly sober, and full of a kind of majesty and reverence, with hands held up indifferent high, her eyes very broad open, said to one, *he is come*.[72]

Mary then turned and repeated this phrase over and over to various assembled godly folk, all of whom grasped the significance of her channeling of that holiest godly age. It surely helped draw a clear line between a glorious Puritan past and Glover's present, with a convenient parallel between the suffering her grandfather faced at the hands of his persecutors and the antagonism she faced from skeptical Anglican officials.

After demonstrating the right amount of eloquence in prayer and fashioning herself as a blameless soldier in the battle against the Devil, Mary recovered. At that moment, "one, I think a kinsman, went to the maid (sitting still in her chair) saying with joyful tears, *welcome Mary, thou art now again one of us*: the father also in like sort took her by the hand, as not being able to speak a word: and the mother went, and (putting away the handkerchief wherewith her daughter sat covering her blubbering face) with like watery cheeks kissed her." Then Mary "was bid to go near the fire: and so she went and sat . . . where she took her place at her first entering into the room."[73] Thus Mary brought her performance to its necessary conclusion by becoming once again a recognizable member of her family, safely within the bounds of contemporary social expectations. Mary's own experience in the aftermath of her possession, when few would welcome her eloquent preaching however closely it reflected her grandfather's unimpeachable pedigree, was likely fraught with uncertainties. But her reintegration at the conclusion of the published narrative had considerable symbolic power. It enabled Swan's account to be many things: a narrative of witchcraft-possession that told a cracking good story, a piece of propaganda aimed at bolstering Puritan legitimacy, and a way to discredit the Anglican establishment that sought to repress such incidents and to punish ministers who carried them out. It also provided her attendants with an opportunity to present themselves as guardians of the proper order. Although the religious and political dimensions of that order were especially divisive, its foundation in patriarchal hierarchies was not.

Concluding the Possession Script

Each of the possession cases reviewed here demonstrates why such relatively rare episodes could easily become disproportionately influential. The behavior of these frequently young demoniacs became the center of attention of their families and communities, took on cosmic importance, and sometimes captured the attention of the highest leadership of the land.[74] Mary Glover's case reignited the flurry of contentious dispossessions that had erupted between 1599 and 1602, and attracted renewed negative attention from representatives of the Church of England. As the ensuing controversy intensified, the first new witchcraft statute was instituted since the Act of 1563; the Act of 1604 made witchcraft a capital offense and included Canon 72, which effectively acknowledged the existence of possession but forbade anyone from using "fasting and prayer under the pretense of casting out devils" unless they received permission from a bishop.[75] Whatever had prompted Mary's symptoms and speeches, her body became a battleground first for godly and demonic forces and then for ministers and high-ranking officials. Although they agreed on little else, both Mary's sympathetic godly community and the Anglican men who sought to disprove her dispossession shared a sense that the performance must come to an end and that chaos must give way to an order structured by patriarchal authority.

Participants in these disputes expended great energy debating the implications of these complex phenomena for medicine, religion, and politics, and at the core of all of these matters lay gendered cultural assumptions, language, and strategies. Just as such cases involved real female and male subjects, at the discursive level they engaged both womanhood and manhood as a way to evoke the qualities of godly or devilish subjects. Across this period, individuals who acted as if they were possessed continued to capture the attention and fears of observers local and—through print—far removed. Attending to the gendered foundations of these controversies provides a fuller sense of their early modern meanings and reminds us that there is no complete picture without both women and men, or womanhood and manhood, and that the power to control and declare bodies' meaning lay at the center of these struggles.

Engendering English Witchcraft-Possession:
The Samuel Family in Warboys

One of the most famous English witchcraft-possession cases of the late
sixteenth century began in Warboys, England, in 1589.[1] According to
the published account, the troubles originated among the daughters and
servants in Throckmorton household, when "Mistress Jane, one of the
daughters of the said Master Throckmorton, being near the age of ten
years, fell upon the sudden into a strange kind of sickness and distem-
perature of body."[2] Her symptoms included loud and vehement sneez-
ing, trances and swoons, a swelling of her belly that heaved her above
the restraining arms of observers, and a traveling palsy throughout her
body. After two or three days, neighbors came to visit the child, among
whom was "Mother" Alice Samuel, who lived nearby. Jane sickened
upon her arrival and said, "Look where the old witch sitteth (pointing
to the said Mother Samuel) did you ever see (said the child) one more
like a witch than she is?"[3] The child's mother evidently rebuked her and
laid her down to rest, where she remained unsettled. Alice Samuel was
an elderly neighbor of lower social status and, if the authors were to be
believed, a woman with some reputation for having a disorderly tongue.
Perhaps she had frightened Jane and her sisters, either in their imaginings of her as a witch or through actual criticism or threats. That part of
the story is unknown, but the response of the Throckmorton parents and
community members overall suggests that however the girls chose their
target, they had chosen wisely.

The Warboys episode was the first major English case to link posses-sion symptoms with witchcraft, and it both reinforced existing popular beliefs about possession and codified certain practices within the genre. Published as *The most strange and admirable discoverie of the three Witches of Warboys* in 1593, it was widely read and subsequently used as a kind of manual by both demoniacs and observing authorities. As a crafted text, the published narrative may not provide a reliable represen-tation of what "really happened," but its biases, presumptions, and argu-ments still reveal a great deal about the evolving engagement of godly Protestants with the preternatural realm. In her discussion of "neces-sary" versus "trivial" witchcraft pamphlets, Marion Gibson has noted that *Witches of Warboys* is "perhaps the most officiously 'necessary' of all the pamphlets" because of the great effort its handful of authors took to make the text appear to be a seamless, reliable narrative somehow both scrupulously documented and casually assembled.[4] Gibson notes several reasons why the text is neither a transparent account nor a coherent representation of witchcraft and possession beliefs. But even as a constructed composite, the text communicates myriad ideas about male and female behavior and trades in explicit and implicit gendered presumptions. Its influence on subsequent articulations of witchcraft-possession also recommends it for close reading. Barbara Rosen explains that the Warboys text "more than any other was the book which fixed the unhappy tradition of Puritan witchcraft—a tradition still valid and unchanged at Salem in the seventeenth century."[5] By taking the narrative seriously, even if we question the authors' claims about the meaning of key events, it becomes clear that gender—meaning manhood as well as womanhood—was a central medium for the struggles that took place. Given the overarching continuity in patriarchal culture, imagery, and language, the case was a rare particular that nonetheless illuminated its broader world.

While *Witches of Warboys* was published anonymously, it appears to have been the work of more than one godly writer on the side of the pros-ecution. The likely authors—Throckmorton himself, and at least three of the children's uncles, Gilbert Pickering, Henry Pickering, and the vicar of Warboys, Francis Dorrington—were strongly Puritan, which indel-ibly shaped the narrative's tone and priorities.[6] At one point, for example, someone posed questions to one of the girls, "or rather the Spirit in her," targeted to provide spectral corroboration for godly Protestantism. Her afflicting spirits caused her to respond with great shaking when asked if she loved the word of God, but they "seemed content" when asked, "love you Witchcraft?" and "love you Papistry?" The author concluded that "what good thing soever you named, it misliked, but whatsoever concerning the Popes paltry, it seemed pleased and pacified."[7] Possession cases drew power from such testimony, since the demons' allegiances neatly fitted the participating clergy's expectations, although this also could also open them to sectarian challenges.

Though it incubated a rare witchcraft-possession outbreak, the village of Warboys was largely similar to the four other adjacent villages that "comprised a wedge of land projecting from the gently rising uplands of Huntingdonshire," characterized by "extensive fens, lush marsh grass and meadow at one place, and marshy bog and turf at another."[8] As in most early modern villages, the residents of Warboys experienced mobility but were suspicious of itinerants and strangers.[9] The question of belonging did not apply only to poor itinerants, however. Historian Anne Reiber DeWindt has shown that Robert Throckmorton arrived in Warboys after a thirty-year period in which no adult male representative of the family had lived in the village. Once installed, Throckmorton sought to establish himself by wielding influence, asserting his authority, and expecting deference from its residents in ways that strained relations in the community.[10] Comparatively less is known about the Samuels—Alice; her husband, John; and daughter, Agnes—who were tenants to Sir Henry Cromwell, a knight in neighboring Ramsey (and grandfather of Oliver Cromwell). John Samuel participated as a member of the community, if not always positively. Over time he was fined for a series of infractions that included insufficiently trimming his hedges, reaping contrary to the ordinance, and revealing the business of the village jury—an act that got him barred from future service.[11] The precise nature of the relationship between the Samuels and the Throckmortons is unknown, but their conflict took place within a turbulent context. Long-term economic trends, such as increases in rent and decreases in lease length, accelerated after 1580. While some yeomen and husbandmen benefited from the increased demand for agricultural products and rising prices that came with population growth, many small tenants faced greater insecurity. As Keith Wrightson explains, although many English tenants "had shared with the yeomanry the initial benefits" of "rising agricultural prices, by the early seventeenth century the fortunes and interests of the two groups among the manorial tenancy were diverging."[12] With an unmarried daughter and no recorded allies in the community, Samuel may well have feared for the security of his landholding.

The Throckmorton family's interconnected economic and social superiority in relation to the Samuel family helped grant credibility to the published narrative, and its resulting widespread influence makes it particularly worthy of a close reading. Both the moral and material aspects of their greater credit factored in the case's legacy,[13] as demonstrated by references to the Warboys case that appeared six years later in the high-profile possession propaganda war between Samuel Harsnett, the chaplain to the bishop of London, and Puritan minister John Darrell over Darrell's dispossession of the fraudulent demoniac William Somers. Harsnett wrote that Somers confessed that he "had heard and read some part of a very ridiculous book, concerning one M. Throgmorton's children (supposed to have been bewitched by a woman of Warboys) whereby he saith, that he learned some points."[14] Darrell noted in 1600 that although Harsnett heaped his scorn on the participants in other possession cases, he was comparatively subdued about Warboys. Darrell tartly suggested that Harsnett believed the Throckmorton children were frauds, "yet he thought it best and most for his safety because they were the children of an Esquire, not to say so in plain terms."[15] Darrell also informed his readers that public opinion was on his side, because the Warboys case "is notoriously known, and so generally received for truth, as [Harsnett] himself dareth not deny it, though fain he would, as appeareth by his nibbling at them."[16] Their debate underscored the importance that a family's status played in determining a case's legitimacy and, consequently, of its potential to serve as religious and political propaganda.

If the Warboys case emerged at a time of economic and political pressure, its initiation in 1589 and resolution in 1593 also placed it at a significant moment for witchcraft and possession in England and in Europe.[17] The case against the Samuel family became recognizable as witchcraft-possession because these aforementioned pressures combined with inherited witchcraft beliefs and the kind of quotidian tensions that took on greater significance in times of crisis. In Warboys, the Throckmortons found receptive neighbors and magistrates who shared the same cultural views of witchcraft-possession and used a shared script as a lens through which to perceive the girls' affliction. The authors thus recorded the dramatic details of the case not simply because they were astonishing but also because they made the case culturally decipherable. The core of the narrative rested on the onset of the girls' possession symptoms and the initial suspicion of Mother Samuel. By beginning with her and moving on to her daughter, Agnes, the authors grounded the narrative in primary female suspects and provided the foundation from which John Samuel was subsequently unmade.

This chapter begins with the story of the accusations and campaigns against primary suspects Mother Alice Samuel and Agnes Samuel. The Throckmorton girls' possession performance was especially convincing because of the way they modeled their symptoms on preexisting scripts, and the girls were at their most formidable when they articulated the wishes of their afflicting spirits in ways that manipulated the Samuels into participating in their own destruction. Historians have speculated about which earlier possession cases may have been most formative, but what the girls gleaned from their own religious instruction and broader cultural beliefs about witchcraft-possession mattered just as much; there was no single script for a viable possession, but demoniacs adapted their actions to increase the likelihood that observers and authorities would recognize them as innocent sufferers of preternatural malice.[18] Second, this chapter argues that while actors in the episode wielded gendered power very flexibly, it remained at the center of the case. For example, underlying beliefs about female bodies supported the girls' performance of possession symptoms and the apparent guiltiness of the accused. In addition, Mother Samuel's inconsistent capitulation to the role of "witch" meant that control of her compliance invoked broader questions of manly power and mastery. Finally, I argue that Alice's husband, John Samuel, was differently unmade, as a man, before his conviction and execution. Compared to his wife and daughter, John Samuel was able to access power differently in the crucial settings where the drama unfolded, and he and Robert Throckmorton found themselves locked in struggles over credit, claims to legitimate authority, and control of the female Samuels. Ultimately, the Warboys narrative reveals how the prosecution of witches of both sexes operated within a patriarchal system, and that keeping both sexes in view further illustrates gender's complex role in English witchcraft-possession.

The Female Witches in Warboys

Jane Throckmorton's question, "Did you ever see . . . one more like a witch than she is?" indicates how closely Mother Alice Samuel, as an older, socially marginal woman, resembled the traditional witch image. But it took a great deal more than a likely suspect to make a witchcraft-possession case viable in the eyes of the neighbors, religious and legal arbiters, and a reading public. The authors of the text described the girls' symptoms in familiar terms and took care to bolster their claims by emphasizing that the adults who observed their fits followed sanctioned procedures. For example, the Throckmortons initially sought the assistance of physicians rather than "cunning people" or priests, something that highlighted the family's resistance to both popular and popish superstitions.[19] The doctors' diagnoses and ministrations, as well, reflected seventeenth-century attitudes about the body, its humors, and the boundaries between ailments natural and unnatural.[20] After evaluating the girl's urine, the doctors considered possible natural causes for her affliction, such as worms or "the falling sickness" (epilepsy).[21] But they could help neither Jane nor, after the symptoms spread to her sisters and some of the servants, any of those suffering in the household. Both their failure to pinpoint natural cures and the progression of fits and visions among young family members strongly suggested that the episode resulted from preternatural causes.[22] By the time it was published, the narrative had passed through several interpretive layers; adult observers reacted selectively to the children's astonishing performances and later honed the narrative arc to reflect a viable witchcraft-possession script.

An audience presently gathered in the Throckmorton home to observe the girls' affliction and consider the cause. Along with the Reverend Francis Dorrington, the children's uncle, they witnessed the girls' suffering, cries, and antics that demonstrated an almost mad indifference to their own safety. The one constant underlying the girls' rapidly changing symptoms was their naming of Mother Alice Samuel as the one who harmed them, and over time the sheer repetition of this charge must have reinforced observers' sense of its validity. Elizabeth, age ten, now joined her sisters Jane, age nine, and Joan, age fifteen, in setting the tone. Their fits, which varied in length and intensity, only worsened when adults attempted to calm them. Joan soon introduced a pivotal development by reporting that a spirit spoke in her ear, foretelling that all five sisters and seven servants "should be bewitched."[23] Thus Joan introduced the dynamic of communication with the afflicting spirits, something that fascinated observers and ultimately proved so devastating to the accused. These spirits, named "Smacke," "Catch," "Pluck," "Blew," "White," "Callico," and "Hardname," appeared frequently to the girls and spoke with them at length. They were, as the girls described them, figures of considerable ambivalence. At first the spirits did little other than enact the malice of she who had allegedly sent them, causing the girls to argue dramatically with them. In time, however, the spirits claimed that "they now waxed weary of their Dame mother Samuel," and they took on roles more like accomplices than torturers. The spirits still had to do their Dame's bidding, but they also provided the girls with information that helped them resist her. In fact, the girls reported that the spirits ultimately communicated the terms under which they would be delivered. Similarly, Joan's prediction about the number of afflictions in the household served as a kind of directive for the others, since those who lived in close quarters were highly suggestible. Joan and her sisters envisioned a household struck down by the malice of a neighbor and managed to convince their parents, ministers, doctors, and judges to share their vision.

Once the case was under way the girls' uncle Gilbert Pickering arrived and compelled Alice Samuel; her daughter, Agnes; and one Cicely Burder, "who were all suspected to be witches, or at least in the confederacy with Mother Samuel," to come to the Throckmortons' house.[24] Thus began a long process of tests, fits, prayer, and countermagic that ultimately sealed the fate of the Samuel family. Soon after Pickering arrived, Lady Cromwell, to whose husband, Sir Henry Cromwell, John Samuel was tenant, also joined them. The arrival of Pickering and Lady Cromwell changed the case's direction and significantly raised the stakes. The Throckmortons' close relationship with the Cromwells established their reputation, provided ammunition in struggles over the Samuels' compliance, and forestalled potential accusations of fraud or popery.

After Lady Cromwell observed their fits she demanded to see Mother Samuel, who "durst not deny to come."[25] Lady Cromwell warned Mother Samuel to stop harming the children, something in which the old woman denied having any part. Later, Lady Cromwell snipped a lock of Alice Samuel's hair and gave it to Mistress Throckmorton to burn, a traditional countermagical practice that was believed to interrupt a witch's capacity to harm.[26] According to the narrative: "Mother Samuel, perceiving her self thus dealt withall, spake to the Lady thus. Madam why do you use me thus? I never did you any harm as yet." After leaving Warboys, Lady Cromwell was haunted by this perceived threat, fell ill, and in a little over a year she died. During this time she suffered from fits that resembled those of the Throckmorton girls, and "that saying of Mother Samuel which she used to her at Warboys, which was, 'Madam, I never hurt you, as yet' would never out of her mind."[27] Whatever combination of physical and psychosomatic factors caused Lady Cromwell's death, it bolstered the Throckmorton girls' legitimacy and brought the case to the felony level because the witchcraft statute in its current incarnation did not count the bewitchment of the girls a capital offense in itself.[28] The girls would probably have heard the news of Lady Cromwell's suffering and death with considerable fear but also vindication. It surely increased the onlookers' certainty that her death resulted from powerful witchcraft. The authors' tone subsequently shifted, as well, reflecting greater momentum and a clearer accounting of the girls' strategies to ensnare the woman they accused.

At this point an author reported: "Now did the spirits manifestly begin to accuse Mother Samuel to the children in their fits, saying it was she who bewitched them and . . . that whensoever they were in their fits and were either carried to Mother Samuel's house, or she caused to come to them, they should be presently well."[29] After a long period of experimentation and enforced proximity to the girls, Mother Samuel appeared to lose her will to resist the proceedings. The Throckmorton family allowed her to believe that a confession would provide a way out of the nightmare. The girls said they "would forgive her from the bottom of their heart, if she would confess it that they might be well . . . that they would entreat their parents and their friends (so much as in them lay) clearly to forgive and forget all that was past." The parents likewise said that they "would freely forgive her from their hearts, so be it their children might never be more troubled."[30] Their manipulation was accompanied by great pressure—they occasionally denied Mother Samuel food and subjected her to long periods of intense prayer, weeping, exhortation, and promises to end the ordeal if only she confessed and asked for forgiveness.

As the prayer and weeping sessions began to have their effect, Alice Samuel wept uncontrollably along with the girls. Finally, broken, she confessed to Master Throckmorton. Realizing that he had no impartial witnesses, he summoned neighbors to hear her confession, and then, satisfied, he let her return home on Christmas Eve. The next day, however, under the influence of her husband and daughter, she retracted her confession.[31] The ensuing struggle over her compliance, explained in greater detail below, led the Throckmortons to shift their attention to her daughter, Agnes. Despite the relative scarcity of evidence against Agnes beyond guilt by association, and Mother Samuel's attempts to protect her, both women were taken away to the bishop of Lincoln. There Mother Samuel was examined and eventually confessed two more times. At this point the narrator breezily commented, "Now that we have brought Mother Samuel to the jail, we will let her there rest in God's peace and the Queene's, until the next general assizes day."[32] His tone expressed satisfaction that Alice Samuel's confession of guilt resolved one of the text's central tensions, after which the authors reduced her to a type, or witch-figure, that stood in for the more ambivalent character she had provided before. This may have been how her contemporaries saw her as well, as it was easier to convict an archetype than a neighbor.

The second part of the narrative describes the transformation of her daughter, Agnes, into a witch, in the final weeks of 1592, in a way that served to conflate the women in the reader's mind. In an assured tone, the narrators reported that the Throckmorton girls' spirits now offered new information about the source of their bewitchment, prompting their father to spring into action: "And to come unto the daughter, Agnes Samuel, who now cometh upon the stage with her part in this tragedy, you shall understand that she was left with her mother in the jail . . . [until] Master Throckmorton made his request to the high Sheriff and the Justices to bail this maid, and to have her home to his house, to see, if it might please God, whether any such evidences of guiltiness would appear against her, as had before appeared in the children against her mother."[33] Given the success of these methods so far, and because a failure to convict Agnes might have threatened the legitimacy of the entire case, there was little doubt that "evidences of guiltiness" would appear. The girls' investment in their possession performance gave them little choice but to continue, and their parents, uncles, and neighbors similarly turned to the rest of the Samuel family with strong presumptions of their guilt. That the Throckmorton girls were strategic and manipulative in their building of the case against the Samuel family does not preclude their sincerity; there is no evidence to suggest that they were attempting to perpetrate an intentional fraud rather than simply coming to believe what needed to be true. Rather, the girls and observing adults reacted to fearful phenomena in line with inherited cultural presumptions about witchcraft and possession that were shaped by the godly Protestant inclinations of their community.

Once Agnes was installed in the Throckmortons' home, the girls continued to advance upon the new target. Their pressure and demands escalated much as they had for her mother, only now the girls appeared more confident in their ability to persuade those in authority. They demanded that Agnes remain nearby so that they could perform the same experiments that had implicated her mother. These experiments included coercing her to repeat formulaic commands to the spirits and brutally scratching Agnes's face and arms, discussed below. In the first instance, the Throckmorton daughters, led by Elizabeth and Joan in particular, demanded that Agnes utter oaths that culminated in a command that the spirits depart. These oaths, presumably a manifestation of the popular belief that only the source of the bewitchment could call off the afflicting devils, amounted to a form of coerced confession. By submitting, the accused individual essentially admitted to being a witch and to having bewitched others, sometimes to their death. It was taken as proof of the test's validity that the girls' fits continued when bystanders repeated the oath but would cease when the accused was made to say it.[34] Each of the Samuels was subjected to this experiment, but the oaths played a particularly important role in the girls' campaign to prove Agnes's guilt. These are some of the passages that seem the most transparently manipulative, and Agnes's pitiable situation comes across in the text despite the authors' great pains to depict the Samuels as persecutors and not as victims.

Joan Throckmorton beckoned to her sister Elizabeth to join her in "listening" to the spirit's instructions. After succeeding in getting Agnes to repeat the oath, and recovering at that moment from her fit, Joan saw the significance the adults lent to this test and reported that the spirit would torment her until additional oaths were taken. Joan quickly grasped that Mother Samuel's guilt provided an ideal foundation for the pursuit of Agnes. She informed Agnes, "the thing saith . . . that mine Aunt Pickering should have been well before this time, had you not bewitched her again since your mother confessed,"[35] which effectively merged Agnes's culpability with her mother's. A full three weeks before the assizes session, Joan's spirit reported that Agnes would be required to repeat three oaths in front of the judge, which Joan helpfully enumerated: "The first must be as she is a worse Witch than her mother in bewitching the Lady Cromwell to death: The second as she hath bewitched mistress Pickering of Ellington, since her mother confessed: And the third, as she would have bewitched mistress Joan Throckmorton to death in her last week of great sickness: and the Spirit said all this is true, and shall be proved true hereafter."[36] The coerced oaths were so effective that they played a central role in the hearing at the court of assize on April 4, 1593. Justice Fenner compelled Agnes to repeat them, and, as always, the girls recovered on cue and only when the suspects spoke the words. The oaths greatly facilitated the Samuels' convictions by implicating them in a variety of offenses, most notably the death of Lady Cromwell, which carried a capital sentence.

The coerced oaths, unchecked by the observing adults, represented the apex of the Throckmorton girls' manipulation and implicitly revealed the perils of legal receptivity to spectral evidence. The oaths also effectively undermined norms of gender and hierarchy by forcing members of the Samuel family to testify against each other, as when Jane reported that only John Samuel's attendance and pronouncement of an oath would heal her. Despite Robert Throckmorton's attempts to procure him, Samuel refused to appear, and the girl had no choice but to persist in her affliction. The next day, Jane adjusted her strategy to take advantage of Agnes's presence and compliance. Jane stated that her spirit laid out only three possible ways for her fits to cease:

> Either your father (speaking unto the maid [Agnes]) must come and speak these words to me, even as he is a Witch, and hath consented to the death of the Lady Cromwell: or you must confess that you are a Witch, and have bewitched me and my sisters: or else you must be hanged: then the maid was willed to ask the child whether she should come forth of her fit, whensoever, or wheresoever her father did speak these words to her: then the childe asked the spirit, and the spirit answered, that she should.[37]

By interweaving the implications of the daughter's speech with her father's, Jane strengthened the case against them both. In sum, either Agnes or her father had to confess to capital witchcraft, which would result in certain execution. This strategy undoubtedly sought to bring about Agnes's confession, as this was the best possible proof of witchcraft and the next logical step in the unmaking of the Samuel family. Although Agnes never did confess, she acceded to the demands of the Throckmortons and the court to repeat these oaths, and ultimately the result was the same. The conventions of witchcraft-possession and the official legitimacy given to the Throckmortons' claims subverted the duty that Agnes owed her parents—and especially to her father. Because the Throckmorton girls were able to compel the Samuel women's speech and behavior, they forced them past standard family relations and denied them the chance to perform the degree of deference of authority appropriate to their age, sex, and status. Their compliance only further distanced them from any resemblance of propriety and facilitated their undoing.

By this point the Samuels may have sensed the futility of the situation, and when the time came for the general assizes trial they alternately defended and implicated each other. Throughout, Mother Samuel seemed consistent only in her insistence on her daughter's innocence. Once Alice stopped trying to retract her confession to save herself, she notably rose to the defense of her daughter and not her husband. When Alice Samuel's interrogators demanded to know "whether her husband was a Witch, or had any skill in witchcraft: She said, he had, and could both bewitch and unwitch: but touching her daughter, she would in no sort confess any thing, but sought by all means to clear her."[38] Once on the ladder, Mother Samuel confessed to every remaining charge. Though Agnes did not resemble a witch as neatly as her mother, she also succumbed to the quandary of witchcraft-possession conventions. If Mother Samuel was the pivotal witch figure, Agnes corroborated the children's claims that their suffering was caused by a broader conspiracy. Once the court was convinced of the legitimacy of Mother Samuel's guilt, there was little Agnes or John could do to save themselves, and all three were hanged in April 1593.

After the Samuels' executions, the girls' immediate recovery legitimated the veracity of the judgment and encouraged the authors to assemble and publish the narrative. The lord of the manor assured the ongoing resonance of the case by giving the money accrued from the Samuels' goods to the corporation of Huntingdon to support an annual sermon on witchcraft.[39] There is little evidence to show how resolution came to Warboys after the Samuels' executions, but the Throckmorton girls' reintegration into the community surely reaffirmed crucial social hierarchies and allowed the village to solidify its commitment to order and stability. The tone of the text suggests that the witchcraft-possession script provided townspeople and elites alike with a satisfactory explanation for the Throckmorton girls' troubling behavior, since it confirmed that those who were executed had been the Devil's, and those who remained were God's. The published narrative also demonstrated the crucial role of power in the creation of a viable witchcraft-possession outbreak, especially as it allowed certain men to wrest authority from others. Because gender provided a perennially flexible lens though which such claims were made legible, the authors made the most of the myriad ways it shored up the credit of some at the expense of others.

Gender and Power in Warboys

In Warboys the young accusers provided the most explicit demonstration of disruption to norms of gender and hierarchy through their performance of possession symptoms. The narrative ably demonstrates the extent to which the Throckmorton girls managed to wrest control of daily life from those whose solemn charge it was to maintain order. This upheaval was what made possession cases so compelling and, ultimately, so ominous. For example, by noting that "above all things Elizabeth delighteth in play; she will pick out some one body to play with her at cards, and but one only, not hearing, seeing, or speaking to any other; but being awake she remembereth nothing,"[40] an author demonstrated how the girl's fits enabled her to shrug off the tedious responsibilities of a godly life without having to accept the responsibility for having done so.[41] While their chores were rarely mentioned in the text, it is certain that the normal household routine was significantly interrupted by the girls' and servants' affliction. It made theological sense that the afflicted girls shunned prayer and thrived during frivolous activities, as the Devil would as a matter of course encourage the opposite of godly behavior. Such lapses represented the sins of temptation, and adults interpreted these symptoms as proof of Satan's ability to exploit natural weaknesses. When Elizabeth was asked to read, and faltered, she received correction from someone nearby. But the authors noted that "she could not hear any that corrected her, though he had spoken never so loud, yet if he had pointed to the place with his finger, or given some other sign, she would have gone back and read over the place again, sometimes reading it true, sometimes not."[42] Elizabeth's possession symptoms allowed her to rebuff the correction of her elders and superiors without consequences, and although the girls did not become possessed simply in order to rebel, the more dramatic the resistance the greater the likelihood that observers would interpret it as originating in the preternatural realm. The witchcraft-possession script made this subversion possible, even as it remained flexible enough to encompass the girls' innovations and the observers' interpretations.

While the demoniacs' challenges to hierarchies of gender and authority took center stage, accused witches faced similar struggles over the meanings of their embodiment and the implications of those meanings for their culpability. Two instances particularly reveal these tensions. The first was the scratching experiment, which ascribed to female bodies the power both to disrupt proper hierarchical relations and to provide the evidence needed to restore them.[43] The second, which especially highlighted the centrality of gendered power, was the struggle between men over the compliance of Mother Alice Samuel. The outbreak of witchcraft-possession in Warboys disrupted customary expectations of gender and hierarchy in a variety of ways, not least of which was the unsettling potential for female bodies to serve as both passive and active manifestations of bewitchment. The scratching experiment conducted on the bodies of the accused, and the competing demands for the presence and obedience of the Samuel women, starkly revealed the ambivalent centrality granted to women by the circumstances. In both instances, John Samuel's access to the prerogatives of manhood—however circumscribed—interrupted the proceedings. The Warboys narrative reveals the extent to which the gendered meanings of the bodies of the accused were profoundly implicated in competing claims to power.

The alternatively curious and sickening ritual of scratching is especially revealing because of the way it juxtaposed, and made mutually dependent, the innocent bodies of the girls with the devilish bodies of the accused. Like burning the hair of a suspected witch, scratching to draw blood, usually from the face or hands, was believed to limit his or her power to harm.[44] Ostensibly used to relieve the symptoms of the afflicted, in Warboys the scratching tests carried out in the spring of 1593 became a way for the girls to reinforce belief in the Samuels' guilt. Laura Gowing has explained that "women's touch was one of the controlling mechanisms of early modern society, and one of the most intimate instruments of patriarchal regulation,"[45] something amply demonstrated by the importance of touch in witchcraft-possession cases. When groups of mature women searched the bodies of accused witches, and when demoniacs responded selectively to the touch of observers and those they accused, both the act of contact and its broader cultural resonances worked to transform suspects into confirmed enemies. The scratching tests highlighted the ambivalent powers of female bodies both to operate beyond the purview of patriarchal interests—beyond, even, the realm of the natural—and also to draw authority from and ultimately reinforce those interests. As with the coerced oaths, this experiment was first tried successfully with Mother Samuel, and once her fate was sealed, the girls turned their attention to Agnes. Joan first expressed desire to scratch Agnes in a conversation with the spirit Smacke, saying, "You have told me many times that I should scratch Agnes Samuel, tell me now, when shall I scratch her?"[46] Before long the spirits' suggestions transformed into commands, which highlighted the girls' maneuvering for power while denying agency and responsibility. To gain an advantage over the accused, the girls had to get within close range and lay hands upon the bodies of those they perceived as their torturers.

Joan introduced the need to scratch, but it was Mary, now nearly fifteen years old, who took up the charge by attacking Agnes so vehemently that she shocked onlookers. Agnes wept as Mary dragged her nails across her face but did not move away, prompting Mary to say, "I know you cry, but the spirit said that I should not hear you, because I should not pity you." After removing a shilling-sized piece of flesh from Agnes's face, Mary excused herself by reporting that she would not have done it except the spirit "told me that I should do it, and forced me thereunto."[47] The girls continued to express their unwillingness to harm Agnes even as they escalated their violence against her, and the authors emphasized this conflict as a sign that their actions were prompted by their afflicting spirits and not their own malice. When Elizabeth, now fourteen, followed suit, she said to Agnes:

> O thou young Witch, fie upon thee . . . who ever heard of a young Witch before? and thus she cried with such vehemence of speech, and eagerness of scratching, so that both her strength and breath failed her. When she had breathed a while she fell upon her again, and said that this was her sister Joan's devil . . . that made her to scratch her, for said she, I would not have scratched you, and it was full evil against my will to do it, but the devil maketh me to scratch you, stretching out my arms, and bending my fingers, otherwise I would not do it.[48]

In addition to revealing the degree of cruelty that witchcraft-possession cases made possible, the ritual enabled the girls to lead observing elites inexorably toward their desired conclusion. That the spirits supposedly named Mother Samuel, and later Agnes, as their "mistress" bolstered the allegations and set an unavoidable trap for the accused. Joan and Elizabeth, under the watchful eyes of Henry Cromwell and supporters, staged an astonishing scratching performance with Agnes in which they merged their reluctance and eagerness to scratch. They seethed with fury at Agnes just moments before kneeling beside her to pray and exhort her to renounce her evil ways.[49] They demanded that the adults present them with the maid's hands, drew copious amounts of blood, and then made a production out of washing, cutting, and burning their nails as a precautionary measure. In essence, they ran rampant as Agnes, sidelined by the narrator but unforgettably at the center of the madness, simply wept and begged for mercy.[50]

Jane Throckmorton instigated an additional scratching experiment with Agnes that reinforced her sisters' claims and made some new ones as well. At first Agnes backed away from Jane's advancing fingers,

> but the child followed still upon her knees, saying to her, that [it was] as good to take it now, as at another time, for she must fetch blood on her, and she must have her pennyworths of her, saying farther, that she knew that [Agnes] did now cry, (which indeed she did) but she could not hear her (for so much the spirit told her

before) because she should not pity her, when the child was weary and windless she left scratching, and wiped that little blood and water together, which came from [Agnes's] hand upon her own hands.[51]

This gruesome image helps to reveal the complex psychological realm inhabited by the afflicted girls, particularly in Jane's assertion that she must not feel pity for the woman she assaulted. Instead, she articulated a sense of entitlement to Agnes's flesh and blood that was buoyed by the adults' acceptance of the authority of the spirits' voices. Mother Alice's confessions may have spared her further tests, but Agnes remained to be broken. Although Agnes never did confess, one can only imagine the trauma of these events, held as they were in front of the community that every day became more confident in her guilt. In Warboys, the bodies of the accused were sites of power and weakness, of malice and vulnerability. The basis for the efficacy of the scratching test resided in the truths held and revealed by the women's bodies. Because the girls' response to the witches' blood was presumed to be natural, their bodies served as anchors for their increasingly conclusive claims of resistance to devilish malice.

Even after the scratching, oaths, confessions, and executions, the dead bodies of the accused women continued to prove their guilt. Lest the reader fear the possibility of a wrongful conviction, the writers described the way that Mother Samuel's body irrefutably told its own story. Directly after the Samuel family was hanged, the jailer and his wife stripped their dead bodies and found on Alice Samuel "a little lump of flesh, in manner sticking out as if it had been a teat, to the length of half an inch." They declined at first to make their discovery known, "because it was adjoining so secret a place, which was not decent to be seen: yet in the end, not willing to conceal so strange a matter, and decently covering that privie place a little above which it grew, they made open show thereof unto divers that stood by."[52] The spectacle of Mother Samuel's body, marked as it was by devilish influence, provided witnesses, judges, and readers with assurance that her guilt—and by extension that of her family—was unquestionable. The presence of an apparent teat on which familiar spirits were believed to suck, and its location near her genitals, suggests the sexual component of witchcraft-possession infrequently seen in English cases.[53] In addition, by stripping and displaying the bodies the jailer and his wife achieved more than a confirmation of guilt. The Samuels' exposure also dehumanized the corpses and emphasized for viewers that they were no longer afforded the dignities of proper folk. Having been proved witches and murderers, the community could now perceive their expulsion in material as well as spiritual terms.

If the scratching experiments revealed the interconnectedness of bodies and preternatural power, struggles between John Samuel and Robert Throckmorton over Mother Alice Samuel demonstrated that witchcraft-possession cases hinged upon who held power over bodies. Under normal circumstances the person with the most immediate authority over Alice Samuel was her husband, to whom she owed certain deference. However, the Warboys narrative suggested that John Samuel might have overstepped the bounds of proper manhood by treating his wife too violently. It was a husband's right to physically reprimand an unruly wife, so long as the abuse was neither so frequent nor brutal that it came to be viewed as excessive and destructive to the community.[54] Because access to lived power was not so simple as legal and patriarchal custom dictated, the Samuels' conflicts both reflected and contradicted hegemonic prescriptions about the allocation of power among men and women.[55] The Samuels' marital relationship, invisible to the historical record until the witchcraft accusations, was additionally compromised as outsiders became increasingly invested in observing and judging their behavior.

Throughout the text the authors cited both threatened and actual violence committed by John against Alice Samuel. When a group of Cambridge scholars visited the Throckmortons, for example, they sought out Alice Samuel for interrogation. Finding her away from home, they "determined rather to follow her whither she went, than stay her return, because her husband was a froward man, and would not suffer her to talk with any, if he might know it." She begged them to let her return home, saying that "her husband would beat her for long tarrying."[56] Later, when Alice Samuel confessed, her husband gave "her a foul term—and with that would have striken her, had not others stood betwixt them."[57] When John Samuel discovered that his wife had disobeyed his order not to go to the Throckmortons', he "utterly forswore the matter, and presently fell upon his wife and beat her very sore with a cudgel—many being present—before she could be rescued by them."[58] It was a bitter irony that in this instance her accusers and others committed to her conviction served as her protectors, since she threw her lot in with those whose pious intentions resulted in her execution. In other circumstances, Alice Samuel might have expected some intervention if her husband's violence was perceived as excessive. Her characterization as a witch, though, and the case's inexorable progress toward her conviction, diminished her claim to assistance.

The Cambridge scholars pursued Alice Samuel in the street and insisted upon speaking with her about the case despite her clear desire to evade them and their knowledge that her husband might punish her for doing so. There was little she could do to defy them, given the circumstances of the case and their entitlement, as elite men, to her attention. Unfortunately, her attempts to assert herself and resist her own unmaking only increased her resemblance to a witch. The narrator, likely the girls' uncle Henry Pickering, complained that "she was very loud in her answers, and impatient, not suffering any to speak but her self: one of them desired her to keep the woman's virtue, and be more silent: she answered, that she was borne in a mill, begot in a [kiln], she must have her will, she could speak no softlier." While this defiant speech might have helped Alice Samuel to resist her interrogators in the moment, it only cemented their certainty that she was a lewd and disorderly woman, quite like the sort who might be tempted to use preternatural forces to harm. Furthermore, the narrator reported that she railed against Robert Throckmorton and his children, saying "that he did misuse her, in suffering his children so to play the wantons in accusing of her, & bringing her name into question," and that "the children's fits was nothing but wantonness in them, & if they were her children, she would not suffer them to escape without punishment one after the other."[59] Both constructions of Mother Samuel, as abused victim of her husband or as a malevolent witch, were refracted through gendered expectations. If she had been able to withstand the temptation to defend herself rudely and vent her resentment at the Throckmortons' treatment of her, she might have more convincingly resembled a woman with a rough husband, and a woman to be pitied. But no matter how successfully she might have performed piety and submission, the existence of the witchcraft charge—given its association with wickedness and malice—undermined her claims for sympathy and protection.

Mother Alice Samuel was neither simply a victim nor an agent, and her uncertain position shifted throughout the narrative. Clearly, her husband, the Throckmorton children, and the community at large victimized her, and her eventual confession and execution demonstrated the extent of her tragedy. Nevertheless, the witchcraft-possession framework allowed her fleeting moments of self-assertion, and her volatility granted her what little opportunity she had for self-preservation. The beatings she endured suddenly captured the attention of observers who intervened despite their suspicion that she had harmed several children with demonic powers and bewitched a woman to death. None of the bystanders seems to have questioned why a woman with access to the powers of Hell would allow herself to be abused by her husband, though if they believed John was a witch as well, his violence would not have seemed incongruous. Mother Samuel may not have been able truly to assert her own will in the case, but by alternating her allegiance between her husband and Master Throckmorton, she kept both men uncertain about the implications of her downfall for them.

Though Alice's confessions sealed her fate, the timing of her admissions, retractions, and reaffirmations suggested a desire to protect her daughter that overrode her obligations to either her husband or Throckmorton. There is too little evidence of Mother Samuel's inner life in the narrative to know her motivations with any certainty, especially given the authors' emphasis on her inconsistent testimony. However, the arc of her confessions begs the question of whether or not they were her last attempts to assert control over the proceedings for Agnes's sake. When Mother Samuel returned home after her first confession, her husband and daughter convinced her to retract it. The narrator recorded Master Throckmorton as saying to Alice Samuel, "I will not let pass this matter thus, for seeing it is published, either you or I will bear the shame of it in the end."[60] When Throckmorton found that she still refused to confess the next morning, he took her by the hand and let her know that his suspicions now extended to her daughter, Agnes. He declared that both Alice and Agnes must go with him to the bishop, and he sent for the constables and charged them to transport both women: "When the old woman perceived preparation for the journey, and the Constables in a readiness, Master Throckmorton also putting on of his boots, she came to him and said, Master if you will go with me into the parlor, I will confess all to you alone."[61] Alice Samuel's submission likely stemmed from a desire to prevent her daughter's transport to the jail, and she may have thought a full confession would distance her daughter from the taint of the case. After her confession was overheard by some neighbors who hid out of view, Throckmorton "caused the old Woman with her daughter to be carried the same day to my Lord, the Bishop of Lincoln, and there he examined her with her daughter."[62] In this instance, Alice's efforts to exert her will within the confines of the case proved futile. Much as in the instances of abuse by her husband, Alice Samuel both exploited and was exploited by those who oversaw the case. In her willful moments she redirected procedure and resisted the control of others, even though her actions played into her enemies' hands. Throckmorton's success depended on his ability to convince Mother Samuel not to act as a proper wife, which the authors then took as a sign of her degradation. As the case progressed, the role of gendered power remained central, not despite its perennially shifting and inconsistent operation but because that flexibility provided useful tools to all competing parties.

Once Alice Samuel accepted the role of witch and admitted in her final confessions that she used preternatural powers to harm, she gained the community's supportive attention. These last compromises, though they made her easier to execute, provided her with a psychological alternative to utter powerlessness—especially after it became clear that she could neither escape conviction nor save her daughter. Having a claim to the Devil's power may have proved more attractive than admitting to having so little of her own. So while Mother Samuel's fate ultimately reinforced patriarchal views of women and witchcraft, her attempts to alter her relations with those in power, selectively internalize the charges against her, and participate in judicial matters demonstrate how even the victims of witchcraft-possession cases could assert themselves. In addition, Alice Samuel's choices held great implications for her husband because however much he resisted the content of the witchcraft-possession script, his standing as a successful head of household rested on his ability to maintain a dominant position in relation to his family and dependents. The Warboys case pitted John Samuel, who was already seen as disorderly, against Robert Throckmorton—a wealthier, well-connected, and powerful man. The contest for her submission was played out between the two men as a contest of manly prerogative, and her refusal to obey her husband helped secure Throckmorton's victory. The authors' treatment of these conflicts demonstrated that witchcraft-possession conventions contained inherent challenges to gender and authority, and that the actors' ability to prevail on these terms could shape the outcome.

Struggles for dominance in Warboys, as seen in the scratching tests and the contest for mastery over Alice Samuel, were inextricable from the wider cultural investment in gendered power that was typical of early modern witchcraft-possession. Female bodies, in themselves exemplars of and justifications for female subordination, represented weakness and permeability to preternatural influence. Yet these same bodies could also contain enormous power, even in the clippings of hair and nails. From the contortions of the possessed to the power of blood to halt them, the Warboys case was a battle largely played out by female sufferers against other female sufferers.[63] Because of the ways they blurred the boundaries between weakness and power, witchcraft-possession conventions created an ambiguous social terrain that compelled men as well as women, and accusers as well as accused, to contend with and contest gendered power. Thus the eradication of witches, who had been unmade as proper women or men, ultimately allowed communities to recommit themselves to customary hierarchical relations. The elimination of male witches, especially those related to primary female suspects, turned on related questions and allowed for the same catharsis.

John Samuel: Manhood in Warboys

The construction of a witch was a complex undertaking, and those who suspected that the Samuels had caused the girls' possession symptoms relied upon more than bodies and speech for evidence. As we have seen, the Samuels' relations with the Throckmortons, Cromwells, and wider community greatly influenced their evolution as likely witches. However, the published narrative also demonstrated the extent to which the Samuels' internal family dynamics contributed to their unmaking. Even though John Samuel had to be forced to comply with the rituals that confirmed his depravity, the authors presented his failure to maintain patriarchal mastery of himself and his dependents as suggestive of his guilt. As the case ran its course, his inability to maintain order in his household pitted individual family members against each other, to the detriment of them all. John Samuel became plausible as a witch in part because he could not provide an alternate account for himself—as a head of household, husband, or father—powerful enough to counter the Throckmortons' charges.

If Mother Alice Samuel most closely fit the traditional witch image, Agnes was the lynchpin that linked her mother's guilt to her father's. The authors of the narrative, as if they felt more was needed to convince the reader, described Agnes's scratching and oath-making tests more comprehensively than her mother's. Agnes was even compelled to state their connection explicitly in terms of their shared guilt: "I am a witch and a worse witch than my mother." John Samuel was a still more difficult case; he was both everywhere and nowhere in the text. For example, he was the first to be mentioned in the title, which promised "Witchcraft, practiced by John Samuel the Father, Alice Samuel the Mother, and Agnes Samuel their Daughter" and the "notable arraignment and examination of Samuel, his wife, and daughter."[64] His status as head of the household likely explained his primary position in these lists rather than the perception that he was the principal witch of the family. At other times he disappeared behind his female relatives, a condition replicated in accounts like John Stearne's 1648 treatise about the preponderance of women among malefic witches. Stearne consigned John to a supporting role, explaining that "those of Warboyes were women, and but one man."[65] The narrative demonstrates that John came to resemble a witch alongside his wife and daughter, but only after negotiating a different set of expectations and interactions. His viability as head of household, along with the questionable nature of his control over his wife and daughter, remained open questions in the text. The authors' attention to the discrepancies between John Samuel's behavior and ideals of proper manhood demonstrate how such shortcomings contributed to the apparent guilt of men accused of witchcraft.

The process of transforming men and women into witches involved gauging the extent to which their disorderly behavior compromised their potential claims to proper manhood or womanhood. Despite the enduring link between witchcraft and women, John did not need to be feminized in order to resemble a witch. Instead, the narrative highlighted his gendered failings—both deficiencies and excesses—as a man. Even more than in the case of his wife, John was characterized as disorderly and depraved, though his faults primarily came across as aggression and reluctance to give due deference. The pamphlet stated that John Samuel "spoke bluntly (as his manner was)" and "was rude in his behavior and . . . lowed in his speeches."[66] Keith Thomas and Alan Macfarlane have argued that suspected witches were often abrasive types, and E. J. Kent has outlined the ways that the disorder of accused men, though distinct from those of accused women, contributed to their apparent guilt.[67] The behavior of the accused was surely relevant in witchcraft accusations, especially as it had the potential to mark some individuals out as excessively destructive to the community peace. But with so many cantankerous villagers to choose from, it is clear that other factors needed to emerge for witchcraft suspicion to persist.

While a man's disorderliness and litigiousness could contribute to his undoing, the established view of what constituted a man's unruly speech was less evident than a woman's. The image of the female scold, for example, had a long association with witchcraft, while its male counterpart—the barrator—had less cultural resonance.[68] As a result, it is difficult to gauge at what point John Samuel's troublesome speech may have come to resemble a witch's malice. Despite the conflicts and censures he had received, his peers nonetheless would have expected him to defend the viability of his own household. One of the first major threats to this viability came when Robert Throckmorton brought his afflicted children to the Samuels' home, hoping to convince John to hand over his wife, whose presence relieved the girls' fits. When John Samuel resisted, Throckmorton "offered very largely for it; which was to allow him (if it came to ten pounds in the year) for the board and wages of the best servant in Huntingdonshire to do his business, if he would, in her stead, besides his promise and bond, if he would require it, for the well using of his wife while she was with him: he could find no other remedy for the health of his children but to carry them thither, which he did, who as soon as they came into the house were all presently well."[69] Given the eventual outcome of the case, it seems incredible that Throckmorton initially sought John Samuel's permission to remove his wife from their home and made an offer that so explicitly denoted the value of a wife's labor. Such an affront, made possible by the conventions of witchcraft-possession and Throckmorton's higher social status, suggested Throckmorton had a superior claim to Alice Samuel than did Samuel himself. For these men, the case was waged not only at the girls' bedsides or in the courtroom but also in the front yard of Samuel's home. As a result of the community's sanction of Throckmorton's interference, Samuel stood to lose the right to expect his wife's presence and labor. The offer of money hardly disguised the fact that the effect of Alice's presence on the girls reinforced the charges against her, and that Throckmorton was offering not an amicable labor exchange, but a way to accelerate the dismantling of the Samuel family. These conditions were forced upon John Samuel, but he still paid the price for the ensuing compromise of his claim to one of the privileges of patriarchy.

In the aforementioned confrontation, Throckmorton, armed as he was with his five clear-eyed daughters, had the upper hand by being able to set the terms of the engagement. Nothing in the narrative suggested that he seriously considered the possibility that his daughters' suffering could have originated in divine judgment of himself rather than pre-ternatural malice by his neighbors, which bolstered his conviction that resolution would only come about through the Samuels' confession and prosecution. In actuality, he offered John Samuel a choice of disorders. First, Samuel could allow Throckmorton to remove his wife, thereby establishing Throckmorton's mastery of the situation and unmaking John in the ways central to the early modern definition of an adult man.[70] Alternatively, if John would not release his wife, then Throckmorton and his five girls would invade, which would similarly lend credence to the witchcraft charges and reinforce John's inability to police the boundaries of his household. In sum, either he would lose his real and symbolic power over his wife by its transfer to Robert Throckmorton, or that neighbor with his five fit-prone daughters would overrun his own home. Clearly Throckmorton was the one in the position to insist, as his daughters and the village undoubtedly knew.

In response, John Samuel expressed his resentment of their incursion by quenching the fire and "saying he would starve them, besides very many evil words, which came from him and his daughter at that time."[71] The narrators emphasized Samuel's insufficient piety and deference to aid their construction of him as a flawed and angry man. The language also reveals John's struggle to regain control of his household, which would have legitimated his family's standing, not as the Throckmortons' equals but at least as viable members of the community. Though he was not ultimately successful, his resistance represented an entitlement he held as a man, whose nature, body, and speech were not so easily associated with witchcraft. This discrepancy enabled him to resist his conviction and to remain consistently defiant throughout.

For example, John Samuel made it clear he did not believe the girls were genuinely possessed and took an offensive stance. When he came to the Throckmorton home to check on Agnes, Elizabeth Throckmorton logically extended to him the strategy that had served to implicate his family: she expressed her afflicting spirit's desperate desire to scratch him. But this time it was not so easy to complete the experiment. The author reports that while she crawled toward him, saying, "I must scratch him, I must scratch him, on the sudden she stopped, saying, I must not scratch him, look you here, and showed her hands how her fingers were shut up close together."[72] Faced with John Samuel's resistance, Elizabeth's determination faltered, but she continued to weep and exhort him, saying that "he was a naughty man, and a Witch, and but for him and his daughter, his wives soul might have been saved."[73] In addition to displacing responsibility for Mother Samuel's imminent execution, Elizabeth directed at John Samuel the aspects of the possession script that she could most feasibly apply. It was too intimidating to physically attack him as he glowered defiantly and insisted the possession was a fraud—something she could not countenance. Notably, he was not compelled by the onlookers to submit. Unlike Alice and Agnes, who helplessly withstood the tests, John could not be made to play his part.

John Samuel assertively claimed that Elizabeth and her sisters lied, and he strove to resist the conventions previously established by the observers and ministers. He even said, "she had been taught her lessons well enough," which suggested both a calculated fraud and a darker controlling presence working behind the scenes—not unlike Satan working through witches. Interestingly, the narrator added that Samuel "would not be silent nor suffer the child to speak for anything until he was almost forced unto it by the child's father. Although [Samuel] might perceive very well . . . that the child could not hear him nor answer to any of his speeches, neither yet stayed her words at his talking in anything she intended to speak to him, although he greatly interrupted the same (if she could have heard him); but she neither heard him nor any other in the company, yet she saw him and his daughter and not any other."[74] The passage reveals how extensively the script had been developed before John Samuel entered the Throckmortons' house. As a result, his refusal to accept the rules of engagement as they had been established appeared jarring to the narrators and readers. The discrepancy between his reaction and his wife's might be explained in part by the different position he held as a man in his relations with the authorities. Because there was less convergence between his appearance and behavior and the witch image, he could more easily afford to act aggressively in the Throckmorton house. There are ways that such behavior could have been interpreted as a representation of his innocence, whereas his wife's aggressive speech only hastened observers' certainty of her guilt.[75]

Just as contradictory gender expectations interrupted observers' perceptions of John Samuel's scratching test, his oath tests also operated differently than they had for Alice and Agnes. Robert Throckmorton, ever-mindful that prosecution would require successful demonstrations in front of witnesses, told Samuel that Agnes had succeeded in commanding the spirits to depart from his children and demanded that he do the same. But John "said he would not, neither should any make him to speak them, and he would not be brought to it for any thing." Throckmorton countered by saying that for as long as Elizabeth continued in her fit, Samuel would not be permitted to leave the house, even if it should take a week. In an attempt to persuade him to follow suit, various onlookers repeated the oath "until in the end [Samuel] perceived that Master Throckmorton was resolute, not to suffer him to depart until he had spoken them, then he began to speak. . . . [T]he man had no sooner spoken the words, but the child presently arose, and was very well."[76] In the face of demands from Master Throckmorton, the minister, and esteemed neighbors, Samuel was ultimately coerced into his de facto confession, which gave Throckmorton what he needed. Unlike Alice and

Agnes, however, John's coercion sprang not from the girls' prayers and exhortation but from direct orders from superiors in the eyes of the community at large. For all of his rights as a man and force of personality, John Samuel was compelled to participate in a ritual he believed to be false and a trap. Even though John remained the most consistently recalcitrant of all the Samuels, Throckmorton must have realized at this point that he had won.

Rather than let the viability of the oath test stand alone, the girls helpfully provided corroboration from the spirit world. One of Joan's spirits reported not only that John Samuel was a witch but that he would be "worse than either this young Witch is, or the old witch her mother was, when they two are hanged, for then all the spirits will come to him, and he will do more hurt then any have yet done." The spirit added that Samuel had "already bewitched a man and a woman, and to prove this, if the young witch [Agnes] shall charge the devil to depart from you [Joan] at this present, [saying] even as her father hath bewitched two parties, you shall be presently well: so [Agnes] Samuel did, and Mistress Joan was well."[77] Here again, the girls relied on the oath of one Samuel to implicate another and emphasized that the ones who least resembled a witch were in fact the most evil. They used Agnes against her own father in a way that provided an interesting counterpart to the choice she had been granted earlier: either confess or implicate your father. Her compliance thus constituted a further failure of John Samuel's dominance over his family, since he was undercut in this situation not only by his wife, who confessed despite the fact that he forbade it, but also by his own child, over whom he ought to have had authority. John Samuel was truly undone at this point as a head of household.[78] In the eyes of his accusers, the narrator, and early modern readers, all that remained was the formality of securing official recognition of the experiments' significance.

Once they were all gathered in the court, Judge Fenner summoned John Samuel from among the other prisoners and had him stand in front of Jane Throckmorton. The judge had been told about the oath tests, and he first asked Samuel if he believed that he could by any means cause Jane to come out of her fit, which he denied. The judge then told Samuel that he had been informed of a "charm made of certain words," and that if he spoke them the child would be well. Samuel, however, "refused the same and said, I will not speak them. The Judge persuaded him, and entreated him, insomuch that the said Judge, the rather to encourage the said Samuel, spake himself openly the charm, so did also master Doctor Dorrington, and others then present . . . yet he refused."[79] Even as the case progressed in this favorable direction, the girls continually reinforced the proceedings with their fits and proclamations. After many prayers the judge willed John Samuel to pray to God for the child's comfort, but whenever he invoked the name of God or Christ, the children's heads, shoulders, and arms shook violently. Through each of these developments the girls further embellished their claims and convinced the authorities of Samuel's guilt.

In what must have been the final blow to John Samuel's hopes, the judge told him

> that if he would not speak the words of the charm, the court would hold him guilty of the crimes whereof he was accused: and so at length, with much ado, the said Samuel (with a loud voice) said in the hearing of all that were present: As I am a Witch, and did consent to the death of Lady Cromwell, so I charge the devil to suffer Mistress Jane to come out of her fit at this present. Which words, being no sooner spoken by the old Witch, but the said mistress Jane . . . wiped her eyes, and came out of her fit: and then seeing her father, kneeled down, and asked him blessing, and made reverence to her uncles that stood near her . . . and wondering said: O Lord, father where am I?[80]

Once Samuel learned that he would be found guilty whether he spoke the oath or not, he relented in a loud tone, perhaps to maintain his dignity despite his capitulation. In addition to legitimating the court's methods, the narrative's dramatic culmination completed Jane's transformation from one who relayed the words of devils to one who offered reverence to her godly father and uncles. Perhaps this appropriately submissive offering served as a kind of atonement not only for her previously outrageous behavior but also for the way she and her sisters had so masterfully dismantled the deference John Samuel might have expected of his own wife and daughter. Jane's restoration to proper patriarchal order required not only the Samuel family's destruction but also her transition from one who directed action with her speech to one who awaited instruction.

The conclusion, much like the narrative overall, placed the most emphasis upon Mother Alice Samuel's confessions. After all, her surrender was the strongest proof the Throckmortons had, and her willingness to implicate herself and her husband—if not her daughter—was crucial to the case. Interestingly, John Samuel's submission to the oath test, which had been the focus of a most determined campaign, did not have pride of place at the end of the narrative. As husband and father to witches, he could have figured as a kind of master and director of their malice, second only to the Devil, whose work ultimately lay behind their downfall. Instead, as if sensing John Samuel's imperfect resemblance to the witch image, the writers wove him into the narrative but never let the readers' attention rest with him for long.

Even as they worked to overcome the tacit disjuncture between their evidence and the overwhelming cultural association of witchcraft with women, John Samuel's particular voice emerged disconcertingly from within the confines of a narrative dedicated to the certainty of his guilt. The series of jarring discontinuities in his part of the narrative reminded the reader that even some with reasons to support a society based on patriarchal premises, and some who tangibly benefited from that system, could come to represent the ultimate disorder. After all, his guilt represented something other than the traditional image of the usurpation of power by a discontented woman, or even the customary belief that men could be witches; it demonstrated that witchcraft-possession conventions had allowed one granted a degree of patriarchal rights and responsibilities to be undermined by the rebellion of his wife and surrender of his daughter. Thus the writers unmade him as a man not only to justify his death but also to reassure the reader that John Samuel deserved to be discarded, rather than the system that arranged familial power as it did. Once that had been accomplished, his guilt, and hence the legitimacy of his trial and execution, were assured.

A Family Unmade

Over the course of the Warboys episode, one family was destroyed and another indelibly transformed by the onset and progression of witchcraft-possession phenomena. Although no one case exemplifies all the ways that witchcraft-possession operated in early modern England, this one reflected and codified several key aspects of the traditional script. Its notoriety assured that it remained largely uncontested even as the social climate for such cases grew less receptive. *Witches of Warboys* even became the basis for a ballad, now lost to the record but recorded in the Stationers' Register. Some later publications made offhanded references to the Warboys case, as if it were unnecessary to outline the specifics of something so commonly known, or placed it alongside similar cases to lend credence to those that resembled it.[81] Because it was so well known and factored in future possession cases, its reflection of the gendered assumptions that governed interactions among the accusers, the accused, and those who interpreted their performances influenced wider thinking far beyond Warboys.

Witchcraft-possession cases provided opportunities for the disruption of a wide range of social norms, and their grounding in hierarchies of gender and age was particularly striking. While these cases allowed communities to rally around common values, externalize transgressions, and ultimately reinforce traditional patriarchal standards, they also retained latent disorder. Individuals in low social positions could vault to positions of great influence at these moments, however ambivalent or self-defeating that influence might prove to be. At the end of *Witches of Warboys,* the authors inadvertently reminded the reader of the danger that John Samuel's downfall represented. When Samuel heard the judge pronounce the indictments, he said "to his wife, in the hearing of many: A plague of God light upon thee, for thou art she that hath brought us all to this, and we may thank thee for it."[82] His claim was all the more threatening for its truth; Alice Samuel's capitulation to the demands of her captors facilitated her husband's accusation and conviction. Despite her subordinate position, he was unable to control her confessions and complicity in the experiments. She implicated him as a witch in his own right even as she sought to preserve her daughter from the same judgment. Whether this demonstrated the consequences of women's subversive power or the potential for witchcraft-possession conventions to encourage female subversion even as they repressed it, both possibilities threatened instability and lay dormant in the text.

On the morning of the executions, John Samuel gave voice to his resentment in a final moment of retribution. When godly men visited the family in prison to exhort them to confess and repent, they likely sought not only hope for the Samuels' souls but also the ultimate justification for their imminent executions. The narrator recorded that when one asked Mother Alice Samuel if she had bewitched Lady Cromwell, she denied it. But then "her husband old father Samuel, standing behind, and hearing her deny the same, said, deny it not, but confess the truth: for thou didst it one way or other."[83] Perhaps the long, oppressive ordeal had finally convinced him that his wife was in fact a witch, or at least that she had somehow harmed the girls. It is more likely that his statement conveyed resentment toward his wife and frustration with the futility of his resistance. His accusation might also have referred to the way that her concession to the Throckmortons' demands had bolstered the case against them. However filtered by the authors, John Samuel's final statement blamed his wife for their defeat and expressed resentment of his own inability to better leverage his potential authority.

The unmaking of John Samuel as a man and head of household was central to the process of differentiating him from his neighbors and sealing his fate within the confines of the witchcraft-possession script. And although he charted a different path than his wife or daughter, all three of them came to resemble a witch through a process that centered on gendered views of their bodies, comportment, and power. John did not cease to be a man, or appear as a feminized man, but he was undone as a proper man because he exhibited excessive hostility further undercut by inadequate mastery. By stripping him of the prerogatives of manhood, his adversaries transformed his destruction into a way to reinscribe patriarchy's priorities; the successful conclusion of the case reinforced the authority of the Throckmorton family, their elite neighbors, the magistrates who pronounced judgment in 1593, and the ministers who reiterated that judgment in yearly sermons thereafter. On the other hand, the narrative's account of a respectable family's victory against wickedness nonetheless left the implicit question of patriarchy's vulnerability in the context of possession unresolved. As a whole, the published narrative reveals how questions of power, patriarchy, and claims to legitimate authority operated through the prosecution of witches of both sexes. Even in a phenomenon overwhelmingly associated with womanhood, manhood and its particular claims to power were wielded—if unevenly—by people struggling to control the events' essential meaning.

3 / Disputing Possession in England: Samuel Harsnett versus John Darrell

In London in 1603, Samuel Harsnett—chaplain to the Anglican bishop Richard Bancroft—published a long diatribe against Catholic priests and Puritan ministers who claimed to have cured people who were possessed by the Devil.[1] Despite the fact that godly Puritans dispossessed the afflicted through prayer and fasting rather than by the Catholic rite of exorcism, Harsnett saw both groups as fraudulent, disruptive, and dangerous. Harsnett further dismissed both sorts of participants as a "route, rabble, and swarm of giddy, idle, lunatic, illuminate holy spectators of both sexes, but especially a Sisternity of mimps, mops, and idle holy women, that shall grace . . . the devil, with their idle holy presence."[2] Harsnett's book was ostensibly aimed at Catholic priests who had performed an infamous series of exorcisms back in 1586, but his principal target was actually John Darrell, a Puritan minister against whom he had been writing since 1599. At that time, in response to pamphlets published on Darrell's behalf, Harsnett had reported that it was through public dispossessions that Darrell "hath won his spurs in the opinion of many, especially women." Furthermore, he wrote that those who published in Darrell's defense were "children indeed: to what ripeness in railing think you they will grow, by the time they be men?"[3] Harsnett further claimed that those who supported Darrell's "juggling" did so in order to pursue a factional "Presbyterian" agenda: "It were to be wished, that at the last they would leave this giddiness, or . . . think more reverently of those that be in authority."[4] When Darrell sought to defend himself, he countered that any who believed Harsnett's charges were like "Italian women" and the "credulous popularity" in France who accepted their priests' descriptions of Protestants as monsters, "whereupon the poor women and silly multitude, never . . . examining the matter any farther, fell straight to a kind of hissing & clapping their hands, with most bitter out cries and hateful exclamations against them."[5] Throughout the pamphlet war waged from 1599 to 1603, Harsnett, Darrell, and their supporters used gendered language to bolster their arguments about the validity of demonic possession in a postapostolic age and the legitimacy of those who presumed to remove the Devil, or devils, from the bodies of those who acted as if they were possessed.[6] Over the course of the debate—which consisted of fifteen publications—questions about the nature of the Devil commingled with questions about the authors, and about the extent to which either side exhibited qualities that revealed them to be more like women, youths, or Catholics than honorable Protestant men. In this way, gender was an essential tool in the debate as the authors' invocations of manhood contributed to explicit arguments about the implications demonic possession cases held for religious authority and legitimacy.

Early seventeenth-century challenges to demonic possession were possible in England partly because of initial uncertainty about King James's opinion of bewitchment, and partly because Richard Bancroft and Samuel Harsnett had the support of the anti-Puritan archbishop of Canterbury, John Whitgift (until his death in 1604, after which Bancroft took his place).[7] The political and religious context for possession, though, had been set long before. The traditional possession script had a series of classical, biblical, and European precedents that varied over time but maintained considerable continuity in popular belief. The Devil was believed to prey upon people's weaknesses and to tempt them into sin and damnation, and townsfolk recognized a potential demoniac by his or her symptoms—such as the aforementioned convulsions, demonic utterances, and spectral appearances.[8] Historians have rightly focused on the ways that the controversy over Darrell's dispossessions was an outgrowth of struggles for political and religious dominance between the Church of England and godly Protestants who found the official church's policies too popish for comfort.[9] While debating the validity of demonic and witchcraft-possession phenomena, participants in the controversy not only forwarded their religious and political aims but also worked to persuade readers that their opponents, wittingly or unwittingly, had failed to discern and respond appropriately to the manifestation of evil in society. It was in these failings, and in each side's defenses against such charges, that gendered language and strategies were most evident.

The roots of the controversy over Darrell's involvement with possession cases in 1599 can be traced to Darrell's first case in 1586, when he was only twenty-two years old. At that time he helped dispossess one Katherine Wright, aged around seventeen, whose severe fits had raised the concerns of her family and Derbyshire neighbors. Darrell went on to gain something of a reputation for his successful treatment of demoniacs. In 1596, he and fellow minister George More traveled to Lancashire to aid the seven possessed members of the Starkie household. Mr. Starkie had relied on a cunning man, Edmund Hartley, who treated the children for a few years before he himself became the focus of their accusations of bewitchment and was executed. Later in 1596, Darrell was called to perform another dispossession in Burton-on-Trent. This time the sufferer was Thomas Darling, age thirteen, whose crisis of faith fueled an intense struggle with the Devil. The woman accused of bewitching Darling confessed, which lent the proceedings further credibility. In addition to leading prayers and fasts, Darrell exhorted the demoniacs, observers, and the communities at large. The news of these remarkable instances of God's triumph over the Devil spread and reinvigorated piety. More broadly, Darrell's success disproved Catholic claims that members of the Roman Church were the only ones to whom God granted this wondrous skill. In fact, Darrell's success suggested to some observers that God might favor the "hotter sort" of Protestants for their efforts—a message that frustrated and concerned officials in the Church of England.

Given these successes, and Darrell's certainty that God called him to this work, it is understandable why in 1597, at the behest of the mayor of Nottingham, he agreed to provide his assistance once again. At first, the Nottingham case proceeded much as the others had, but its aftermath proved disastrous for Darrell and his colleagues. The demoniac in question, William Somers, was a twenty-year-old musician's apprentice who was unsatisfied with his position. Like his predecessors, Somers's symptoms included dramatic fits and contortions that observers swore could only have been caused by preternatural means. Darrell managed, with the help of George More and godly neighbors, to dispossess Somers through prayer and fasting. Though Somers became repossessed shortly afterward, Darrell facilitated a final dispossession that left many of Nottingham's residents mindful of the fearful power of God. Unlike the other communities Darrell had served, some in Nottingham and—importantly—London did not allow this success to stand. The Commission of Ecclesiastical Causes in Lambeth convicted Darrell of fraud in 1599 and imprisoned him in Westminster. Darrell was eventually released without a license to preach, and although he appears to have been welcomed into godly circles, his work with demoniacs was over. The controversy, and the publications it produced, forever changed the climate for possession cases in early modern England by galvanizing the Church of England's response to what it perceived as an internal conspiracy against its authority.[10]

A key element of the debate over Somers's possession centered on Darrell's ability to discern the presence of the Devil in the youth, especially after the apprentice later claimed that the minister had coached him to fake his symptoms. Although this accusation allowed Harsnett to question Darrell's integrity as well as his judgment, it also allowed Darrell to assert that by erroneously dismissing what happened at Nottingham, Harsnett was "smothering the work of God."[11] Of the many extant pamphlets published between 1599 and 1603, this chapter focuses on the principal publications written by Harsnett and Darrell because of the way they forwarded the arguments and strategies that characterized the debate as a whole. After a few of Darrell's anonymous supporters defended him in illegally published pamphlets, Harsnett used biting sarcasm to articulate the official anti-Darrell position in *A discovery of the fraudulent practices of John Darrel* (1599).[12] Darrell pointedly entitled his response *A detection of that sinnful, shamful, lying, and ridiculous discours, of Samuel Harshnet. . . .* (1600), in which he inverted Harsnett's accusations in an attempt to convince the reader that the chaplain's abuses of power represented the greater threat to order. Later, in 1603, Harsnett's *A declaration of egregious popish impostures* forcefully reiterated the Anglican position.[13] Harsnett and Darrell both invoked gendered language in the debate—not simply as a reflection of the gendered nature of possession and witchcraft phenomena but in the very essence of their challenges to each other and to other men.

As opponents, John Darrell and Samuel Harsnett engaged in gendered contests of self-assertion that rested on their ability to align their cause with proper manhood and demonstrate the failure of their opponents to do the same. They expressed their respect for authority and denounced (feminized) disorder and vain self-interest. Their enemies, however, they depicted as inversions of honorable men; instead of deferring to appropriate authority, these men refused to accept the wisdom of their betters, were reckless in their emotions and actions, and eager to push themselves forward at the expense of others. These charges reveal more about the rhetorical construction of viable manhood than they tell us about "real" characteristics of the individuals involved, but neither should one read these texts as nothing more than scurrilous slander. In calculated propaganda about issues of profound importance, authors on both sides were deeply invested in defending the inherent legitimacy of their views in comparison to those of their opponents, which led them to align the other side with base interests. In the end, the men who conducted and championed accounts of dispossessions could come to share with accused witches a vulnerability to being unmade as proper women and men. Significantly, the sources demonstrate that even men of high status could be unmade on account of their participation in or defense of such cases. Thus the disorder of possession cases, which had customarily led to a reinscription of patriarchal order, could damage even men who could reasonably claim to represent and defend that order. John Darrell in particular became a casualty of the struggle with other, politically powerful men who sought to divest possession cases of their spiritual implications.

This chapter examines four central ways that Harsnett and Darrell articulated their positions and attacked those of their enemies; in each strategy, representations of viable and degraded manhood served as media for the authors' own claims of legitimacy. The first strategy was their effort to establish their credit at the expense of their opponents, whom they aligned with Catholics, atheists, and other disreputable forces. This sort of credit relied upon a man's relationships with other men, the common report of his character, and his ability to claim the traits of honorable manhood: independence, piety, and appropriate deference for authority. A second strategy consisted of the writers' attempts to represent their enemies as having a dearth of reason and surplus of passions revealed through emotional, linguistic, and humoral excess. While asserting their scriptural and manly authority, the writers distanced themselves from the unruly passions attributed to the bodies and temperament of women and youths. A third strategy, which Harsnett used to great effect, consisted of references to trade and occupation. By associating Darrell with "exorcists," "tinkers," and "peddlers," Harsnett compared him to enemies and nuisances viewed as potential threats. Because popular literature commonly ascribed crass motives to these tradesmen, Harsnett was able to mark Darrell and his supporters as similarly outside the community of respectable gentlemen. The fourth strategy involved the characterizations of one's enemies as a threat to social order, specifically as a result of having seduced subordinates away from their proper relationship to authority. Such accusations evoked a set of explicit and implied crimes nefarious enough to make them particularly inimical to honorable manhood. These four themes illuminate gender's intricate operation in early modern English possession propaganda, particularly in the ways it appeared and disappeared alongside sex, age, status, and reputation. As part of their larger project to forward their religious and political objectives, writers on both sides attempted to discredit the legitimacy of their opponents by attacking, in various ways, their manhood.

Manly Credit

The concept of "credit" was a crucial mechanism by which an early modern Englishman's relationship to his community was defined and evaluated. Craig Muldrew has investigated this "highly mobile and circulating language of judgement," which he calls the "currency of reputation."[14] He traces the social and cultural significance of credit to its origins in economic pressures. As more and more people failed to meet their debts, and litigation soared from 1580 to 1640, credit provided an important alternate way to determine the nature of one's relations with others. As a result, an individual's inclusion within a community was "increasingly defined in more negative and competitive moral terms."[15] Credit's social and economic meanings were inextricable from one another, and because "households were the basic economic unit, reputation had definite competitive economic implications, and this is why credit became synonymous with reputation." In possession cases—especially those that involved accusations of witchcraft—the same "competitive piety in which householders sought to construct and preserve their reputations for religious virtue, belief and honesty" that Muldrew describes could hold grave consequences for demoniacs, those they accused of witchcraft, and even the attending clergy.[16] Although Alexandra Shepard's analysis of court records reveals that men and women evaluated their worth by emphasizing material wealth more often than the model of competitive piety suggests,[17] authors of possession narratives strove to shore up both the moral and material foundations of their subjects' credit. Possession propaganda on the whole exhibited considerable strategic flexibility in these matters, as authors tailored their challenges or defenses to each case's participants and the immediate political climate.

A man gained honor and credit through piety, wisdom, and self-moderation. Even though not every man served as a household head, relations between masters and servants, and among neighbors and economic competitors, all reflected the legitimacy of a man's credit. As Elizabeth Foyster explains, men and women in the seventeenth century did not speak of "masculinity" or "femininity" when pressing suits in church courts. Rather, "honour, reputation, credit, or a good name could be the rewards for men and women who upheld the ideals of patriarchy." Foyster concludes that "learning how to achieve credit and avoid shame was essential in the process of becoming a man in early modern England."[18] In addition, Susan Amussen writes that credit's "equation of wealth and worth" served to clarify the boundaries of respectability, particularly for members of the "upper sorts."[19] Not all men had access to the same degree of "patriarchal notions of credit and worth," as Alexandra Shepard points out, especially for those men excluded from householding entirely.[20] But credit played a role in all sorts of possession cases because, as Marion Gibson and others have argued, controversies over Puritan dispossession held both symbolic and concrete implications for state-controlled religion, the autonomy of the localities, and the faith and allegiance of the people.[21] Legitimate religious governance, like viable manhood, rested on a foundation of rationality, self-control, respect for authority and moderation. Accordingly, in the pamphlet war between Harsnett and Darrell the players relied upon shared cultural expectations and gendered language to press their claims. At times this gendered language operated indirectly, through invocations of "gentlemen" or "ministers," roles so inextricably male that they merged connotations of gender with social status, piety, and honor broadly conceived. Though the writers did not place manhood per se at the center of their publications, their efforts to degrade or augment the reader's confidence in Darrell's reputation as a sober and godly man remained central throughout.

For both Darrell and Harsnett, manly credit was a foundation upon which to build their main arguments. In Harsnett's *A discovery of the fraudulent practices of John Darrel* (1599), for example, Harsnett did his best to depict Darrell as a self-promoting impostor who was wicked, degenerate, aligned with Papists, and an utter hypocrite. In his related effort to defend the commission's preferential treatment of young William Somers at Darrell's expense, Harsnett used a combination of insinuation and nice distinctions. Harsnett lacked any corroboration for Somers's most damning claim—that Darrell had worked with him to orchestrate a fraudulent possession—but he presented what he had as if it established the truth of the whole. Harsnett was a frequent and clever user of "it seemeth," "in all likelihood,"[22] and other phrases that hinted at the limits of his case against Darrell. Still, Harsnett's maneuvers provided a kind of justification for the elevation of Somers's word over Darrell's, however the commissioners' tactics diverged from conventional social and legal practices. Harsnett's main task was to contradict the protestations of the pro-Darrell camp that malicious officials had wrongfully targeted a godly minister who had powerful and respectable friends. Thus Harsnett repeatedly called Darrell a "dissembler" and "pretender" and invoked an image of degraded and hypocritical manhood by presenting Darrell as lacking the support of credible, gentlemanly allies. By doing so, Harsnett reached past Darrell to malign by extension the credit of his supporters, the demoniacs whom Darrell claimed to have cured, and sympathetic readers as well. Harsnett's criticism of Darrell's "adherents"—a synonym for "supporters" with more sinister and partisan connotations—was an important component of this strategy. According to Harsnett, Darrell's adherents were simple-minded townspeople (namely women), slavish disciples, or respectable men who had been misinformed. By transforming a community of respectable, godly gentlemen into base adherents, Harsnett painted their allegiance to Darrell as a sign not of his legitimacy but of degradation. This approach allowed Harsnett to adapt his critique to the status of Darrell's individual supporters, without allowing any to escape his critical gaze.

One of Harsnett's main assaults on Darrell's cohort consisted of a claim that the majority of them were uncreditable. Harsnett dismissed most of these as women and fools who supported Darrell blindly, irrationally, or wickedly. For example, he wrote that after the first dispossession of Katherine Wright, Darrell was "thereby into some small credit with the simpler sort: he became very pert and proud in that respect." And, as mentioned above, Harsnett also claimed that this had allowed Darrell to win "his spurs in the opinion of many, especially women."[23] He also suggested that Darrell attempted to renew enthusiasm for his scam by convincing residents of Nottingham that Somers's sister, Mary, was also possessed. Harsnett wrote that this new development, however ridiculous, "was very zealously followed by certain wives in that town."[24] According to Harsnett, Darrell "doubteth not (it seemeth) but that if the worst fell out, his credit would be sufficient to overweigh the boy's. Howbeit therein he hath overshot himself."[25] Even though Darrell's reputation ought to have protected him from such indignities as being likened to silly women, the Church of England's greater political power brought a lifetime of godliness into question. In attacking Darrell's status by accusing him of being both a duplicitous exorcist and a fraudulent man of credit, Harsnett made it nearly impossible for Darrell to invoke his reputation in his own defense.

To leave no stone unturned, Harsnett also impugned Darrell's ability to judge the credit of others, as when he related how quickly Darrell accepted the news of Somers's likely possession "upon the rude report of a simple man, one Hugh Wilson, and upon a letter received by Wilson from his sister in law, one Mistress Wallys."[26] Harsnett later wrote that "M. Darrell was so confident upon so light a report," that he reportedly told someone before witnessing the boy's fits that Somers was possessed and that he, Darrell, would be able to dispossess him. "This M. Darrels confident bragging . . . being joined to his rash credulity, doth make it probable, that either he had laid his plot with the boy before, or else that he knew very well, how by his cunning to draw on the boy, for the serving of his turn, as he himself list."[27] Harsnett moved from Darrell's failure to prudently judge the validity of others' reports to the insufficient honor and reason of his (lowly and female) supporters, which brought the minister into focus as foolish, overtly self-promotional, and conniving. At first glance, Harsnett appeared to have made little more than a witty critique of Darrell's judgment, but it amounted to a far more serious charge. How, Harsnett asked, could one trust Darrell's ability to discern the presence of a possessing demon if he could not even discern a reliable witness?

Having effectively dismissed Darrell's lowly adherents, Harsnett made sure to address the minister's more esteemed supporters as well, such as Master Ireton of Nottingham.[28] Harsnett took pains to undermine their association by shifting the blame onto Darrell. Ireton, he wrote, "(being a man of very good parts, and yet somewhat overcarried in this cause, being unacquainted with the proceedings in it, & suspecting no evil) is one of the men, of whom M. Darrell and his friends have greatly bragged. And it is true, that his credit wrought some inconvenience, through his faculty in believing those things which were told him. . . . Besides some indiscreet opposition in points of learning, did make him to say something, whereof more hold was taken, then peradventure he meant."[29] This quotation exemplifies Harsnett's ability suggestively to lead the reader toward desired conclusions. He treated Ireton with greater respect than Darrell's other supporters and appeared unusually willing to grant him positive motives. Still, the passage reads as a kind of cautionary tale for men who would involve themselves with possession cases. Despite his position and reputation, Ireton came off as having acted foolishly or, at the very least, as having suffered a lapse of judgment. By taking the word of unreliable men, he invited damage to his own credit. Even though Harsnett closed with a reference to Darrell's unnamed supporters, the lasting impression was that Ireton allowed his words to be twisted and misused by dishonorable men. Harsnett appeared to apologize for Ireton, but the reader grasps that Darrell was not the only man made vulnerable as a consequence of standing against the established church in this matter. With the authority of the Church of England and its commission at Lambeth behind him, Harsnett thus spelled out the stakes for men who might consider throwing in their lot with the godly: they, too, could be unmade.

In Harsnett's formulation, Darrell's manipulation of the fools who supported him constituted a corruption that infected them all. The contingent nature of manly credit allowed Harsnett to suggest that Darrell's associations with rude people proved his degradation. Once again, Harsnett's invocation of unnamed "adherents" provided a profitably vague site for the laying of blame. For example, Harsnett wrote "there was a rumor cast about the town one evening, that the Devil had . . . dashed out [Somers's] brains against a wall. This was of likelihood a simple device of M. Darrel's grossest friends: but yet such as it was, it wrought for the time."[30] Rumor, hearsay, and the attribution of the worst deeds to unnamed subordinates allowed Harsnett to fling all the mud he wished. Ever astute, Harsnett anticipated and averted complaints about the esteem given to Somers's oath. He wrote that Darrell "thought himself to have won such credit, as he might say anything, were it never so absurd, without suspicion of falsehood or juggling."[31] Harsnett's sheer repetition that Darrell intentionally misrepresented himself allowed him to suggest that Darrell's credit rested on fraud, and that instead of keeping exemplary company, he relied upon base lackeys to pursue his interests. Thus Harsnett demonstrated, at Darrell's expense, the ways a reputable man and his associates could be collectively unmade.

By challenging Darrell's credit, Harsnett was able to underscore Darrell's failure to judge accurately Somers's character and the reliability of other witnesses. This allowed Harsnett to make two contradictory but equally effective accusations. Harsnett first claimed that Darrell was a scheming and ambitious trickster who orchestrated a false performance along with the supposed demoniac. But he also suggested that Darrell had, perhaps even in a sincere attempt to interpret Somers's affliction, grossly misjudged both Somers and the phenomenon of possession. As a result, even for a reader predisposed to defend the minister's intentions, Darrell's lack of discernment of both the natural and preternatural marked him as unreliable and uncreditable. The Devil was known to be a liar and clever adversary, but Harsnett presented the narrative so that even the best possible interpretation of Darrell's behavior had him taken in not by God's foremost enemy but by a dissembling apprentice. These arguments gave Harsnett an upper hand in claiming greater access to the "truth" of the Somers case, which in turn allowed him to claim political and religious authority for his construction of a postapostolic age without room for such wonders as possessions.

When Darrell responded to Harsnett's accusations in 1600, he addressed many of the same questions of scriptural and relational legitimacy in an attempt to redeem his credit. In his rebuttal, *A detection of that sinnful, shamful, lying, and ridiculous discours, of Samuel Harshnet*, Darrell expressed frustration and bewilderment at the commission's indifference to his testimony, petitions, and offers to produce reputable witnesses. Harsnett was his particular enemy, but Darrell used William Somers's problematic credit to highlight the commission's inexplicably unjust proceedings. Darrell described Somers as "a young man about the age of 22 years: who first is known to be a notorious and infamous liar: for 4 times hath he varied with that double and false tongue of his: sometimes affirming, at other times denying all counterfeiting."[32] Being both young and a known liar, Somers ought to have posed little threat to a minister with as solid a reputation as Darrell's. Despite Darrell's formulaic self-deprecation, his distress was palpable.

Darrell's indignation led him to write energetically on the subject. He maintained that Somers was genuinely possessed, as this was central to his larger argument about the harm done by Harsnett and Bancroft's refusal to recognize God's work. Unfortunately for Darrell, Somers's capitulation to Harsnett made this claim nearly impossible to maintain. Accordingly, Darrell was forced to address the possibility that Somers had faked his possession. He wrote that if Somers had counterfeited, then he was not only a liar but also a blasphemer. This ought to have rendered Somers's credit doubly useless, but Darrell found himself nonetheless in the awkward position of trying to convince those in authority to reject their star witness. Darrell complained that Somers was the only witness against him, stating, "Me thinketh were I a private man, in regard of my education, years and life, I should be credited rather than Somers: much more being a minister of Christ Jesus and preacher of his gospel."[33] Darrell went to great lengths to undermine Somers's undeserved credit as a way to illustrate the injustice of the proceedings at Lambeth and the hypocrisy of Harsnett's position. He asked if Somers's "words be of such credit with [Harsnett] & some few others (for with few or none that are wise and godly I hope they be not) why should not his words sealed at other times with oaths and execrations be of like value?"[34] Even if the commission would not accept Darrell's view that Somers was truly possessed, the minister was determined to force his accusers to acknowledge the boy's inadequate credit. For such a youth to hold sway among learned commissioners, Darrell suggested, amounted to a concession of proper manly authority to the hopelessly disordered.

Darrell expanded this strategy to emphasize the risks of subverting standard hierarchies of gender and authority. He complained that the case against him "resteth only and barely upon Somers's credit, which I think is long ago shamefully cracked, and shivered both with wise men and with fools . . . were Somers's credit better than it is, yet the tale which is told us, is so unsavory or rather so absurd, & senseless, that me thinketh it is more than strange that any man of wisdom and judgment should ever harken unto it. . . . For mark I pray you: here is a paltry boy brought in deliberating and consulting, as if he were a grave man of great deliberation and advisement."[35] By presenting Somers's credit as "cracked, and shivered" even with fools, Darrell echoed Harsnett's invocation of unreasonable adherents, modeling for the reader a more proper interpretation of events. To treat this "paltry boy" as if he were "a grave man" disrupted not only conventional hierarchical relations but also the gendered conceptions on which a man's character could be weighed in order to determine his rightful place in the social hierarchy. Moreover, Harsnett's policies made elite men, such as the judges and magistrates who oversaw the convictions of witches in Darrell's cases, similarly vulnerable. By implicating Harsnett and the commissioners in these ways, Darrell provided not only a spiritual justification for his actions but a worldly one as well. If the commissioners' tactics were allowed to stand, Harsnett would have elevated a subordinate above his natural station. Darrell's sympathetic reader might thereby have come to see Harsnett and the commission as representing a disorder nearly on par with possession itself.

Harsnett and Darrell's arguments demonstrated significant gaps in Protestant consensus even on the fundamental nature of the Devil. In Harsnett's writing the Devil appeared as an adversary found in Scripture and in the fevered imaginations of evangelizing Catholics and Puritans, whereas Darrell's Devil was a real and powerful enemy allowed by God to torment individuals as a warning to the rest of humanity. Even as they invoked different versions of the Devil, both men shared a sense of what constituted credit and accepted without question its central role in establishing an intelligible truth. By invoking manly credit, Darrell, Harsnett, and their supporters used a gendered language of order against disorder, and legitimacy against degradation. The concept of credit shifted in and out of gendered space but remained inseparable from its foundation in patriarchal principles. The degree to which manly credit relied upon relations with other honorable men was both its strength and weakness; in this controversy both sides could reasonably invoke the right to a degree of authority, and the contest between them came down to institutional power. The ability to discern the true nature of people and of devils became a central question around which Harsnett and Darrell staked claims to reason, legitimacy, and respectable manly authority.

Manly Reason, Unmanly Excess

Just as both sides of the propaganda war invoked manly credit, the participants employed other, equally flexible, gendered strategies to strengthen their arguments. One such strategy was to emphasize that one's opponent shared the weaknesses of women and youths, particularly insufficient reason and immoderate language and physicality. These same characteristics reflected long-held views that these populations were the Devil's most likely targets, because it was presumed that they would be less capable of resisting temptation and sin. As with manly credit, the ability to refute such accusations hinged upon an individual's ability to call upon the support of a community of respectable peers, and a man's deficiency likewise could be proven if his supporters were themselves irrational or given to excess. Writers also invoked irrationality and excess to discredit their enemies, depict them as inversions of proper men, and invoke gendered assumptions about bodies and the humoral foundation of character. If an honorable man subjugated the passions that characterized women and youths, then adult men who demonstrated excessive malice and passions revealed themselves to be unfit.

Darrell directed these accusations against Bancroft and Harsnett, whose *A discovery of the fraudulent practices of John Darrel* (1599) had so effectively challenged Darrell's interpretation of Somers's dispossession. Darrell stressed both the irrationality and excess of Harsnett's claims and ultimately linked these faults to a disorderly and wicked agenda on the part of the Church of England. He feared that some readers might, "in their simplicity and rash credulity verily believe that [quoting Hars-nett] *Somers & the rest have counterfeited, & I instructed them*, because of the silly reasons printed & published to that end by the Bishop of London and S. Harsnet."[36] Darrell's references to "simple and rash cre-dulity" and "silly" reasons evoked a strong customary association with women and fools.[37] Both Darrell and Harsnett augmented their religious and political accusations with culturally resonant gendered ones, and because gendered strategies permeated the arguments of both sides so thoroughly and spurred rebuttals that were as fervent and intricate as those meant to address less overtly gendered challenges, the gendered arguments clearly constituted more than a medium for "truer" agendas.

After noting the "silly" reasoning underlying Harsnett's book, Darrell portrayed Harsnett and his writing as revealing an unmanly degree of excess. He complained, for example, that Harsnett "behaveth himself so ridiculously . . . with his colors of rhetoric, fine quips, & multitude of words & depositions."[38] To invert Harsnett's depiction of dispossession as a theatrical illusion, Darrell presented himself as a more reasonable man who did not need to rely upon such sleights and slippery words. Darrell stated that Harsnett "doth not only here but . . . elsewhere . . . prattle and flourish with empty words" and, later, "used many words to small purpose."[39] In Darrell's formulation, Harsnett the man became as excessive and irrational as his accusations; he reduced Harsnett's arguments to "pretty jests . . . wherewith he desired belike to delight his reader."[40] Darrell wrote, "I cannot be persuaded (for all this impudent & shameless discourse of S. Harsnet's, so bedecked and adorned with my Lord of London's flowers) that they themselves in their consciences do believe this knack of knavery against me in that sort as they have set it down."[41] Darrell invoked gendered concepts of legitimacy in an attempt to associate Harsnett's excessively flowery writing with his character, thereby undermining his credit. Clearly, neither side's case was reducible to a challenge to manhood, but invoking the manly qualities of unbi-ased, plain-speaking rationality provided both with familiar and power-ful arguments.

If excessive passions were the antithesis of measured reason, they also threatened to compromise one's powers of discernment. In addition to highlighting Harsnett's unmanly excess in language, Darrell suggested several ways in which Harsnett and his confederates not only failed to recognize true instances of demonic possession but also came to resem-ble devils themselves. One of the principal signs of this devilish orien-tation was Harsnett's excessive vitriol. According to Darrell, Harsnett's snide depiction of Darrell's supporters stemmed more from hatred and partisanship than from concern about actual fraud and compromised both Harsnett's and the commission's judicial impartiality. Darrell stated that Harsnett's "whole book from the first leaf to the last, is written of such scoffing and railing characters, that it might seem rather to have been compiled by Nash's Pasquil . . . then any other of sobriety & judgment."[42] Pasquil was a character created by Thomas Nashe, who published satirical, anti-Puritan tracts during the Marprelate controversy of 1588–90 and who responded, on the Anglican side, to several Puritan pamphlets that satirized the Church of England under Archbishop John Whitgift. By comparing Harsnett's vehemence with Nashe's avid anti-Puritanism, Darrell argued that the chaplain's partiality deprived him of the reasoned temperance required for discernment, the authority to adjudicate, and honorable manhood.

Highlighting Harsnett's immoderate fury also allowed Darrell to liken the Anglican leadership to biblical enemies such as the Pharisees. This allowed Darrell more effectively to depict any dismissal of dispossession as a rejection of God's works. He explained that "as the Pharisees because of their extreme malice against Christ, which must needs extend itself to his disciples . . . so also for that they could not endure that the people should *believe in him*, but when any miracle was done that might cause or help forward that same, they were ready to burst for anger."[43] By aligning Harsnett and the commissioners with the Pharisees, Darrell managed momentarily to sidestep such sticky theological questions as whether dispossession was a wonder or a miracle, and whether one could reliably discern the presence of the Devil based on a demoniac's symptoms as well as on scriptural precedent. Instead, by presenting himself as a defender of God's judgment and saving mercy, Darrell managed at one stroke to paint Harsnett as a dangerous, atheistic force and himself as a humble martyr for Christ. This tactic also allowed Darrell to undercut Harsnett's claims to those central components of manhood, reason, and moderation. Like the Pharisees, Darrell argued, Harsnett was governed by an extreme malice that had transformed his antagonism to Darrell into an antagonism to God.

Darrell extended this strategy to many of the men who testified against him as well, by depicting them as the same sort of nefarious "adherents" Harsnett had ascribed to him. Just as Harsnett had claimed that Darrell's supporters were irrationally steadfast in their delusion, Darrell depicted Harsnett's witnesses as driven by immoderate and excessive passions. Darrell wrote that Harsnett discounted the testimony of his godly supporters "because they were brought to pass by such as [Harsnett] despiseth and hateth, and would fain have all men to hate and despise."[44] That hatred did not extend to Darrell's detractors in Nottingham, of course, who had been treated with respectful attention. One of Darrell's principal opponents there was an alderman named Freeman. According to Darrell, Freeman was motivated not only by family loyalty—he was related to the accused witch—but also by "malice," which led him to want to be "revenged" of Darrell. Indeed, Darrell wrote, Freeman "hated extremely" and refused to attend church services while Darrell led them. Similarly, he described the testimony of the town clerk, M. Gregory, primarily as the result of "malice." To this characterization Darrell added that Gregory was "(a popish mate) against the work of god."[45] Darrell represented a final opposing witness along similar lines, claiming, "I did not know any living that did more deadly hate me then M. Walton."[46] In Darrell's formulation, these men's fury marked them as ineligible for participation in impartial judicial inquiry. By juxtaposing himself against these detractors, Darrell took the part not only of a martyr for Christ but also of a moderate man of reason. By noting that "The *Discoverer* sure taketh me to be a very impatient man . . . yet he shall see that I will answer him without any great choler,"[47] Darrell merged gendered images of order and legitimacy alongside political, religious, and cultural ones as a way to elicit the reader's sympathies and present himself as a man of reason.

At times, Darrell invoked bodily humors to illustrate his enemies' unseemly emotionality. In the humoral model, women's bodies were cold and wet, whereas men's were hot and dry, conditions believed to explain men's superior intellect and rationality.[48] But because excess constituted a failure of moderation in its own right, an overly heated man risked losing his rationality. Darrell instructed the reader to note Harsnett's and Bancroft's "doting partiality, that would be so hot and sweat so much" about certain possession cases while allowing the participants in others to escape relatively unscathed.[49] Darrell argued that Harsnett's excessive heat made him irrational: "It may very probably be gathered, that the thing which hath vexed the *Discoverer* and made him sweat so much about counterfeiting, is not the counterfeiting . . . nor his hatred and abomination to sin . . . but his hatred against the instruments which God used in these great works of his."[50] Darrell wanted the reader to see that Harsnett's misuse of his official position with the commission proved that he lacked the temperate logic and moderation necessary in a man of authority. These quotations demonstrate that, even as political and religious concerns remained central, these writers embedded gendered strategies in their efforts to protect themselves and undo their enemies.

Published defenses of Darrell alerted male readers to the fact that the commissioners could unmake Darrell despite the fact that his manly credit rested largely on the same components as the readers' own. Pro-Darrell pamphlets further suggested that the commission's disorder, as an extension of Bancroft and Harsnett, threatened godly men and the community at large. Because gendered notions of manly reason and moderation—and their problematic inversions—were so fundamental to articulations of legitimate power, the language of honorable manhood was an important weapon in the political and religious struggles between the Church of England and godly nonconformists. Instead of resembling foolish and manipulative exorcists, Darrell and his associates recast themselves as men risking all for the sake of English souls whose leadership conspired to keep them unaware of their perilous state.

Trade and Occupation

Authors on both sides of the possession debate invoked collective and individual markers of honorable manhood to dismiss their opponents and support their own political and religious aims. Like manly credit and charges of unmanly irrationality and excess, which applied to individual men but also depended upon relations with others, trade-based accusations had both individual and collective components. Harsnett was particularly adept at exploiting the potential of these strategies and drew upon a rich tradition of occupational stereotypes to vilify Darrell for his attempts to dispossess the purported demoniacs. By invoking commonly held notions of trade, occupation, and profit, Harsnett found a critique of Darrell's honorable manhood that was not so easily inverted as the attacks on manly credit. As Elizabeth Foyster has explained, among "the middling and lower sorts, a man's identity was also closely linked to his occupational status, and the honour of certain trades and occupations was often proudly asserted."[51] Furthermore, the absence of a respectable trade could contribute to a man's degraded status, as Susan Amussen notes in reference to neighbors' complaints about one Bernard Shipabarrow of Outwell in 1606. According to those complaints, Shipabarrow "liveth very suspiciously, not following any trade, or honest means to live as other men do."[52] Darrell's lack of a steady position as settled minister left him open to Harsnett's insinuation that he was not a true gentleman and that he wandered about the country in search of prospects. As with "gentleman" and "minister," trade-based language such as "exorcist" and "tinker" allowed Harsnett to levy accusations that seamlessly merged disparaged social status, piety, and honor into a broader gendered critique.

Harsnett cleverly combined trade-related accusations with explicit references to Darrell's claims to have accurately discerned the presence of a demonic spirit in those he helped by prayer and fasting. "He that will take upon him to cast Devils out of men, must first know whether they have any in them, or else he may peradvanture lose his labor," Harsnett quipped. One of the central occupations that Harsnett attributed to Darrell was that of "Exorcist," a term with damning connotations of popishness, insincerity, and lewdness. "It seemeth to be a matter very pertinent to the dignity of an Exorcist," Harsnett continued, "that he be able to declare who sent the Devil into his patient. For men of that trade do affirm, that sometimes it is God, sometimes holy men, and sometimes witches, that do send them. . . . Whether witches can send Devils into men or women (as many do pretend) is a question amongst those that write of such matters & the learneder and sounder sort do hold the negative."[53] Harsnett questioned the very possibility of witchcraft-possession in a way that aligned Darrell with the "grossest sort of the popish Exorcists." Just as priests made false claims of having God's special dispensation for the adjuration of spirits, so Darrell sought to exploit the ignorance of the people for personal gain. By labeling exorcism a "trade," Harsnett undermined Darrell's status as a gentleman and suggested that Darrell's piety was nothing but a hypocritical screen for his ambition. To divide and conquer his opponents on this important point, Harsnett argued that Darrell had more in common with Catholics than with moderately godly Protestants: "When M. Darrell, with his fellows, and all other Exorcists, or Devil drivers are agreed, & . . . can make it apparent unto us without their gross and palpable forgeries: that they are able to discern who is possessed: then let them tell us, that they have dispossessed them."[54]

Images of trade and occupation also provided Harsnett with a way to counter Darrell's invocations of Scripture, claims to greater piety, and accusations that the commissioners were atheists and contemporary Pharisees. Harsnett used the language of trade to introduce the reader to the important theological question of whether prayer and fasting were truly sanctioned by Scripture as appropriate means for Protestant dispossessions, or whether they replicated the follies of Catholic exorcisms. Harsnett claimed that while prayer was not so central to Catholic exorcism, priests were "as earnest to make a trade and merchandise of it, as

Master Darrell."[55] Labeling the act of prayer as "merchandise" allowed Harsnett to align Darrell with papists and tricksters who swindled gullible customers. This juxtaposition of central theological points with images of occupational hypocrisy capitalized upon widely held notions of dishonorable manhood to reinforce the case against Darrell and godly dispossession more generally.

By referring to trade and occupation, Harsnett managed to apply the debased characteristics of others onto Darrell. He wrote that when "these cosening merchants, do tell men nowadays, that they have cast devils out of any their children, servants or friends: it is hereby manifest, what credit their words do deserve."[56] He further asserted that, because possession cases were relatively rare, "the trades-men in that skill, have devised many ways to keep themselves in work."[57] Trade-related disparagements allowed Harsnett to strike at credit, manhood, and character at once, for surely no man with such manipulative business dealings would be credited among reasonable peers.[58] Furthermore, the popular image of the profane, wandering tinker provided a familiar image for readers of the period's satirical pamphlet literature and cast a questionable light upon Darrell's motivations. Harsnett painted Darrell as little more than a charlatan, much like Catholic priests. These "Exorcists of both kinds," he wrote, "for want of work are driven to their shifts: and like Tinkers walk up and down from place to place, seeking to be employed. It is a matter of some difficulty to discover their shifts, and sleights to that purpose, they have so many; and by their experience do manage them so craftily."[59] Rather than a sober and well-respected minister, Darrell became a lowly, itinerant swindler. Vagrancy laws of the period show the suspicion with which itinerants were commonly regarded, and by this point in Harsnett's text Darrell came to resemble, at least rhetorically, a character that every reader would recognize and scorn.

Harsnett found several opportunities to link images of dishonorable trade to the allegedly popish aspects of Darrell's "work" with demoniacs. In one sarcastic passage, he provided a long list of objects that priests in Rome presented as holy relics, such as "the crib that Christ was born in: the thorns of the Crown that Christ was crowned with: our Lady's hair: the Chin of Saint John Baptist's father: some of Mary Magdalene's hair: a piece of the fat of Saint Laurence: a piece of the arm, and some of the brains of Saint Thomas of Canterbury, with many such trinkets." Harsnett then asserted that "many credulous and superstitious people are drawn to admire them. It is the manner of the Mountebanks in Italy, resembled by some of our Peddlers, when they open their packs, to set out their ware with many great words. Unto which kind of people, and seducing Mirabilists, Master Darrell in his practices with Somers, may well be resembled."[60] Clearly enjoying the comparison he was drawing between Darrell and both foreign and local hucksters, Harsnett went on to state that while Darrell "was thus jetting up and down the place where Somers was playing his pranks, and setting out the boy's actions, as his chief Wares . . . a man may well remember the said Romish Priests in extolling their feigned Relics, and the said Mountebanks, and Peddlers, in lying and cogging, to make the best of their packs."[61] By merging the theatrical falseness of Catholic priests with the conceits of common swindlers, Harsnett instructed the reader that the path away from such superstitious foolery required a repudiation of the potentially powerful spectacle offered by demonic possession.

Harsnett soon returned to this effective device and aligned Darrell yet again with priests and lowly vagabonds. He contended that when Darrell "commanded" Somers, a term that evoked the Catholic practice of commanding the devil to depart, the "simpler sort of people, ascribed great virtue and holiness unto him. If the resemblances before made of M. Darrel's practices in this point, to *Peddlers, Mountebanks*, and the Relic-mongers of Rome be not so fit: then as you remember, Somers and Darrell dissembling and colluding together, think upon the pretty feats, betwixt Banks and his horse. Indeed it was one of the greatest wonders that happened in those actions at Nottingham, that so many were seduced by such palpable fooleries."[62] Harsnett dealt a blow both to priests and Darrell by comparing their actions with a well-known image of frivolous entertainment: Banks and his horse. Banks was a Scotsman who trained his horse, Morocco, to dance on his hind legs, stamp out the number shown on a thrown die, and to deliver objects to particular members of the audience. With this comparison, Harsnett effectively transformed the godly witnesses of Somers's dispossession into a gullible, gaping mob.[63] By associating Darrell with exorcists, peddlers, and street performers, Harsnett maintained that the dispossessions were less demonstrations of God's judgment than entertainments calculated to deceive and extort. Using images of trade, occupation, and profit provided Harsnett with a way to evoke customary characteristics of debased manhood such as greed and excessive self-promotion. He depicted Darrell as a disruptive force that wandered into Nottingham and sacrificed its peace and social order to forward his own interests. One only had to consider the controversy and factions that developed among citizens and clergy in Nottingham and London as a result of the case to see demonic possession's divisive effects.

Manhood, Social Order, and Power

Harsnett, Darrell, and their allies in the propaganda war used the aforementioned strategies—citing manly credit, irrationality and excess, and notions of trade—to evoke the gendered failings of their opponents. Each of these failings represented a threat to political, religious, and cultural conventions, which were grounded in patriarchal structures of power and together constituted social order. An emphasis on social order allowed the writers to warn that only their protagonists stood between the reader and the profound disarray that would surely result if the other side—which they aligned with Catholics, immoderate men, women, youths, and even the Devil himself—prevailed. It was relatively simple for Harsnett and his allies to emphasize the disorderly nature of witchcraft-possession, which forced Darrell's side to adopt a defensive posture. While addressing the theological and factional import of the witchcraft-possession controversy, particularly the question of whether Darrell claimed to have worked a miracle, Harsnett and Darrell relied upon these gendered strategies to mark their enemies as those who subverted proper hierarchical relations. Because the enforcement of order had such a central role in the writers' agendas, it was particularly damning to accuse one's opponent of seducing subordinates away from their proper places in that order.

Once Darrell came under fire, his entire career as a dispossessor of demoniacs—from his first interaction with Katherine Wright to the final debacle with William Somers—became vulnerable to accusations that he used forms of seduction to manipulate the social order. In *A discovery*, Harsnett claimed that Darrell had behaved lewdly during his dispossession of Katherine Wright back in 1586. Specifically, Harsnett reported Wright's testimony that the young minister had lain upon her body as she convulsed. There were two ways in which this accusation harmed Darrell; in the first place it suggested there was an unwholesome if not lascivious tone to his services to demoniacs, and in the second it suggested Darrell's immoderate elevation of himself as one who claimed the ability to direct divine power through touch. The first accusation was easy to invoke, given the routine depiction in contemporary anti-Catholic propaganda of exorcisms as opportunities for mendacious priests to slake their lusts. By casting aspersions on Darrell's comportment with Katherine Wright, Harsnett thus managed to paint Darrell as a lecherous fraud and simultaneously to conflate Puritan dispossessions with much-derided Catholic exorcisms.[64] Even if the reader dismissed the idea that Darrell had lewd intentions, to have lain upon Wright in an attempt to heal her rather than simply contain her—perhaps in emulation of those who healed in Scripture by that method—would have represented a shocking presumption.[65] By linking these accusations, Harsnett depicted Darrell as a kind of degraded solicitor who led young people into lies and disregard for their responsibilities to parents, clergy, and even the law of God.

When the commission first questioned Darrell about the incident with Wright, he claimed not to recall it—after all, the case had taken place fourteen years earlier. Later, he testified that once his wife had reminded him of the circumstances he recalled that she and a few others had been present when it occurred. The company of these observers ought to have helped Darrell deflect accusations of impropriety, but Harsnett recorded this explanation as if it only enhanced their collective dissipation. Darrell's attempt to rebut these charges was made more difficult by his own inconsistent testimony about the event:

> In all this my dealing with *Kat. Wright*, I had not (I thank God) so much as an unclean thought: neither did I lie on her in such manner as *Elias & Paul* sometimes did in the restoring of two to life, nor yet in imitation of them: all which I directly deposed before the *Bishop*. And that there was no uncleanness in act, every one may be assured hereby, in that this said lying were there present, and eye witnesses thereof, my own wife with other women, and for that another man also . . . lay together with me upon her.[66]

Darrell appeared desperate to rectify his initial confusion, to deny Bancroft's implications and discredit Harsnett's damning repetition of them. According to Darrell, Harsnett used this "shift (a sluttish one) thinking thereby utterly to shame me, and disgrace me forever viz. to make the world believe that I am a vicious and unclean person."[67] As much as Darrell contradicted the charges, however, his lengthy parsing failed to overcome Harsnett's sensational allegations. Darrell was caught because he lacked the influence to convince the commission to credit his supporters' testimony rather than Harsnett's poison pen. Gendered language and strategies, such as those used in this instance, provided participants with a powerful discourse that readers could quickly grasp. The accusation of seduction was effective not only because it suggested sexual impropriety but also because it reinforced customary associations between corrupted manhood and women's concupiscence, and between the hypocritical men who spoke of heaven to hide base agendas and the youths whose immoderate passions they exploited.

Several negative associations about dissolute youth, particularly the turbulent passions that made young men, like women, unsuitable for independence, circulated in the pamphlet war.[68] Like womanhood, youth was that against which manhood was defined, and William Somers's youth was frequently invoked by both sides when they wanted to discredit him. Nonetheless, the limitations of youth also allowed Darrell to mount a kind of defense in the matter of his behavior with Katherine Wright. When Bancroft initially pressed him for an answer about that day fourteen years earlier, Darrell recalled, "I told him that for the present I *did think* or imagine that I did it in some childish, foolish, and indiscreet imitation of the Prophet and Apostle: For quoth I unto him, I was then young and had studied divinity but a little while, and therefore it may be [I] did fall into such an error and childish part."[69] Darrell's invocation of his youth here served both as a way to condemn the act and also to excuse its commission: "But suppose this latter were true: yet seeing it was done so many years since, when I was little better then a child in understanding, and that now being of riper years I am as far from approving thereof, or practicing the like as any man whatsoever, it must needs be I take it, and cannot be excused to be in the highest degree of malice."[70] While Darrell was willing to acknowledge the seriousness of the indiscretion, he begged the reader to reflect on his spotless reputation as a man. This appeal to honorable manhood largely fell short, however, because Harsnett had so convincingly undermined his credit. Because the commissioners denied Darrell the opportunity to make use of his esteemed supporters and in fact made support of Darrell dangerous for them, they managed to isolate and unmake him.

The specter of the seduction of subordinates, however, did provide Darrell with opportunities to invert Harsnett's accusations, as when he painted the bishop and Anglican chaplain as the true manipulators of the demoniacs who were less willing than William Somers to implicate him, namely Thomas Darling and Katherine Wright.[71] Whereas Harsnett wrote of Darling as a lewd and fraudulent boy, Darrell cast him in a more sympathetic light:

> Here it must not be forgotten how Darling a young stripling of
> those tender & unsettled years was dealt with and ensnared. He was
> for the space of a month in the Bishop's house: during which time
> the Bishop and his Chaplain with all their searches and devices
> were daily and hourly in hand with the boy to wring this confession
> from him . . . and then presently perceiving him not to be for their

purpose as Somers was, they retaining Somers, turned him out of the doors. . . . Men sometimes of greater years and riper judgment, have in such case been too easily drawn from the truth to affirm that which is false and erroneous. How easily then might such a weak boy be perverted and seduced?[72]

Darrell's passage reinforces how closely concepts of reason and strength were linked to age as well as sex. He invoked a kind of simplicity here for Darling; instead of dismissing him as a fool, he presented him as guileless and vulnerable to influence. Such simplicity, the early modern reader would know, made one susceptible to the temptations of Satan or, in Darrell's formulation, more worldly tempters. It was only through perversion and seduction, Darrell averred, that Harsnett managed to manipulate Thomas Darling into a new interpretation of his dispossession.

Darrell suggested a similar dynamic between Harsnett and Katherine Wright: "I trust S. Harsnett did thereunto by his slights and devices draw her and entice" Wright to change her testimony. By emphasizing Harsnett's unwholesome and unseemly influence over Wright, he reinforced his claims that Harsnett misused his authority in service to his malice and to his lord bishop. Darrell inverted Harsnett's images of seduction and manipulation and managed to conflate preternatural devils—such as those who afflicted the demoniacs—with earthly ones like Harsnett himself. Interestingly, Darrell often appeared to be at his strongest when he followed Harsnett's lead by posing pragmatic arguments rather than strictly theological ones. For example, Darrell demonstrated not only that he lacked motive to manipulate Wright's case but also that Wright's own interests would hardly have been served by such an arrangement:

If K. Wright have counterfeited, she hath therein spent the prime of her life, from the age of 17 until about 30 thereby depriving her self of many, if not all the comforts of this life, as society, marriage etc. Who can now in any reason think, that a young damsel to my remembrance of a comely feature and personage, desirous enough (if not too much) of the pleasures of this life, would wittingly, and willingly, deprive her self of them all, and that for so many years together, and to such an end as here is pretended.[73]

Darrell's reader likely would have found this a convincing argument. Because the ideal of honorable womanhood entailed marriage, motherhood, and the management of a household, an intentional fraud would not only have required Wright to deny herself social viability but would also have left her as a vulnerable dependent in her stepfather's home.[74] Why, Darrell asked, would Wright have intentionally deprived herself of all worldly pleasures, and all that would grant her credit as an honorable woman, in order to act out painful contortions for years after the crowds subsided? The pains Darrell took to praise her attractiveness and healthy orientation toward marriage, while cautiously sidestepping any suggestion of immoderate lust, exemplified the dangers inherent in invocations of gendered character. It shows that the charges of exploiting this young woman, whether for seduction or hubris, had to be rebutted. It further reveals how gendered strategies such as these linked the credit of men and women, so that Darrell's attempts to defend himself from the commissioners' charges required that he fluently address accusations of gendered weaknesses on behalf of those he dispossessed, as well as himself.

The nature of dispossession imposed a kind of mutual engagement between demoniacs and the ministers who attended to them that made it very difficult to avoid these kinds of struggles. This was especially true for Darrell, who was plagued not only by Harsnett's allegations about his behavior with Katherine Wright and Thomas Darling but also by Harsnett's gleeful reiteration of William Somers's obliging testimony to the commission that Darrell had promised him a release from service if he would counterfeit. Given the general anxiety with which contemporaries viewed the disorderliness of apprentices, the charge that Darrell sought to entice Somers away from his service only compounded the offense. In *A discovery*, Harsnett added that Somers maintained his claims to having been truly possessed until he was "got out of M. Darrel's hands," which further suggested Darrell's nefarious and controlling influence over the young man.[75] Somers's capitulation allowed Harsnett to argue strongly that this last case could stand in for them all. By linking accusations of lewdness, the seduction of subordinates, and ambition, Harsnett contended that Darrell—like Catholic exorcists—made a show of piety while gratifying his unseemly desires within the disorderly context of witchcraft-possession.

Harsnett and Darrell expertly used gendered language and strategies in defense of their competing visions of legitimate authority in a time of religious and political controversy. These linguistic strategies, including accusations about the seduction of subordinates, were nuanced enough to allow them to invoke a series of implicit meanings alongside the explicit ones. Harsnett's criticism of Darrell's prior conduct with the Seven of Lancashire provides a good example. Harsnett claimed that the ministers had impressed upon the recently delivered demoniacs the idea that the Devil would strive to repossess them, and that Darrell and George More "told them such tales of a lewd purpose, thereby to draw them to pretend the like." There was no question, he wrote, that "if these absurd mates had gone on, they would have proved as gross deluders, as any of the popish or Jesuitical Exorcists, if not more gross."[76] By repeatedly describing the ministers' actions as "lewd" and "gross," Harsnett cleverly intertwined a set of explicit and implicit accusations that worked together to cast them as wily seducers of the young and impressionable. Beyond its connotation of sexual wickedness, "lewd" suggested one who was unlearned, rude, common, base, ignorant, and ill bred.[77] These qualities painted Darrell as a likely candidate for the inveigling of subordinates from their proper places, as the associated meanings dismantled nearly all aspects of honorable manhood for a gentleman. The exceptionally flexible term "gross" allowed Harsnett to draw together myriad insults; most of the time he took advantage of its use "in concord with [nouns] of evil import, and serving as an intensive of their meaning: Glaring, flagrant, monstrous." But "gross" also allowed him to evoke other meanings, as in things "uncleanly or repulsive in quality; lacking in delicacy of perception; dull, stupid, or brutally lacking in refinement or decency." Interestingly, "gross" also denoted "things material or perceptible to the senses, as contrasted with what is spiritual, ethereal, or impalpable."[78] This pungent mixture of connotations, which ranged so effortlessly between bodies, social quality, and earthiness, suited Harsnett's intentions perfectly.

Participants in the propaganda war used all of the aforementioned strategies—invoking manly credit, irrationality and excess, trade imagery, and the specter of seduction—to emphasize the gendered failings of their opponents. Because Harsnett was able to make such strong charges about the disorderly nature of demonic possession, Darrell was forced to adopt a defensive position. The inherently disordered nature of witchcraft-possession provided the foundation of the commission's concerns about Puritan dispossessions, and Harsnett took pains to ensure that the reader recognized the Church of England's greater claim to authority and stability. The propaganda war waged between Harsnett, Darrell, and their supporters came to an end after other godly ministers revealed their doubts about Darrell's discernment and his view of the possibility of dispossessing demoniacs in a postapostolic age.[79] The aftermath of the pamphlet war, and Darrell's defrocking, demonstrated that his credit indeed rose and fell based on his relations with other men. Of course it is tempting to take a side in the debate and attempt to answer the question of Darrell's guilt in training demoniacs to fake their symptoms. On the whole, I side with scholars who absolve Darrell from the worst of these accusations.[80] Nonetheless, the aim here is not to determine "truth" so much as to call attention to the kinds of gendered argumentation that illustrate how pervasively gender figured in the enactment, interpretation, and contestation of witchcraft-possession.

A broad reading of gender in these publications reveals how pervasively the participants contested meanings of manhood at the same time that they argued over the cases' profound implications for political and religious authority. References to manly credit, reason and excess, trade imagery, and accusations of seduction provided both sides with means by which to interpret Darrell's dispossessions, but it was Harsnett and the commission's greater institutional power that enabled them to unmake Darrell despite the fact that his credit outweighed that of his primary accuser. Their gendered strategies coexisted with, and at times were subsumed into, broader concepts of social order applicable to all of the participants—all of whom risked being demeaned and unmade. Harsnett and Darrell's propaganda thus illuminates the extent to which the ambiguities of manhood shaped the destinies of men who became involved with those who acted as if they were possessed. Darrell's undoing, for example, reinforced patriarchal order even as it demonstrated one man's vulnerability within that order. Over time, it became increasingly difficult to sustain local wonders in the face of broader skepticism, a tension that ultimately led to the dismantling of official sanctions for witchcraft prosecution as well as dispossessions. This represented an important change for those who saw possessions as tools for conversion, and for those whose lives were saved by the greater difficulty in achieving convictions for witchcraft. But it ultimately represented continuity in patriarchal control, as those in power defended their right to proclaim the meaning of witchcraft-possession cases against those who would use those cases as a platform from which to usurp the right to regulate the existing order.

Engendering New England Witchcraft-Possession:
George Burroughs in Salem

In Boston, Massachusetts, in 1689, Puritan minister Cotton Mather published *Memorable Providences Relating to Witchcrafts and Possessions*,
his account of preternatural wonders intended to shock all atheists and
"sensual Saducees" who denied the existence of angels or devils back to
a godlier frame of mind. Mather reminded his reader that "God is therefore pleased . . . to suffer [allow] *Devils* sometimes to do such things in
the world as shall stop the mouth of gain sayers."[1] The centerpiece of the
text was Mather's narrative of the dramatic witchcraft-possession episode involving the children of John Goodwin that had taken place the
year before. Mather explained that the children—in particular Martha
(thirteen years old), John (eleven), Mercy (seven), and Benjamin (five)—
had been religiously brought up and that "it was perfectly impossible
for any Dissimulation of theirs to produce what scores of spectators
were amazed at." Next, Mather went on to explain that after the eldest
daughter had an altercation with the daughter of a notorious woman she
was "visited with *strange Fits*, beyond those that attend an *Epilepsy*, or a
Catalepsy, or those that they call *The Diseases of Astonishment*."[2] Mather
provided startling examples of the children's "exquisite pain" and fits
that rendered them deaf, dumb, blind, and wracked by numbness and
contortions. They cried piteously, barked, purred, sweated, panted, shivered, and even flew like geese, "carried with an incredible *Swiftness* thro
the *air*, having, but just their *Toes* now and then upon the ground, and

their *Arms* waved like the Wings of a *Bird*. One of them . . . [flew] the length of the Room, about 20 foot . . . none seeing her feet all the way touch the floor."[3] The Goodwin children's possession performance was remarkable for the way that it reflected elements of the traditional possession script, and for the way that their affliction's translation of local pressures ultimately reinforced the godly patriarchal authority of their minister. It certainly helped Mather's case that the woman they named as the cause of their troubles, another Mary Glover, had the low social status, long-standing reputation as a witch, and Irish (and possibly Catholic) background that made her a most likely suspect. But even after her confession, Mather took care to point out that just to be sure, "The Court appointed five or six Physicians, one evening to examine her very strictly, whether she were not craz'd in her Intellectuals, and had not procured herself by Folly and Madness the Reputation of a Witch."[4] Thus Mather eliminated fraud, illness, and madness, the three main pillars of skepticism in matters of witchcraft and possession since Reginald Scot's infamous skeptical text of 1584.[5] Having neutralized these objections, Mather continued confidently to describe the story of the children's affliction, their eventual delivery by prayer and fasting, and the witch's lawful execution. Mather's preface therefore demonstrates the considerable continuity of the witchcraft-possession script, tenets of skepticism, and these cases' power as propaganda across the seventeenth century.

Most of Mather's narrative focused on Martha Goodwin, whom he brought into his home to observe and to facilitate her delivery. Martha exhibited a particular flair for the dramatic and the kind of ingenuity seen among the Throckmorton children at Warboys. Because the preternatural skills with which demoniacs were endowed came from the Devil, most ministers warned against experimenting with their knowledge of secrets or having them demonstrate the devils' preferences among competing religious groups. This latter tactic had been derided when Catholics used it, as in the case of the very widely published narrative of William Perry, known as the "Boy of Bilson," who was the subject of a fraudulent exorcism in England in the 1620s. In that case, one of the attending priests wrote that he

> commanded the divell to shew by the sheet before him, how he
> would use one dying out of the Romane Catholicke Church? [Perry]
> very unwillingly, yet at length obeyed, tossing, plucking, haling,
> and biting the sheet, that it did make many to weepe and cry forth.
> Then I commanded him to shew how hee did use Luther, John

Calvin, and John Fox; which unwillingly he did performe after the same manner, but in a fiercer sort. Then I commanded him to shew what power he had on a good Catholicke that dyed out of mortall sinne? hee thrust downe his armes, trembled, holding downe his head, and no more.[6]

Mather scorned such Catholic perfidy and was surely aware of how John Darrell had suffered similar accusations a century earlier, but when faced with a live demoniac of his own, he could barely contain the urge to test the reality of the devils by the reality of his religion.[7] His testing of Martha's reactions to godly and worldly books provides a notable example. A Quaker book, "she could quietly read whole pages of; only the Name of God and Christ she still skipt over, being unable to pronounce it." And when he showed her "a Jest-Book . . . she could read them [without] any Disturbance, & have witty Descants upon them too. I entertain'd her with a Book that pretends to prove, That there are no Witches; and that she could read very well. . . . I produced a Book to her that proves, That there are Witches, and that she had not power to read."[8] Unsurprisingly, Martha happily read "popish books" but stumbled over anything that Mather considered profitable, notably those by his "grandfather Cotton"; his father, Increase; himself; Samuel Willard; and others. Some of the texts appeared to be almost tangibly endowed with holiness, as merely touching them would cause her to fall into a dead faint. Mather added coyly, "I hope I have not spoil'd the credit of the Books, By telling how much the Devils hated them."[9]

As sometimes happened in the intense environment of a possession, participants managed to internalize contradictory evidence without allowing it to diminish their faith in their overarching interpretation. There was one "certain Prayer-Book" that Martha could not only read well but that she reverenced above the others and called "Her Bible." He noted that "If she were going into her tortures, at the offer of this Book, she would come out of her fits and read; and her Attendants were almost under a Temptation to use it as a Charm, to make and keep her quiet."[10] The book was certainly one of Mather's own, especially since merely entering his study was usually enough to bring Martha to her senses. Despite the contradiction between the lessons drawn from these different reading tests, and as much as Mather knew that he should not be searching for answers from devils, Martha's behavior appeared to provide proof of his fundamental beliefs and all that mattered most to him.

Cotton Mather and Martha Goodwin mutually constituted her possession performance by building on their shared conception of how these phenomena worked. Because witchcraft-possession lent itself so powerfully to propaganda, Mather was able to use the truths that Martha and her devils revealed to shore up his godly worldview. The following long concluding passage demonstrates how seamlessly he claimed the status of proper arbiter of how to discern and interpret preternatural cases:

I have related noting but what I judge to be true. I was my self an Eye-witness to a large part of what I tell; and I hope my neighbours have long thought, That I have otherwise learned Christ, than to [lie] unto the World. Yea, there is, I believe, scarce any one particular, in this Narrative, which more than one credible Witness will not be ready to make Oath unto. The things of most Concernment in it, were before many Critical Observers; and the Whole happened in the Metropolis of the English America, unto a religious and industrious Family which was visited by all sorts of Persons, that had a mind to satisfy themselves. I do now likewise publish the History, While the thing is yet fresh and New; and I challenge all men to detect so much as one designed Falshood, yea, or so much as one important Mistake, from the Egg to the Apple of it. I have writ as plainly as becomes an Historian, as truly as becomes a Christian, tho' perhaps not so profitably as became a Divine. But I am resolv'd after this, never to use but just one grain of patience with any man that shall to go to impose upon me, a denial of Devils, or of Witches. I shall count that man Ignorant who shall suspect, but I shall count him down-right Impudent if he Assert the Non-Existence of things which we have had such palpable Convictions of. I am sure he cannot be a Civil, (and some will question whether he can be an honest man) that shall go to deride the Being of things which a whole Countrey has now beheld an house of pious people suffering not a few Vexations by. But if the Sadducee, or the Atheist, have no right Impressions by these Memorable Providences made upon his mind; yet I hope, those that know what it is to be sober, will not repent any pains that they may have taken in perusing what Records of these Witchcrafts and Possessions, I thus leave unto Posterity.[11]

This passage, written a few years before the outbreak at Salem, joined Mather's sensitivity to criticism with his marshaling of his own best defenses against it. He reminds the reader of his ample credit and asserts that the case's origin in "the Metropolis of the English America, unto a Religious and Industrious Family" ought to preclude any undue suspicions. His subsequent challenge to any who doubted him merged an attack on their character with the automatic elision of such criticism with un-Christian Sadducism and atheism. Having defined such critics as outside of the bounds of decent men, he reinforced his view of himself as a representative and defender of godly rectitude. Each step in this highly strategic conclusion fortified Mather's position as the rightful godly authority in contrast to his detractors, who were necessarily rendered ignorant, impudent, uncivil, dishonest, and frivolous.

After completing his dramatic account of the children's possession and dispossession, Mather appended a short reflection on the experience by their father, John Goodwin. Goodwin outlined several passages from Scripture and interpreted them as a sign that his own sins had resulted in his children's suffering. By taking on a great deal of the blame and modeling an acute awareness of the propriety of heeding ministers' counsel, he showed godly introspection and affirmed Mather's view of the affair. Regarding the legitimacy of pursuing popular folk remedies or consulting cunning people when confronted with his children's debilitating fits, Goodwin explained: "you must think it was time of sore temptation with us, for many did say (yea, and some good people too), were it their case, that they would try some tricks, that should give ease to their children: But I thought for us to forsake the counsel of good old men, and to take the counsel of the young ones, it might ensnare our souls, though for the present it might offer some relief to our bodies."[12] Here Goodwin, echoing Mather himself, assured the reader that prayer and fasting were the only appropriate method for countering witchcraft-possession symptoms, and that accepting the counsel of ministers over neighbors was the correct choice. By invoking the expertise of "old men," he reaffirmed the customary association between age and wisdom. Mather must have found it gratifying to be grouped with the old men, not least because he was only twenty-five years old at the time, and many referred to him as "Mr. Mather the younger" to differentiate him from his famous father. Sober maturity occupied the positive pole of the binary with rash youth, just as Englishness, godliness, and honorable manhood constituted the superior conditions in relation to their opposites.

In 1689, Mather expressed full awareness of the skepticism that had accompanied accounts of witchcraft-possession for more than a century, but his overall tone was one of pious confidence; with other divines like Richard Baxter in England, he believed that wondrous providences like these would bring worldly people back to a profitable fear of God and the Devil. This sense of community and shared purpose spurred on his efforts, as demonstrated by his fulsome but revealing introduction to the text:

> But I can with a *Contentment* beyond meer *Patience,* give these rescinded Sheets unto the Stationer, when I see what pains Mr. *Baxter,* Mr. *Glanvil,* Dr. *More,* and several other *Great Names* have taken to publish Histories of *Witchcrafts* & *Possessions* unto the world. I said *Let me also run after them;* and this with the more Alacrity because, I *have tidings ready.* Go then, *my little book,* as a *Lackey* to the more elaborate *Essayes* of those learned men. Go *tell* Mankind, that there are *Devils* & *Witches;* & that tho those *night-birds* least appear where the *Day-light* of the Gospel comes, yet *New-Engl.* has had Exemples of their *Existence* & *Operation;* and that not only the *Wigwams* of Indians, where the pagan *Powaws* often raise their masters, in the shapes of *Bears* & *Snakes* & *Fires,* but the *Houses* of *Christians,* where our God has had His *constant Worship,* have undergone the Annoyance of *Evil spirits.*[13]

Mather's book went out to tell the world that terrible preternatural assaults were real and plagued Indian powwaws, the religious leaders (or "wizards," in Mather's view) whom many New Englanders presumed to be the Devil's agents. That the Devil could be found in New England not only among Indians but also in the homes of Christians was a great chastisement for the godly colonies. Mather's presentation of his little book's role in this global mission reached for modesty, but there was no disguising his conviction that he spoke on behalf of what was right. He wrote when his status in New England was at its pinnacle, which allowed him to invoke unreservedly the community of honorable men who would attest to the veracity of his narrative.

Mather also drew from a tradition of English witchcraft-possession writing, from the controversies of the late sixteenth century to the cases that had emerged across the seventeenth century. Despite fluctuations in the volume of printed cases, and the dramatic political, religious, and social turmoil of the period, claims to interpret preternatural phenomena remained closely implicated in claims to patriarchal authority and order. Continuity did not mean stasis, particularly because the role of gender in men and women's lived experiences could fluctuate considerably. But at the cultural level, manhood and womanhood continued to factor significantly for demoniacs, witches, and propagandists whose language shaped the meanings of witchcraft-possession cases. Cotton Mather drew upon this shared culture from his desk in New England, and when the witchcraft-possession outbreak began at Salem and spread throughout Essex County, familiar patterns emerged in the claims of those who acted as if they were possessed, among accused and confessing witches, and from the magistrates and ministers who passed judgment on the outbreak's meanings.

Because case studies so ably illuminate preternatural texts' explicit and implicit use of gender to support claims to proper authority, this chapter and the next focus on two significant cases. First, after reviewing possession phenomena that arose across the seventeenth century on both sides of the Atlantic, this chapter focuses on the Reverend George Burroughs, a man accused of witchcraft during the Salem witchcraft-possession outbreak, whose downfall reflects several aspects of John Samuel's a century earlier. Chapter 5 centers on Margaret Rule, a young woman from Cotton Mather's own congregation who became possessed in September 1693—just over a year after Burroughs's execution—and the controversy that erupted in 1700 over Mather's interpretation of Rule and of Salem. The two case studies highlight some of the lesser-known ways that gender, language, and power operated in and through the outbreak. These individuals' cases, both at the time of their trials and in their written legacies, reveal a familiar reliance upon gendered language that suggests both Salem's transatlantic continuities and a more pivotal role for manhood than has been previously recognized. In both cases, the gendered language of witchcraft-possession cases reveals the persistence of patriarchal models of authority across the seventeenth-century Anglo-Atlantic.

Transatlantic Witchcraft-Possession, 1620–1690

The profound turmoil of the transatlantic seventeenth century, and the intermittent appearance of viable witchcraft-possession cases, make the continuity in the patriarchal aspects of their symptoms and argumentation all the more notable. The controversies at the turn of the seventeenth century, particularly the aforementioned propaganda wars that the Archbishop Richard Bancroft and his chaplain Samuel Harsnett waged against Puritans and Catholics, had a dampening effect on English witchcraft and possession cases. This suppression lasted for decades and was reinforced among judges and magistrates by some high-profile witchcraft cases that were judged to have been fraudulent.[14]

The relative dearth of successful witchcraft-possession cases extended from the 1630s—spanning the reign of Charles I, who replaced James on the throne in 1625, soon after the planting of the Plymouth colony in 1620—until the outbreak of the English Civil War in 1642.[15] This trend was definitively broken by a resurgence in dispossessions and a major witchcraft outbreak in Essex, England, from 1645 to 1647. This outbreak emerged during the upheaval of the Civil War, when communities lacked the assize judges who traditionally restrained the progression of witchcraft cases, and at a moment when the removal of censorship led to an explosion of printed material and propaganda.[16] At that time, Matthew Hopkins and John Stearne oversaw a godly campaign to root out demonic influence, which resulted in more than 250 accusations and, astonishingly, more than 100 executions. When the panic ended, Hopkins's self-justifying tract *The Discovery of Witches* (1647) could not prevent the collapse of his reputation and the ridicule he would have felt most acutely had he not died just a few months after its publication.[17]

The second half of the seventeenth century saw the gradual reappearance of published witchcraft-possession cases, between the 1650s and 1670s, as England transitioned from the Interregnum and the reign of Charles II to that of James II.[18] In New England, the first decades of the "Great Migration" of colonists had resulted in the transplantation of more than twenty thousand English settlers, primarily to Massachusetts and Connecticut. In these building years, New England settlements were predominantly Puritan in nature.[19] Tensions over the future viability of this "errand into the wilderness" coalesced when James II suspended Massachusetts's charter in 1684 and absorbed the region into the Dominion of New England under royal authority.[20] Colonists chafed at this loss of autonomy until Protestants on both sides of the Atlantic, alarmed by James II's Catholicism as much as his authoritarianism, fomented the Glorious Revolution and installed William and Mary in his place.[21] Even though the possession script remained largely consistent, the English climate for witchcraft-possession cases after the Hopkins witch-hunt was clouded by demonological and philosophical sources that emphasized fraud and natural causes, such as melancholy, to explain demoniacs' performances and witches' confessions.[22] Nonetheless, many more English possession pamphlets emerged in the period from 1680 to 1700 and reignited the bitter controversies that made the advocacy of preternatural claims dangerous for men and women's credit and lives.[23]

As one would expect, it took some time before official prosecution of preternatural phenomena like possession and witchcraft emerged in

New England. While the colonists came with an already intact cultural tradition of wonders that included demonic and witchcraft-possession, the colonies lacked the dynamics of settled communities and relatively unfettered print trade that enabled the spread of published possession tracts in England. Between 1620 and 1700 New England was planted, expanded, and struggled to assert godly Protestant rule over the European and Indian populations. English migration to New England involved the movement of many people, largely but not entirely Puritan, who brought with them a sense of Englishness despite their remove. They had a millennial view of their mission, famously likened by John Winthrop to the "city on a hill" from Mathew 5:14, and imbued even everyday occurrences with providential significance.[24] In the first years of New England's settlement, few cases of witchcraft or possession proceeded through the courts, and straightforward demonic possession was extremely rare. Indeed, Cotton Mather provides the only unambiguous reference to a demonic possession, by the "Boy of Tocutt," that involved neither witchcraft nor sectarians like Quakers or Baptists. Increase Mather did attribute the trembling fit of a troubled man who visited him in 1682 to "a sign of Satanical Possession,"[25] but it was Cotton Mather's relation of the story of the Boy of Tocutt, so called for his residence in that town in Connecticut, that provided the fuller record. The story emerged from his grandfather Richard Mather's papers and was supposed to have happened "many (perhaps Thirty) years ago," or around 1659.[26] The story of the Boy of Tocutt followed his descent from dissolute and worldly behavior in the Netherlands to full-blown possession in New England. For years, he vacillated between confessing his sins and reveling in them, and eventually admitted to having familiarity with the Devil. Notwithstanding this compelling example, however, in New England the enactment of the possession script was almost always accompanied by the naming of a human agent as the cause.

When witchcraft-possession cases did occur, they were most likely to find their way into print as published sermons or as part of godly tracts that invoked these phenomena to support the tenets of faith. These texts informed and were informed by the transatlantic relationships that many eminent New England Puritans maintained with nonconformists back in England, usually Neoplatonist divines who committed themselves to use remarkable providences to eliminate atheism and Sadducism. Ministers like the Mathers circulated letters, manuscripts, and published tracts, and this transatlantic flow of texts was the primary source for printed material even after the development of a colonial printing press by 1639.[27]

Cotton Mather's correspondence with noteworthy men such as Richard Baxter considerably influenced his own writings on witchcraft.[28] Works by Meric Casaubon, Henry More, and Joseph Glanvill were also formative for Mather; these men, as Barbara Shapiro writes, "applied the proof of fact to establish the existence of spiritual phenomena. Their concern was fueled not by a zeal to prosecute witches but by an aspiration to show the existence of spirit to an age that appeared to them overly attracted to mechanism and materialism."[29] Cotton Mather's drive to locate and record instances of wonders that defied natural explanation derived in part from the example set by Glanvill and More, and like them he argued that the possibility of fraud should not subject all reports of spirits to suspicion.[30] The Mathers can hardly be considered typical of New England's population, but they loom largely in the polemical articulation of witchcraft-possession under consideration here.

New England's Puritan establishment had greater control over printing and book shipments than their counterparts in England, but although the colony imported a preponderance of Bibles, prayer books, almanacs, and instructional texts, a considerable number of jest books and romances circulated as well.[31] Published controversies between Puritans and Anglicans, and by extension Catholics, reverberated in New England—particularly during the period from 1679 to 1685, when the lapse of the Press Act in England led to a proliferation of printed material. Although literacy may ultimately have undermined the Puritans' power in New England,[32] during this period it usually reinforced a godly conception of authority that adapted to suit its current political state. Witchcraft-possession tracts were especially attractive for transatlantic sale because both godly and worldly audiences counted as likely customers. John Dunton, a London bookseller who visited New England and the Mathers in the 1680s, later reprinted a variety of modified editions of both ministers' books. There was a market for books about witchcraft and possession on the eve of the Salem outbreak, in part because of the shared script that conveyed a language of order and authority in response to chaotic and bewildering events.

Because these links were strongest in Boston and its environs, it makes sense to focus this cultural analysis on the Salem outbreak rather than on singular cases that took place farther afield. While the historiography of American witchcraft has worked to move beyond New England,[33] Salem continues to attract both scholarly and popular attention because of the way its extant sources evoke a society caught up in extreme circumstances. Much of the literature on "Salem," which remains convenient shorthand for the broader crisis that spread from Salem Village and Town to Andover and nearby communities in Essex County, treats it as an exceptional event in early American history. To be sure, various factors made Salem unusual; key among these were the pressures resulting from years of Indian wars that rendered magistrates unusually willing to enforce the accusations of afflicted female accusers, which Mary Beth Norton highlights as a sign of Salem's exceptionalism.[34] But Salem emerged alongside an increase in the number of witchcraft-possessions in both England and New England after 1680, and despite the Puritans' greater institutional power in the colony, they had to address the same debates and controversies.[35] New England's particular political pressures influenced published demonic and witchcraft-possession cases, of course, but did not transform them by the turn of the eighteenth century into something substantively different from their earlier configuration.

Scholars have charted local specificities and various causes that contributed to the Salem outbreak, but these two chapters focus on the degree of transatlantic continuity that surpassed these differences. In the broader colonial project, gender, in all of its explicit and implicit forms, was one of the central systems through which various parties consistently negotiated contact, coexistence, and conflict. For example, differences in gender norms structured Puritans' antipathy for Native Americans and Quakers, whose differences made them seem devilish in the former case and possessed in the latter.[36] These "others" were two of the primary challengers to the Puritan sense of order, but myriad other enemies and worldly sins contributed to the instability that fueled the Salem outbreak. Most New England colonists in the seventeenth century shared an investment in the maintenance of order and social hierarchy in which gender was a primary contributor.[37] And, as in England, published texts and circulated manuscripts about witchcraft-possession perpetuated the reliance upon gender as a central organizing principle for power and authority. Even given the reversal of Puritans' relation to institutional power in New England compared to England, where Anglicans had the upper hand, the struggle to make stable meaning from embodied witchcraft-possession performances largely replicated the context in which John Darrell had struggled a century before.

Over the course of the seventeenth century the nature of demoniacs' symptoms, and the manner with which authorities attempted to wrest meaning from their bodies, continued to evoke the binary conceptions of order and disorder that both reflected and reconstituted patriarchal power. Seen within this broader context even the outbreak at Salem, which diverged from previous instances of preternatural harm in New England, takes its place on a continuum of events that wracked both sides of the Atlantic during this century of struggle over political and religious authority. For demoniacs and the authors who described their afflictions, gender provided a durable yet malleable language because of its rootedness in cultural understandings of possession and witchcraft. The continuities in demoniacs' symptoms, gendered invocations of patriarchal authority, and cases' implications for power and propaganda appear all the more compelling given the extent of the political and religious change that occurred in the seventeenth century.

Unmaking a Minister: Manhood in George Burroughs's Trial

The Essex County witchcraft-possession outbreak began in January 1692, in the home of Salem Village's minister, Reverend Samuel Parris, against a backdrop of widespread instability: the colonial charter had expired leaving governance in flux, warfare on the Maine frontier had increased fear of and tensions with Indian and French combatants, and internal divisions had revealed conflict over how best to protect New England's autonomy.[38] Reverend George Burroughs, though living on the Maine frontier in 1692, had served as minister in Salem Village from 1680 to 1683. During that time he lived with his wife as a boarder in the home of John and Rebecca Putnam. When he left Salem Village, Burroughs moved to Casco (which later became Falmouth), Maine, as their minister, where he lived until its destruction by the Wabanakis. Burroughs survived that assault and returned to Maine to live in Casco and later Wells. It was there that the thirty-nine-year-old minister was arrested in May 1692 and transported back to Salem on suspicion of witchcraft. As Mary Beth Norton has shown, there were numerous connections between the accusers and Burroughs, not to mention the likely routes for gossip that contributed to his unmaking.[39] As the case against him progressed, witnesses, magistrates, and clergy came to share a perception of Burroughs as a ringleader of the witches who sought to undermine and destroy godly New England.

While witchcraft-possession in New England was indelibly marked by conditions particular to its colonial location—such as its Indian wars, Puritan intensity, and political uncertainty—preternatural phenomena there retained many of their English cultural roots.[40] Proceedings taken against some of the male witch suspects in Salem, such as John Proctor and John Willard, echoed John Samuel's unmaking in Warboys a century earlier.[41] But Burroughs's conviction particularly resonated in the texts that alternately described, defended, and decried the proceedings. Both trial testimony and published texts record an implicit struggle to reconcile Burroughs's downfall with his potential claim to manly prerogatives, something that required his transformation from minister to witch. To be a minister in Puritan New England was to occupy a complex and important role, and even though much about Burroughs's actual religious belief and practice remains uncertain, he nonetheless retained claims to leadership as a result of his position. Burroughs was a practicing but not ordained minister, which meant that he preached but neither baptized nor administered communion.[42] As a social category, "minister" was so inherently and exclusively linked with men that it denoted "man," which allowed authors to invoke gendered questions of piety, social status, and honor all at once. The earlier fate of Anne Hutchinson, and of Quaker women who presumed to proselytize, demonstrates how Puritan New England regarded any challenges to the exclusive attribution of the role to men. Not coincidentally, Hutchinson's Antinomian heresies had cast her as a kind of witch figure, and Quakers were those about whom Puritan leaders like the Mathers made their most unsympathetic accusations of demonic possession.[43] Whatever Burroughs's failings, he embodied—if ambivalently—a social and discursive position that reinforced his status as a man above others. This might have placed him among those least susceptible to the Devil's overtures, but it also made him especially dangerous once he was believed to have capitulated.

In New England as in England, men and women were unmade into witches in ways that were embodied and enmeshed with power relations.[44] To move the analysis of Burroughs away from causes (why him?) and toward meaning (what did he come to represent?) suggests that his symbolic reversal from minister to witch constituted both a challenge to and exercise of patriarchal power. Burroughs's identity as a minister was dismantled amid a broader crisis that heightened tensions between competing men's claims to religious and political authority. And yet, these fears and conflicts only reinforced the colony's reliance upon men of credit to discern the meaning and implications of witchcraft-possession. Across the Anglo-Atlantic even the destruction of a potential patriarch, once he was sufficiently unmade, could serve to bolster patriarchal conceptions of authority.

George Burroughs's trial, which took place in August 1692, attracted some particularly distinguished members of the clergy. Reverend Increase Mather, who attended no other trials during the witchcraft outbreak, was there, as was Deodat Lawson, another former minister of Salem. Those who lodged formal accusations against Burroughs—not counting the confessed witches who named him as a confederate—were nearly evenly divided by sex and fell into two main groups: one of afflicted female accusers who performed symptoms of witchcraft-possession, and another predominantly male group of accusers who did not.[45] There are several factors that likely contributed to the stark division by sex in this case, such as men and women's different internalization of their complicity in demonic influence, magistrates' and ministers' variable reception of testimony, and the far greater number of women than men who acted as if they were possessed in New England.[46] Historians have shown how possession symptoms provided an outlet for discontent by female deponents who were largely disempowered, and an opportunity to direct fear and resentment brought on by the Indian wars onto one who survived when so many did not.[47] But the central question here relates to how, in witchcraft-possession cases, both groups of accusers invoked constructions of manhood as a way to transform Burroughs from a culturally recognizable man into a witch. Because honorable manhood required a proper balance between mastery and moderation, Burroughs's downfall was facilitated by representations of his manhood as both excessive and deficient.

The first category of accusers, those who acted as if they were possessed, emerged out of the initial manifestations of spectral interference in Samuel Parris's household. Although the afflicted of Salem were not classic demoniacs, their symptoms ably demonstrate the blurred line that existed between witchcraft and possession. They convulsed violently and reported seeing apparitions of the accused witches, of the spirits of dead people, and of animal familiars. They suffered from trances, rigidity, blindness, and dumbness. They reacted to the movements, touch, gaze, and speech of those they accused and said their torment would continue unless their tormentors were detained. These accusers also reported that the specters of the accused cajoled, threatened, and tortured them to sign the Devil's book, thus constituting a sufficiently clear articulation of the diabolical pact that clergy and magistrates were most likely to find actionable. Even without the emission of devilish voices, the vomiting of foreign objects, or knowledge of unlearned languages, the afflicted of Essex County invoked elements of the witchcraft-possession script to present themselves as innocent victims of preternatural torment. The gray area between bewitchment, obsession, and possession provided a way both to admit spiritual weakness—a key aspect of Puritan devotional life—and to displace responsibility for sinful and blasphemous behavior.[48] The most powerful leverage that the afflicted accusers had was their ability to provide spectral evidence. This often took the form of seeing apparitions of those they accused, and reporting the speech and actions of the apparitions in ways that suspects could not rebut without further implicating themselves. Some ministers expressed reservations about the viability of apparitions as a source of evidence, but spectral manifestations greatly amplified the value of the testimony by afflicted persons for as long as magistrates accepted their legitimacy.[49] The afflicted provided extensive and varied evidence against Burroughs, but their identification of and emphasis on him as a man and minister particularly signified a perverted manly authority that constituted a betrayal of both godly and worldly obligations.

Although the fact of Burroughs's sex may have been unremarkable, his afflicted accusers systematically addressed the components of his identity that comprised his manhood. They reiterated his status as a minister first to identify him and then to express both surprise at his fall from grace and a reflexive presumption that his inverted leadership granted him authority among witches rather than Christians. Mercy Lewis, an afflicted accuser who was a refugee from the Indian wars in Maine and a former servant of Burroughs, testified that his specter frequently tormented her to sign his book. Her identification of Burroughs as a minister emerged alongside her depiction of him as a devilish seducer, which further highlighted his inversion of his proper role. She declared that he had "carried me up to an exceeding high mountain and showed me all the kingdoms of the earth and told me that he would give them all to me if I would write in his book and if I would not he would throw me down and brake my neck: but I told him they were none of his to give and would not write if he threw me down on 100 pitchforks."[50] Lewis's vision would have been instantly recognizable to her godly audience as the temptation Christ faced in Matthew 4:8–9, when "the devil took him up to a very high mountain, and showed him all the kingdoms of the world in their magnificence, and he said to him, 'All these I shall give to you, if you will prostrate yourself and worship me.'" Lewis had learned the verse's lesson very well, and she modeled Christ-like resistance by reminding Burroughs-Satan that he had no power to deliver on his promises. Like the Devil, Burroughs's specter represented a tempter who lured discontented sinners with promises of material goods and social influence—a neat reversal of the proper role of a godly minister. Thus Burroughs was rhetorically elevated because of his role as minister but also cast, despite it, in the image of the tempter of souls.

The afflicted who accused Burroughs identified him through this role, calling him "a little man like a minister with a black coat on," and a "little black-haired man . . . in blackish apparel."[51] When Ann Putnam Jr. testified that she saw an apparition of a minister, she said "she was grievously affrighted and cried out 'oh dreadful: dreadful here is a minister come: what are Ministers witches too: whence come you and what is your name for I will complain of you though you be a minister: if you be a wizard.'"[52] Over time the claims of the afflicted echoed in the examinations of confessing witches, reinforcing the idea that Burroughs was a devilish leader set above common witches. He became *the* minister, as his accusers grappled with the question of his misdirected authority. A proper minister was supposed to act as a sober custodian of his family and flock, provide an example to his dependents, and represent godly authority in those little commonwealths.[53] The afflicted accusers' charges effectively unmade Burroughs along these same lines and in ways that supported circulating claims that Burroughs had been promised the role of the king of Hell.[54] Even if the offer was false, as New England Puritans knew most of Satan's promises to be, such a role offered an enduring but transposed authority that made sense in Essex County. In the same way, Burroughs made the witch meeting legible in a New England context; unlike European accounts of orgiastic sabbats, Burroughs oversaw a meeting centered on a devilish Lord's Supper with red bread.[55] For the afflicted accusers, the Devil's profane version of worship in New England did not look quite like Roman Catholicism or a French and Indian alliance, both likely options, but looked very much like an inversion of what they already knew. This constituted a partly veiled critique of New England's clergy,[56] especially since it was Burroughs's status as a minister that made him believable as this leader of witches and future king of Hell.

Part of what made charges against Burroughs effective was that his accusers cast him in the image of a witch at the same time that they unmade him as a decent man; in his case this entailed a set of ideas about ministers, husbands, fathers, and neighbors.[57] This meant that in addition to establishing that he had committed the crimes of witchcraft— harming by preternatural means and encouraging a diabolical compact between New Englanders and the Devil—his accusers also cast him as one who abused the prerogatives of patriarchal authority and who failed to show sufficient care to dependents. From a legal perspective, it was vitally important that the afflicted accusers provided spectral evidence that Burroughs had used preternatural means to take the lives of others.

On April 22, 1692, a witness reported that young Abigail Williams, one of the original afflicted accusers, said that "there was a little black minister that lived at Casco Bay" whose specter told her "that he had killed three wives, two for himself and one for Mr. Lawson: and that he had made nine Witches in this place."[58] The charge that Burroughs had murdered these former wives circulated through the testimony of many of his afflicted accusers, sometimes enabled by the testimony of confessed witches. During the examination of confessing witch Abigail Hobbs on May 9, the afflicted accusers fell into fits and said not only that Burroughs had pressed them to sign in the Devil's book but also that his dead wives appeared in order to name him as their murderer.[59] These claims, especially once they were reinforced by related testimony about his violence against Lawson's family, established not only that he had used witchcraft to kill but also that he embodied the complete inversion of a proper man, minister, husband, and father.[60]

The devilish image of Burroughs portrayed a minister who failed to nurture souls or protect them from devils and Indians and had instead used nefarious means to harm godly dependents and to work against Christian interests both within and beyond the communities in which he resided. To feed the outbreak's momentum, it was important that other ministers not see Burroughs as one of them or feel personally imperiled by his downfall. By attributing the deaths of Lawson's relations to Burroughs, his afflicted accusers established that he was not truly one of New England's godly ministers but was working against them. This sort of testimony effectively identified Burroughs as a minister-yet-murderer of women and children, and a recruiter of witches. This recipe proved particularly effective, and even as others added testimony about his alleged crimes, the most powerful aspect of Burroughs's witch image was his status as a minister on a perverted path. That Burroughs had been a minister in Salem meant that he was an unusual suspect, but it also provided his accusers with gossip that could be used as ammunition against him and allowed his denunciation to feed the momentum of the outbreak by expanding its scope and raising the stakes.[61]

Some of the gossip Burroughs's afflicted accusers used against him emphasized his lack of husbandly care and his excessive correction of his dependents, both charges for which he appeared to have a long-standing reputation. The afflicted female accusers who introduced and developed this charge had surely absorbed the community's attitudes toward Burroughs from his time in Salem ten years earlier. Burroughs's vulnerability was increased by the personal details offered by John and Rebecca Putnam, with whom he had boarded and from whom he had borrowed money when his first wife, Hannah, died in 1681. The residents of Salem ought not to have blamed Burroughs for having to board with the Putnams before the parsonage was built, since it was on their account that Burroughs had not been able to act as head of his own household, but however commonplace complex households were in colonial New England, his boarding with the Putnams constituted a dependence.[62] At the very least, this forced proximity facilitated the spread of gossip about his "sharp" treatment of Hannah and of his second wife, Sarah. Financial strain dogged Burroughs until he left his position at Salem in 1683, and when he returned to town, Putnam had him arrested for his failure to repay the funeral debt. Even though Burroughs's lack of solvency was the result of his withheld salary, it created another point of contention between him and the town he had tried to shepherd for three years.

In 1692 many of these rumors and memories reemerged, catalyzed by the broader suspicion of witchcraft in and around Salem. The domestic component of these charges was augmented by testimony from John Putnam Sr. that Burroughs had been unreasonably harsh with Hannah, despite the fact that she was a good and dutiful wife. Rebecca Putnam attested to the same, adding that the boarding couple had disagreed so seriously that they asked the Putnams to intervene. The argument was allegedly over Burroughs's demand that his wife sign a written covenant promising not to reveal his secrets.[63] As if this were not suspicious enough, several of the afflicted accusers reported Burroughs's spectral confession to having killed his first two wives. Perhaps it is unsurprising that the description of their apparitions provided by the Putnams' niece Ann Putnam Jr. was among the most dramatic. She described "Two women in winding sheets" who "turned their faces towards Mr. Burroughs and looked very red and angry and told him that he had been a cruel man to them. [A]nd that their blood did cry for vengeance against him." The ghostly women further told Ann that he had murdered them, the first by stabbing her under the arm and hiding the wound with sealing wax, and the second reported that Burroughs and his current wife had killed her so that they could be together.[64] This last piece of gossip about Burroughs's relatively swift marriage to his third wife after Sarah's death mingled with earlier rumors about his treatment of Hannah in a way that brought him into focus as a violent man. The afflicted accusers made sure that Burroughs's failings in these crucial relationships, even the parts that might have been hidden from public view, came to light.

There is no question that the afflicted accusers' dramatic fits and spectral manifestations drove the Essex County outbreak forward within and beyond Salem in 1692, but it was the combined effect of testimony from the afflicted and from regular folk that sealed Burroughs's fate. Where the afflicted and nonafflicted accusers overlapped was their depiction of him as a man who showed cruelty toward his dependents rather than the proper degree of moderate correction and care for their physical and spiritual well-being. Manhood, after all, was based—at least in principle—on having dependents rather than being one. As a result, an honorable man at the head of a household balanced his prerogatives with his responsibilities, commanded the respect of those he guided at home, and maintained credit among his fellow men in the community.[65] George Burroughs of Salem had appeared insufficiently independent and yet excessively controlling. Even if the former no longer applied when he moved to Maine, the latter charge followed him there.

In May 1692, Burroughs's newer neighbors and acquaintances—who did not suffer from the symptoms of witchcraft-possession—reported similar suspicions about his behavior as a husband. The court heard testimony about his conduct toward his second wife, Sarah, from one Mary Webber, who had been a neighbor of the Burroughs family in Casco Bay. Webber was not afflicted, but she along with her husband and "negro" servant reported hearing strange sounds and seeing images of a thing like a white calf and of Burroughs himself, in addition to Mary's sensing a terrifying presence in the night.[66] She claimed to have been well acquainted with Burroughs's wife and said that she "hath heard [Sarah] tell much of her husband's unkindness to her and that she dare not wright to her father to acquaint [him] how it was with her, and so desired me to write to her father that he would be pleased to send for her and told me she had been much affrighted" both by her husband and by mysterious happenings at their house in the night." Mary Webber went on to add that she knew nothing of the spectral assaults attributed to Burroughs "except by common report of others," which speaks to the important role that gossip played in this and other trials.[67] Hannah Harris, the nonafflicted woman who testified about Burroughs's ill treatment of Sarah, reported that many times after speaking with Sarah, George Burroughs returned and scolded his wife, saying that he knew what she had said in his absence. Furthermore, Harris said that Burroughs let his wife become seriously ill not long after having given birth and had balked when Harris called on neighbors for help. She also claimed that Burroughs had tried to convince her that if his wife did not get well, she should not tell anyone about it, which she refused.[68] These women's testimony about Burroughs's callous treatment of his second wife echoed what the afflicted accusers of Salem had already established regarding his reputation for cruelty and resulting failure as a proper husband. Notably, Burroughs was not the only male witch suspect who was accused of cruel treatment of a wife; John Willard, who was executed on the same day, faced similar accusations.[69] Of course wife-beaters were not generally accused of witchcraft, and not all male witches faced such allegations, but the charges clearly resonated in these men's cases as they had for John Samuel in Warboys, England, a century earlier. Such unrestrained passions—coupled with malice in the place of mercy, and linked rhetorically with savage and unnatural Indians in New England Puritans' imaginations—further cemented these men's resemblance to witches by unmaking them as proper men.

Besides Rebecca Putnam, Mary Webber, and Hannah Harris, Burroughs's nonafflicted accusers were male peers who reported rumors—sometimes disseminated boastfully by the minister himself—of his remarkable strength that allowed him to brandish heavy rifles at arm's length that other men could barely lift, and handle entire barrels of cider or molasses in the same manner. This testimony emerged when Benjamin Hutchinson related the claims of the afflicted accuser Abigail Williams and was expanded upon by several men who knew Burroughs from Maine.[70] Simon Willard, William Wormall, and Samuel Webber related tales of strength that they had heard about, witnessed, or received from Burroughs himself.[71] Thomas Greenslit offered first-hand testimony about Burroughs's lifting and carrying of a molasses barrel in addition to lifting of the gun.[72] Their testimony reflected the primarily homosocial world in which Burroughs conducted business and served in the militia. That Burroughs boasted about his strength and performed feats to impress his peers suggests a variety of possible insights into his personality, but more pertinent here is the role that this testimony played in making him into a witch. Burroughs's behavior was unusual enough to make a lasting impression, but neither his feats nor his pride in them was patently preternatural; these were the sorts of claims that took on particular meaning once suspicion of witchcraft had been put into motion. Strength and status among male peers were central components of manhood, so it was not their existence but their *excess* that marked him as anomalous. His peers readily reported both gossip and eyewitness testimony about Burroughs's character, behavior, and speech because they shared with the afflicted accusers a sense that his inordinate faculties made him seem less like an ordinary man and more like an enemy within.

It certainly did not help Burroughs's case that he had also apparently reveled in leading people to believe that he had more than usual knowledge of their thoughts and actions. Burroughs may have tried to prevent Sarah from complaining to her male relatives,[73] but Sarah's brother Thomas Ruck contributed testimony that touched upon these supposed skills. Ruck reported that when the three of them walked for some miles together, Burroughs not only seemed to disappear and magically transport himself ahead of them, but he also chided Sarah for what she had been saying to her brother, claiming that "he knew their thoughts." Ruck testified that he had replied at the time that even the Devil did not know so much, but Burroughs apparently said, "My God makes known your Thoughts to me," something later interpreted as a reference to his allegiance to the Devil.[74] Such boasts might have recommended themselves as a means to control others' behavior, but in the climate of 1692 this charge, along with rumors of his mistreatment of his wives and efforts to browbeat his neighbors, took on ominous significance. Most importantly, Burroughs's attempts to demonstrate mastery through excessive strength, control, and knowledge—buttressed by his position as a minister—effectively transformed him into a figure with the power to lead a cabal of witches intending to bring down godly New England.

The same connotations of excess tinged the testimonies of the accusers who depicted Burroughs as one who was particularly exalted: Elizabeth Hubbard said that Burroughs's apparition told her as he pressed her to sign his book that "he was above a wizard for he was a conjuror," a statement that was repeated in later testimony.[75] Elizar Keysar suspected that Burroughs was "the Chief of all the persons accused for witchcraft or the Ring Leader of them all," and along with other helpful embellishments Mercy Lewis noted that Burroughs's spirit said that he had books that enabled him to raise the Devil, and that "the devil was his servant." Furthermore, Mary Walcott said, "I believe in my heart that Mr. George Burroughs is a dreadful wizard," and several accusers agreed that he had led the sacrament at the witch meeting; the preponderance of reports that emphasized Burroughs's eminence made it appear plausible that he had indeed been promised the role of the king of Hell.[76] In these accounts Burroughs achieved all the mastery one could hope for, and more, except that it emerged in an inverted and devilish context. His quest to impress and control those around him was reflected in the representations of him that merged his desire for inordinate mastery over others into the kind of malicious ambition commonly ascribed to witches.

Both Burroughs's excesses—knowledge, correction, strength, and attempts to control—and deficiencies—of husbandly care and pastoral guidance—contributed to his unmaking, but he also suffered from a dearth of supporters who might have spoken on his behalf. Burroughs appeared to have some support from a Captain Daniel King, at least, and of course community support was no guarantee of protection, as petitions in support of condemned and executed witches like Rebecca Nurse and John and Elizabeth Proctor demonstrate.[77] But the lack of supportive testimony on Burroughs's behalf greatly facilitated his transition from a man who ought to have been an unusual suspect into one who might be the worst of them all. It appears that one of Burroughs's supporters, who may have been King,[78] contributed unintentionally toward his unmaking by sending a letter containing some skeptical arguments from a thirty-six year-old English publication, Thomas Ady's *A Candle in the Dark* (1656).[79] When Burroughs read this in court and claimed not to have copied it out of any text, those who recognized it chalked this up to a devilish lie that bespoke other lies. Not only did the use of Ady prove counterproductive to Burroughs's defense, but there do not appear to have been enough people willing to stand by him to constitute the kind of honorable manly community that might have helped him counter the charges. Whatever allies Burroughs had in Salem or who had survived the wars in Maine, they did not provide the volume or type of corroboration that could create a counternarrative. Before long, in the absence of contrary testimony, his specter had already confessed to everything most suspected and feared about this counterfeit man of God.

Reflection upon what Burroughs lacked, however, should not be taken to mean that his gendered failings signaled either feminization or effeminacy. At first, because of the overwhelming number of accused witches who were female and their greater likelihood to progress from accusation and a trial to conviction and execution,[80] it seems plausible that male witches would have been feminized. But like other male witches, Burroughs's "lack" was not a feminization so much as an unmaking as a man. The difference stems from his excessive embodiment of some masculine attributes, and the fact that the Anglo-American cultural association of "witch" with "woman" was dominant but not exclusive. As the trial testimony demonstrated, both the accusers who acted as if they were possessed and those who did not denoted Burroughs as minister and man because the fact of his sex and professed calling lent power to allegations that he represented a perverted version of those roles; his potential claims to patriarchal prerogatives ultimately made him resemble a particularly powerful wizard, conjuror, and future king of Hell. Through their testimony, his accusers deconstructed his potential claims to honorable manhood by using gender as one lens through which the language and meaning of his guilt manifested itself. Both afflicted and nonafflicted accusers invoked his lack and excess of gendered qualities because such language crossed lines of sex, sort, and competing perceptions of witchcraft as a crime. Despite the lack of a simple association between sex and the outcome of witchcraft-possession cases, gendered conceptions of sin fed deeply held shared beliefs of what a man and minister was and reveal the ways that questions of manhood factored in George Burroughs's downfall.

The Published Burroughs and the Restoration of Patriarchy

Because published sources about witchcraft in Essex County were based upon transcripts of examinations, the published Burroughs largely resembled the man invoked in court: a minister-witch whose crimes suited both popular conceptions of malefic witchcraft and elites' emphasis on witchcraft as demarcated by the diabolical covenant.[81] Burroughs never confessed, but the magistrates became convinced of his guilt because his apparition—the very appearance of which suggested that he had permitted the Devil to represent him—pressed the afflicted to sign in the Devil's book, and because of persistent testimony about his leadership among witches and role as a future king of Hell. In contrast to the four other male witches hanged during the Essex County outbreak, there is a range of suggestive references to Burroughs in the corroborative writings of Deodat Lawson and Cotton Mather, in cautionary tracts by John Hale and Increase Mather, and in skeptical accounts by Thomas Brattle and Robert Calef. As we have seen, Burroughs's excessive and insufficient manhood played an important role in the process of unmaking him from a man to a witch during the trials of 1692. In these published texts, though, it was Burroughs's identity as a minister—a man endowed with more authority than most—that took on additional significance. His status as a minister made him noteworthy, yet this also held troubling implications that authors relegated to the background. Each of the six aforementioned authors had a different sense of the pressures that the witchcraft-possession outbreak had placed on the colony, and each crafted an image of Burroughs best suited to their view of how to control the trials' meaning and implications. What made Burroughs appear especially guilty in 1692—his aberrant manhood that nonetheless held potential claims to patriarchal and ecclesiastical authority—made him an important but precarious touchstone.

George Burroughs received the most detailed treatment in sources that supported the claims of the afflicted accusers and the judgment of the magistrates, such as those written by Deodat Lawson and Cotton Mather. In 1692's *A brief and true narrative of some remarkable passages related to sundry persons afflicted by witchcraft*, Lawson explained his return to Salem, where he had briefly served as minister himself, and strove to convince the reader that what he had witnessed could only be explained by devilish interference. In a sermon entitled *Christ's Fidelity the only Shield against Satan's Malignity*, later republished in an extended form in London in 1704, Lawson expressed his support of the official reaction to the Salem outbreak by asserting that officials there had followed proper scriptural precedent.[82] In the sermon, Lawson intoned the familiar verses pertaining to the means by which God allowed the Devil, or lower-order devils, to afflict mankind. He asserted that witches attempted to swell their ranks by pressing others to sign the Devil's book, and that the Devil thereby "having them in his subjection, *by their Consent,* he will use their Bodies and Minds, Shapes, and Representations, to Affright and Afflict others."[83] Having confirmed that the spectral apparition of a person connoted their guilt of having covenanted with Satan, and reiterated the idea that the godliest communities were the Devil's particular targets, he nonetheless assured his audience that God would surely suppress Satan's malice against His own people.[84]

Lawson carefully navigated the unsteady ground between ascribing guilt to any whose apparition had appeared, and allowing that God might permit some innocent people to be so represented to serve His purposes. "It cannot but be a matter of deep humiliation, to such as are Innocent," he wrote, not only that God would permit them to be named, but also that all of New England must wonder that He might allow the Devil to use "at least their shape and appearances, instrumentally, to Afflict and Torture, other Visible Subjects" of God's kingdom.[85] While Lawson's rhetoric was not as overheated as that of the Reverend Samuel Parris, in whose home the first signs of preternatural affliction appeared,[86] Lawson nonetheless cautioned his listeners and readers that it was possible that some "here in the congregation" might have "given up their Names, and Souls to the Devil: Who by Covenant Explicit or Implicit, have bound themselves to be his Slaves and Drudges, consenting to be Instruments, in whose shapes, he may Torment and Afflict their Fellow Creatures." Lawson demonstrated his view of the proceedings through his description of the "Poor Afflicted Persons, that are by Divine Permission, under the Direful Influence of Satan's Malice," and his encouragement of the "Honored Magistrates" to "do all that in you lies, to Check and Rebuke Satan."[87]

After having established these boundaries for the proceedings, Lawson went on to describe the condition of the afflicted, those they accused, and the confessing witches. What he had to say about the accused who did not confess was, of course, derived from the testimony of their afflicted accusers, which emphasized the spectral biting and pinching of the afflicted and relayed testimony about the witch meetings at which the accused supposedly held a devilish Lord's Supper. Most of Lawson's account referred to each group collectively, but among the particular individuals he devoted the most space to George Burroughs. After relating the central aspects of the case against his predecessor—his unusual strength, mistreatment of his wives, and apparent preternatural knowledge—Lawson contributed new material by commenting on Burroughs's comportment in pursuit of his own defense. He wrote that not only had Burroughs failed to answer the charges in any substantive degree but that he also "had the Liberty of Challenging his Jurors, before empanelling, according to the Statute in that case, and used his Liberty in Challenging many; yet the Jury that were Sworn brought him in Guilty."[88] By this time the narrative of Burroughs's suspect character, preternatural capacities, and cruelty as a husband had been compressed into a comprehensible whole, so that every component further reinforced the others. Burroughs's active attempts to control his trial by influencing the composition of the jury were entirely within his rights, but in Lawson's telling his behavior suggests the unwarranted contrivances of a witch rather than the desperation of an innocent man. Like his excessive strength and knowledge, Burroughs's undue suspicion of his peers facilitated his transformation from a minister into one who was no longer recognizable as one. What Lawson accomplished by the end of his excerpt about Burroughs's trial was the resounding verdict put forth by a jury who had already been purged of those against whom Burroughs took exception; this sense of unanimity among the honorable manly community became a cornerstone of Puritan defenses of the witchcraft trials in general and Burroughs's downfall in particular.

Cotton Mather wrote prolifically about the Essex County witchcraft trials and has been the one most commonly accorded blame for the deadly folly of the proceedings. However inappropriate it would be to attribute responsibility for such an extensive and complex episode to any one person, his tendency to suppress the names of suspects while also insisting that they were guilty has complicated the question.[89] The same contradictory impulses appeared in his writing about spectral evidence; he had previously published in *Memorable Providences* (1689) that if "a Person *bewitched* should pretend to see the Apparition of *such* or *such* an one, yet this may be no infallible Argument of their being Naughty people, it seems possible that the Devils may so traduce the most *Innocent,* the most praise-worthy," as had happened in the possession of Elizabeth Knapp in Groton.[90] Still, his utter certainty in the legitimacy of the Goodwin children's possession and the guilt of the woman they accused lent his caution a cursory tone. His sincere determination not to convict innocents ran aground upon his certainty that New England was being buffeted by assaults of witches, devils, Indians, French Catholics, and Quakers. In 1692, feeling personally and collectively targeted led him to praise order and the magistrates above all, and to defend them from any charges that they had acted hastily or maliciously in the colony's time of trial.

Cotton Mather's witchcraft publications increase the reader's sense that Burroughs was both particularly present and also substantively absent in these texts, and that he performed a discursive function apart from his purported confederates. Mather's *The Wonders of the Invisible World* (1692) originated as a sermon delivered the day before Burroughs's trial and evolved into a defense of the trials produced with the blessing of Governor William Phips and bolstered by an author's defense from the lieutenant governor—and chief justice of the Court of Oyer and Terminer created to process the witchcraft trials—William Stoughton. It received considerable attention, including a large advertisement in the *London Gazette*, a review in the *London Compleat Library,* and three English editions.[91] The text is a wide-ranging collection of sermons, memorable providences, and famous instances of witchcraft in Sweden and Bury St. Edmunds, England. Perhaps unsurprisingly, as the volume's main goal was to defend the existence of witchcraft and the proceedings taken against it in Essex County, Mather emphasized cases that allowed him most successfully to argue that spectral evidence had not been the only means by which the accused were convicted. Burroughs's textual presence varied; in one edition his was the only case study, and another imprint placed him at the top of the list of five featured convicted witches, though his was the only name reduced to initials. The

1693 London edition, abridged and republished by London editor John Dunton, reproduced all five case studies with Burroughs in first place.[92] Mather's description of Burroughs did not depart significantly from his characterization of the accused women, but it offered something that Mather needed: a sense of an overwhelming surplus of evidence of guilt that had been supplied by myriad deponents on various elements of malefic and diabolical witchcraft. Burroughs's status as a man and minister lent him infamy and made him appear a particular threat in just the ways that most suited Mather's overarching goals.

Right from the beginning of Mather's account of Burroughs's trial, he makes it clear that his subject was especially odious: "Glad I should have been, if I had never known the Name of this Man; or never had this occasion to mention so much as the first Letters of his Name." Given that Burroughs's name was redacted to "G. B." throughout, Mather nearly implies that its invocation might wield malevolent power, something at odds with his theology but powerfully suggestive nonetheless. Mather then expressed hesitance to write the story, but because "Government" required him to include an account of this trial, it behooved Mather "with all Obedience to submit unto the Order."[93] Having established both his proper deference to government and a formulaic modesty, Mather assiduously detailed all of the ways Burroughs represented the ultimate threat to and betrayal of New England. Mather did not hesitate to use superlative language when describing all five witches; Susanna Martin was "one of the most impudent, scurrilous, wicked Creatures in the World," and Martha Carrier was a "rampant Hag" whom the Devil had promised could be queen of Hell.[94] But Mather enumerated the quantity and type of witnesses against Burroughs with particular vehemence. He reiterated testimony that described Burroughs as "above the ordinary Rank of Witches" and that "he was the Person who had Seduced and Compelled" the afflicted into "the snares of Witchcraft" by promising them fine clothes and bringing them poppets and thorns to afflict and "Bewitch all Salem Village."[95] Mather accorded Burroughs special rank, authority, and malevolence and made sure that the reader grasped the overwhelming nature of the evidence against him.

Mather's main agenda was to defend the executions of convicted witches by emphasizing the preponderance of evidence beyond what was spectral, but he returned to Burroughs's lack and excess of key aspects of manhood because these failings, and the gendered language that gave them meaning, provided an effective way to fashion Burroughs as a faulty man and inverted minister. Mather began by logically connecting the sensational reports of Burroughs's spectral activity with the common report of him, stating that Burroughs "had been Infamous for the Barbarous usage of his two late Wives, all the Country over" and speculating about Burroughs's possible grudge against the Lawsons that had led him preternaturally to murder the minister's wife and daughter.[96] Just as enough smoke likely signaled a fire, Mather invoked Burroughs's gendered failings to convince the reader that spectral evidence and the testimony of confessed witches had confirmed rather than produced the key evidence against him. Mather further unmade Burroughs as man and minister by citing his "Antipathy to Prayer, and the other Ordinances of God, tho by his Profession singularly Obliged thereunto." This, on top of his role as the principal seducer and mastermind of New England's downfall led Mather to make a canny link to one of John Darrell's cases of witchcraft-possession. "When the Lancashire Witches were Condemn'd," he wrote, "I don't remember that there was any considerable further Evidence than that of the Bewitched, and than that of some that confessed. We see so much already against G. B. But this being indeed not enough, there were other things to render what had been already produced *credible*."[97] In his classic style, Mather simultaneously defended the evidence as sufficient even while declaring that it was insufficient. To answer these protestations, he subsequently turned to the signs of Burroughs's immoderate failings that reflected negatively upon his moderation and manhood.

Mather explained Burroughs's "Domestick Affairs" and the various ways in which he had kept his wives "in a strange kind of Slavery," while assuring the reader that the jury had heard sufficient other accounts of Burroughs's murder by preternatural means. After relating Burroughs's excessive control of and insufficient care for his wives, Mather singled out Burroughs as one whose testimony had been especially compromised by inconsistencies: "Now there never was a Prisoner more eminent for them, than G. B. both at his Examination and on his Trial. His Tergiversations [evasions], Contradiction, and Falsehoods were very sensible."[98] While these were only "unlucky Symptoms of Guilt" rather than proof, Mather presented Burroughs's mishap with the portion cribbed from Thomas Ady's skeptical tract as a final indication of his culpability. This catalogue of excesses and emphasis on Burroughs's recalcitrance allowed Mather to avoid entertaining any uncertainty despite admitting that Burroughs had protested his innocence until his death.[99] While others better represented the traditional image of a prideful, malefic crone, Burroughs provided Mather with something more suitable to his larger argument about the presence of a widespread conspiracy to bring down the godly in New England. Even when operating apart from Mather's explicit concern with spectral evidence, gendered conceptions of Burroughs's failings as a man and minister contributed to Mather's unmaking of him because of the power that gendered language had to convey a broad cultural picture of a malevolent, perverted kind of pastoral care from this minister turned witch.

As the Essex County trials waned, ministers Increase Mather and John Hale wrote more openly about their concerns about the use of spectral evidence and the likelihood that that colony had perpetrated a grave miscarriage of justice. Their texts represented substantial challenges to the logic that had fueled the Salem outbreak, while at the same time they sought to defend the magistrates from charges that they had ignorantly or avidly facilitated the execution of innocents. Both authors referred to Burroughs, but the suspect minister played a less overt role than in the earlier publications. Increase Mather, like his son Cotton, struggled to reconcile scriptural certainty of witches and devils with the need to suppress the excesses that had taken place across Essex County. But unlike Cotton, Increase Mather articulated in *Cases of Conscience* (1693) the growing sense among clergy and others in Massachusetts that the reliance upon spectral evidence, in particular, had been erroneous and led to the loss of innocent life. As much as both Mathers rejected the idea that their books—*Wonders of the Invisible World* and *Cases of Conscience*—contradicted one another, there is no mistaking the fact that they substantively diverged.[100] On the whole, *Cases of Conscience* methodically demonstrated that the Devil could take the shape of an innocent person and would strive to do so in order to sow dissension in godly communities. Increase Mather also pointedly criticized overreliance upon the testimony of "bewitched or possessed" accusers because of the Devil's power to deceive. It was only in the postscript and in the appending of his son's "Return of Several Ministers" that the text merged its concerns about the court's procedures with a reassertion of the reality of witches, advocated their "speedy, vigorous Prosecution," and reasserted his confidence in the magistrates.[101]

It was in Increase Mather's postscript that he made his only explicit reference to George Burroughs. After affirming that "there are such horrid Creatures as Witches in the World; and that they are to be extirpated and cut off from amongst the People of God," Mather denied making "any Reflection on those worthy Persons who have been concerned in the late Proceedings at Salem: They are wise and good Men, and have acted with all Fidelity according to their Light." He further averred:

> Pitty and Prayers rather than Censures are their due; on which account I am glad that there is published to the World (by my Son) a Breviate of the Tryals of some who were lately executed, whereby I hope the thinking part of Mankind will be satisfied, that there was more than that which is called Spectre Evidence for the Conviction of the Persons condemned. I was not my self present at any of the Tryals, excepting one, viz. that of George Burroughs; had I been one of his Judges, I could not have acquitted him: For several Persons did upon Oath testifie, that they saw him do such things as no Man that has not a Devil to be his Familiar could perform: And the Judges affirm, that they have not convicted any one meerly on the account of what Spectres have said, or of what has been represented to the Eyes or Imaginations of the sick bewitched Persons.[102]

This passage expresses approval of his son's book and corroborates his son's assurance that there was enough nonspectral evidence— particularly in the case of George Burroughs—to convict. Yet however Increase Mather expressed his support for the magistrates, the overwhelming argument of his book was that they had exhibited the very credulity he had so ably dismantled in the preceding seventy pages. By reiterating the preponderance of evidence against Burroughs from "several" accusers, whom he now characterized as "sick bewitched Persons," Mather crafted a version of Burroughs whose guilt transcended the limitations of spectral testimony. If the references to Burroughs as a minister and likely leader of the devilish sacraments slipped to the background, they nonetheless evoked his presence in the text. Because Burroughs was a minister, Mather needed to show the overwhelming nature of the evidence against him and demonstrate that the court had not executed a man of God. Increase Mather contributed to an ongoing implicit conversation about rightful patriarchal authority in the colony by demonstrating that the clerical peers who mattered most concurred with the magistrates' judgment. For writers who supported the original logic of the outbreak and for those who questioned it, Burroughs provided a serviceable example in the larger project of policing potential claims to patriarchal authority in the colony.

A similarly guarded account of the outbreak appeared in John Hale's *A Modest Enquiry into the Nature of Witchcraft*. Completed in 1697 and published in 1702, two years after his death, it defended the need to prosecute the crime of witchcraft while also expressing dismay at the court's excesses. Hale explained that he had observed the events as they transpired, and he assured the reader that there was "in the Justices, Judges & others concerned, a conscientious endeavour to do the thing that was right." He listed the books of law and treatises on the nature and prosecution of witchcraft they had used but emphasized that those who confessed had provided the most dramatic and conclusive proof.[103] It was in the course of detailing these confessions that Hale made a few succinct references to Burroughs. He recorded Ann Foster's fear "that G. B. and M. C. [Martha Carrier] would kill her; for they appeared unto her (in Spectre, for their persons were kept in other Rooms in the Prison) and brought a sharp pointed iron like a spindle . . . and threatned to stab her to death with it; because she had confessed her Witchcraft."[104] Burroughs and Carrier, as purported king and queen of Hell, fit the narrative that merged malefic and diabolic conceptions of witchcraft in ways that best suited the crime as defined by the magistrates, and it was the element of leadership to which Hale returned throughout.

Hale also included an earlier confession by forty-year-old William Barker, who invoked Burroughs as a principal leader of a devious demonic plot to take over New England. Barker reported seeing not far from the Salem Village meetinghouse "about an hundred five Blades, some with Rapiers by their side, which was called and might be more for ought I know by B and Bu. [ministers George Burroughs and John Busse] and the Trumpet sounded, and Bread and Wine which they called the Sacrament, but I had none; being carried over all on a Stick, never being at any other Meeting." Barker added that their "design was to destroy Salem Village, and to begin at the Minister's House, and to destroy the Church of God, and to it up Satan's Kingdom, and then all will be well."[105] In addition to raising the curious question of how minister John Busse of Wells, Maine, managed to avoid being tried despite being named in this way, Barker's testimony provided a vision of an organized and martial witches' meeting overseen by clergy bent on the colony's destruction. Although Hale did not express Burroughs's guilt in terms as clear as those used by Lawson or Cotton Mather, he reiterated the preponderance of evidence against him that had apparently confounded even Burroughs himself. As Hale recorded, Burroughs "denied all, yet said he justified the Judges and Jury in Condemning of him: because there were so many positive witnesses against him: But said he died by false Witnesses." Despite Hale's caution, and sober demonstration of the myriad ways people could be deceived by the Devil into thinking that witchcraft explained their misfortunes, Burroughs's was one of the main cases Hale used to illustrate his commitment to support the decisions of the magistrates. Although Hale did not ultimately express the confidence that the Mathers had in Burroughs's guilt, he took care to record his conversation with one confessing witch who claimed to have witnessed Burroughs's "Exhorting at the Witch Meeting at the Village." He said to her: "You are one that bring this man to Death, if you have charged any thing upon him that is not true, recal[l] it before it be too late, while he is alive. She answered me, she had nothing to charge her self with, upon that account."[106] Burroughs provided not only a lynchpin between malefic and diabolic witchcraft but also a unifying target against whom legitimate godly ministers could be measured. Even Hale's attempt to express reservations about the proceedings could use Burroughs as a reassuring example, at least for the time being.

In later, more explicitly critical texts, however, George Burroughs's status as a minister continued to cast an uneasy shadow over his legacy. In key challenges to the Puritan establishment's handling of the witchcraft trials that were not written by clergy, Burroughs's presence was profoundly ambivalent, either excised completely or held up as a particular example of folly. Because publication was tightly controlled in Puritan New England, dissenting voices faced considerable challenges getting their works into print. For some, the circulation of a manuscript allowed for the dissemination of controversial views without constituting as direct a challenge to authority. It is certain that Thomas Brattle's critical "Letter" of October 8, 1692, was intended for circulation among potential allies who had an eye on the Court of Oyer and Terminer that was dissolved by the governor later that month.[107] A wealthy merchant and member of the Royal Society, Brattle was a frequent critic of the Puritan leadership who later struggled with the Mathers over the founding Boston's Brattle Street Church.[108] His "Letter" provides a masterful example of how gendered language facilitated challenges against those customarily granted deference and respect. Brattle was not an indiscriminate critic of the colonial powers, and the Essex County outbreak allowed him to express a sharp rebuke of some while modeling enough respect for others to fashion himself as a properly deferential gentleman. Brattle's manuscript dealt extensively in the language of honorable manhood, but he notably omitted George Burroughs when defending other men who were executed the same day. This omission, coupled with Brattle's stronger emphasis on dismantling the credit of the predominantly female possessed accusers, suggests how gender provided a flexible medium for power struggles such as those in the immediate aftermath of Salem.

Brattle directly challenged the "Salem gentlemen" whose credulity had caused them to rely upon methods that were little better than "sorcery,"[109] but before rebuking the magistrates he emphasized his reluctance to challenge those in authority:

> Obedience to lawfull authority I evermore accounted a great duty; and willingly I would not practise any thing that might thwart and contradict such a principle . . . and I am sure the mischiefs, which arise from a fractious and rebellious spirit, are very sad and notorious; insomuch as I would sooner bite my finger's ends than willingly cast dirt on authority. . . . Far, therefore, be it from me, to have any thing to do with those men . . . of a factious spirit, and never more in their element than when they are declaiming against men in public place, and contriving methods that tend to the disturbance of the common peace. I never accounted it a credit to my cause, to have the good liking of such men.[110]

Brattle's self-fashioning here was formulaic but skillfully established his resolve—in terms that neatly countered Cotton Mather's depiction of his enemies—to respect authority and shun those of a more peevish spirit. Brattle's liberal political and religious orientation toward the Church of England may previously have attracted the enmity of some of his contemporaries, but he took care to present himself as driven to write by duty and conscience, lest a few men and "afflicted children" bring further shame to the colony. Brattle further suggested that the reader "be thankfull to God for it, that all men are not thus bereft of their senses; but that we have here and there considerate and thinking men, who will not thus be imposed upon, and abused, by the subtle endeavours of the crafty one."[111]

Having established his support for certain of the gentlemen in the colony's leadership, Brattle shifted the blame directly onto the possessed accusers, confessing witches, and those foolish enough to heed them. Brattle acknowledged that it was misleading to describe the "afflicted children" as such, since "there are several young men and women that are afflicted, as well as children," but he justified the use of the phrase because it "has most prevailed among us, because of the younger sort that were first afflicted, and therefore I make use of it."[112] This formulation also facilitated Brattle's goal to sacrifice the credit of these participants in order to make his challenge to the magistrates more palatable.

He described the "afflicted, possessed children" as "blind, nonsensical girls" who "lye, [or] at least speak falsely," and depicted about thirty of the fifty-five confessors, some of whom "are known to be distracted, crazy women," as "possessed (I reckon) with the Devill, and afflicted as the children are."[113] Culturally, these subjects constituted a more fitting focus for blame and allowed Brattle to critique, if not witchcraft-possession itself, then at least of the methods used in its prosecution.

The most dangerous accusation against the magistrates was that their actions had led to the execution of innocents, and accordingly Brattle treaded carefully when referring to the "late executions" of August 19, at which George Burroughs, John Proctor, John Willard, George Jacobs, and Martha Carrier were put to death. It was the single deadliest day for male witches in colonial Anglo-America; of the nineteen people hanged during the Salem affair, five were men, and four of them died that day.[114] "Some of the condemned," Brattle wrote, "went out of the world not only with as great protestations, but also with as good shews of innocency, as men could do."[115] Brattle recorded their forgiveness of their accusers, their lack of recrimination against those who had condemned them, and their earnest desire for the prayers of the attending minister Cotton Mather. They seemed "very sincere, upright, and sensible of their circumstances on all accounts; especially Proctor and Willard, whose whole management of themselves, from the Goal to the Gallows, and whilst at the Gallows, was very affecting and melting to the hearts of some considerable Spectatours, whom I could mention to you:—but they are executed, and so I leave them." Were it not for competing accounts that accord Burroughs a much more significant role in the events of August 19, Brattle's elevation of Proctor and Willard (not to mention his erasure of George Jacobs and Martha Carrier) might be taken as the full story of the events that day. Brattle's "Letter" represented his best effort at crafting an account that would convince readers that serious lapses in judgment had taken place in Salem and Essex County and that it behooved honorable gentlemen of Boston to accord greater authority to those who had not succumbed to the panic. Burroughs, apparently, did not suit this agenda.

For Brattle's purposes in October 1692, there was little to gain by attempting to redeem Burroughs, the notorious minister-witch about whose guilt both Mathers expressed their complete confidence. The best way for Brattle to navigate the dangerous project of criticizing established authority was to attack the subjects with the least cultural or social credibility—the largely female accusers who acted as if they were

possessed, and the confessing witches—as a way to undermine the legitimacy of the men who had compromised patriarchal order by taking them
seriously.[116] The simultaneous centrality and marginality of Burroughs
in all of these texts attests to the ways that gender provided a flexible
cultural touchstone during and after the outbreak in Salem and Essex
County. Burroughs became legible as a witch on the basis of a broad set
of accusations about his sins as a man, husband, and minister; more than
any of the other male witch suspects (even those also accused of violent
treatment of their wives), Burroughs's accusers highlighted the ways he
exhibited the excesses and deficiencies of a faulty manhood. These failings, and the probity or foolishness of the judges who interpreted them,
drew men across the colony into a complex web of relationships with one
another and with the legacy of Salem.

We know that Brattle omitted Burroughs from his description of the
August 19 hangings because other accounts, both supportive and critical
of the trials, mention the events surrounding Burroughs's execution as
especially noteworthy. The prisoners on the gallows had the opportunity
to pray, confess, or ask for final forgiveness before they were hanged, at
least in part to serve as an example to the people who gathered to witness their demise. On that day, a particularly large and distinguished
crowd gathered, in all likelihood because Burroughs was scheduled to be
hanged; three of the justices were there, and several ministers, including
Nicholas Noyes of Salem, John Hale, Zachariah Symms, Samuel Cheever,
and Cotton Mather of Boston. Judge Samuel Sewall did not attend but
spoke afterward with Mather, who shared the developments that Sewall
recorded in his diary: "Mr. Burrough[s] by his Speech, Prayer, protesta-
tion of his Innocence, did much move unthinking persons, which occasions their speaking hardly [critically] concerning his being executed." In
the margins Sewall added his reflection, "Doleful Witchcraft!"[117] While
Sewall later deeply regretted his role in the Salem trials and was the only
judge to submit a formal apology for his actions therein, at this time he
remained convinced of the validity of the proceedings.[118] The diary entry
that recorded the events as Cotton Mather and Sewall perceived them
granted particular resonance to Burroughs's gallows prayer.

Sewall's account, recorded privately based on his discussion with
Cotton Mather, received corroboration from an unlikely source: Robert
Calef. Calef's *More Wonders of the Invisible World* (1700) later became
the principal published challenge to the Mathers, and he used the events
of August 19, 1692, to depict Cotton Mather as an alternately deluded
and merciless witch-hunter. If Calef was to be believed, Burroughs

provided the most dramatic spectacle of the day, which captivated many in the large crowd. Calef wrote that Burroughs's speech and prayer were "so well worded, and uttered with such composedness, and such (at least seeming) fervency of Spirit, as was very affecting, and drew Tears from many (so that it seemed to some, that the Spectators would hinder the Execution)," possibly because the ability to intone the Lord's prayer had long been used as a test for witchcraft. But at this critical moment the afflicted accusers called out renewed complaints against Burroughs, saying that the Devil had whispered the words in his ear. In response, Calef wrote that Mather, on horseback, reminded the crowd that the Devil often impersonated "an Angel of Light" and urged the executions to continue.[119] However untrustworthy a narrator Calef may have been, the passage suggests the hesitance that New Englanders would have felt at the prospect of executing a minister, who by his profession represented spiritual authority and a bulwark against the Devil's overtures.

Brattle, writing in 1692, could surely have made much of Burroughs's moving gallows speech, but he did not. The strategic omission, while he made a point of mentioning the poignant comportment of Willard and Proctor, suggests how thoroughly Burroughs did not suit Brattle's immediate goals. By the time of his trial, Burroughs the man had already become Burroughs the category of competing meanings, in which gender played its central but malleable role. Although female witches were likewise unmade and reduced to archetypes, in Burroughs's case his claims to some degree of patriarchal authority sharpened the stakes for all of the men seeking to shape the meaning of the Essex County outbreak in print.

Whatever their motivations, for all of these writers the language of manhood and authority—which merged in "minister"—provided an implicit way to fix the meaning of the trials in their aftermath. Written accounts of Burroughs's downfall harbored ambivalent tensions about the implications of unmaking a minister into a witch, but just as the agency gained by afflicted accusers was only fleeting, Burroughs's downfall represented a challenge to the clergy that was effectively shunted aside. Although some men faced greater scrutiny in the aftermath of Salem, written accounts of George Burroughs's conviction and execution invoked a pattern of patriarchal discourse that only underscored the need for proper male authority in the colony. Patriarchy's flexibility was its power; Burroughs had had at least a decent claim to authority, but once this claim was perverted, that potential access to power increased his apparent guilt and shaped the way writers invoked his image.

Burroughs's downfall did not materially threaten patriarchy, but in the broader climate that increasingly criticized those involved, the idea of a minister-witch suggested both the fallibility of the colony's clergy and the need to bolster the central patriarchal premises around which the colony was based. The threat to the colony posed by the witchcraft-possession outbreak in Essex County passed, but its potential for sowing long-term destabilization—as demonstrated by the attacks of skeptics— made important men hasten to recommit themselves to customary power relations.

As we have seen, authors who addressed witchcraft-possession did not concern themselves explicitly with gender, as their goals were over-whelmingly tied to the power these cases had to act as propaganda and to the controversy and risk that accompanied that opportunity. But the ways that authors incorporated hierarchical notions of order and disor-der, along with myriad other cultural premises related to their authority to discern the event, reveal that in large and small ways gender con-tributed to the shifts that led increasing numbers of elite men first to avoid and then to reject and disparage what had long been steadfastly, if controversially, within the realm of Christian doctrine. Throughout the seventeenth century and across the Anglo-American world, witchcraft-possession cases continued to resonate with ongoing political and reli-gious struggles. While myriad changes and reversals like those that took place in Salem shaped published possession accounts, their published forms continued to reflect older suspicions about the meaning that discerning authorities could draw from the bodies of demoniacs and witches.

Patriarchal Continuity in Witchcraft-Possession Propaganda

As time passed, it appeared that Thomas Brattle had correctly pre-dicted that "the reasonable part of the world" would look at some of the evidences brought against the accused and "conclude that the said S[alem] G[entlemen] are actually possessed, at least, with ignorance and folly."[120] And as the publication of John Hale's A Modest Enquiry into the Nature of Witchcraft (1702) demonstrates, the period from the immedi-ate aftermath of the Essex County witchcraft trials in 1693 through the turn of the eighteenth century was marked by ongoing attempts to con-tain and control the meaning of the outbreak for those who remained. For all of Hale's delicate treatment of the magistrates, he concluded with a poignant reflection upon the likelihood that innocent blood had been shed. Hale addressed the "errors and mistakes" committed in 1692, when many who "we may believe were innocent" were put to death. He also expressed his support of the General Assembly's prayer on December 17, 1696, that

> whatever mistakes on either hand, have been fallen into, either by the body of this people, or any order of men, referring to the late tragedy raised among us by Satan and his Instruments, through the awful Judgment of God: He would humble us therefore, and pardon all the errors of his Servants and People. . . . I am abundantly satisfyed that those who were most concerned to act and judge in those matters, did not willingly depart from the rules of righteousness. But such was the darkness of that day, the tortures and lamentations of the afflicted, and the power of former [precedents], that we walked in the clouds, and could not see our way.[121]

The clouds that had darkened Essex County in 1692 cleared quickly, with a suddenness that only emphasized the folly that had overtaken the men in charge. The magistrates and advising ministers had accepted the internal logic of the Essex County outbreak to the extent that nineteen were executed, but very soon after it became apparent to many that the unmaking of a minister, among others, dangerously compromised some of the central tenets of order.

However atypical, unordained, and suspect George Burroughs had been, and however much gossip had followed him from Salem to Maine and back again, he potentially represented the profundity of New England's error: rather than condemn a counterfeit man of God, they had hanged a man who preached the Gospel, thus transforming him from a scriptural enemy to a martyr for Christ. While both Mathers resisted this judgment in Burroughs's case, the general reversal nonetheless left those in the wake of the outbreak suddenly, horrifyingly, on the wrong side of the cosmic battle in which they had been engaged. Consider former judge Samuel Sewall's distress when, in August 1696, he was accosted in the street by Boston constable Jacob Melyen. As Sewall recorded in his diary, Melyen said, "If a man should take Beacon hill on [his] back, carry it away; and then bring it and set it in its place again, he should not make anything of that."[122] His charge, clearly a reference to Burroughs's famously preternatural strength, constituted a sharp rebuke of Sewall for his part in the judges' inappropriate acceptance of testimony against accused witches. Even in 1696, Burroughs haunted the meaning of the trials for those who had participated.

This transition, though experienced unevenly, was sufficiently wrenching to prompt empathy even for those who, like the Mathers, mingled their regret with protestations that they could not have been entirely wrong. What had made Burroughs appear especially guilty in 1692—his aberrant manhood and potential claims to patriarchal and ecclesiastical authority—also made him a perilous reference point. In addition to highlighting the ways in which gendered language and strategies pervaded the trials, Burroughs's case reveals how men as well as women were reduced to ciphers of themselves in their trials. He demonstrates how a man was unmade by male and female accusers and condemned and executed alongside other male and female witches. His case further illustrates that in the Essex County outbreak as elsewhere in the Anglo-Atlantic, witchcraft-possession involved men and women, and ideas about manhood and womanhood, in intricate and malleable combinations. Even when operating implicitly, Burroughs's downfall was both a challenge to and exercise of patriarchal power. As the authorities who oversaw the outbreak of 1692 attempted to accommodate the drastically different view of Salem that had developed at the turn of the eighteenth century, gendered language and strategies remained at the center of the ongoing debates.

5 / Disputing Possession in New England: Robert Calef versus Cotton Mather

Just as George Burroughs's unmaking evoked aspects of John Samuel's experience at Warboys at the turn of the seventeenth century, Cotton Mather's perception of the meaning of demonic afflictions echoed John Darrell's. Neither the men nor the immediate contexts were the same, of course, but the correspondence in gender, order, and authority shows the resonance of New England witchcraft-possession with broad transatlantic trends across the long seventeenth century. The outbreak in Salem and Essex County drew to an uneasy close in the winter of 1692–93 after the special Court of Oyer and Terminer, which had expedited the convictions and executions, was changed into a new court created by the legislature. The new court retained many of the same judges, but the operating procedure had altered so completely that they acquitted all but a few confessors. Lieutenant Governor William Stoughton, still wedded to the judicial model that had propelled Salem's trials while he had been the old court's chief justice, condemned these and a few others to death, but Governor William Phips granted them a reprieve. Clearly, the momentum for witchcraft trials had slowed to a halt. But even as the trials waned, two new possession cases captured Cotton Mather's attention. The first involved Mercy Short, the young servant girl and former captive of the Wabanakis whose fits and visions reappeared in November 1692 and lasted until March 1693.[1] Short's renewed affliction reaffirmed Cotton Mather's belief in the presence of a dangerous witch conspiracy in New England, and he accordingly described the details of her case in a manuscript that he circulated privately. His decision not to publish it outright suggests his desire to avoid provoking criticism from those who merged their dismay about the trials with political barbs aimed at his and his father's influence in the colony. When another possession arose in his Boston congregation in September 1693, involving a seventeen-year-old named Margaret Rule, he recorded her symptoms in a manuscript meant to emphasize its resemblance to previous cases. Compared to the tone of his narrative about the Goodwin children in 1688, the Rule account shows Mather's awareness that he was entering a more explicitly skeptical climate. But just as many in Massachusetts hoped to put the witchcraft trials behind them, the similarities between the Short and Rule cases renewed Mather's conviction that the godly were under siege by witches and devils.

Interestingly, Cotton Mather chose to begin his narrative about Margaret Rule's possession with a story about a Christian Indian man whose brush with evil spirits served as an instructive example for English readers. Mather justified the story of this pious Indian as a "fit introduction" to his narrative of Rule's possession because the man's experience of demonic temptation neatly matched those that had taken place at Salem and among the other demoniacs Mather had attended. The figure of the pious Indian allowed Mather to assure his readers that the witnesses and judges had acted rightly in Salem, and also to offer a familiar moral lesson about the impieties of professed Christians in comparison to a redeemed "savage." He wrote that this man, "notwithstanding some of his *Indian* Weakness, had something of a better Character of Vertue and Goodness, than many of our People can allow to most of their Countrey-Men that profess the *Christian Religion*."[2] Alongside Mather's condescension lay a productive tension with the possibility that the man's struggle against his "Indian Weakness" represented the same ordeal that Mather's English audience experienced as they struggled to follow God's law.

The narrative states that when this Indian man realized he was near death he called his "Folks" around him, urged them to pray and, as Mather put it, "beware of the *Drunkenness*, the *Idleness*, the *Lying*, whereby so many of that Nation disgrac'd their Profession of Christianity." After these noble preoccupations, including the humble acceptance of God's will in the recent death of his son, the Christian Indian saw an apparition of a "Black-Man, of a Terrible aspect, and more than humane Dimensions, threatning bitterly to kill him if he would not promise to leave off Preaching." When refused, the specter softened his approach and told the Indian man that he would leave him in peace if he would only sign in his book. When the Indian called upon God for protection against "the *Tempter* . . . the *Daemon* Vanish't."[3] Mather assured the reader of the story's legitimacy because "I would never have tendered [it] unto my Reader if I had not Receiv'd it from an honest and useful *English* Man, who is at this time a Preacher of the Gospel to the Indians." As much as the devilish encounter resembled English cultural images, the word of an Indian man required the support and greater credit of an Englishman.[4] Mather's relation of this tale managed both to convey a remarkable wonder and to remind the reader that there were certain men—like Mather himself—who could be trusted to pass along true stories about preternatural activity.

Mather's commendation of this exceptional Indian man resembled in some ways his praise for pious Englishwomen.[5] Both Englishwomen and Indian men—for Indian women were largely invisible in Mather's witchcraft writing—had to work against their natural susceptibility to temptation and demonic influence. Paradoxically, their simplicity could also sweeten their faith, allowing them to exemplify an admirable piety. Still, the archetypes of the pious Englishwoman and Christian Indian man were far less compelling than their inversions, which evoked the malevolence of witches and devils. Contact and conflict with Native Americans profoundly shaped colonists' realities both materially and symbolically, including their perceptions and descriptions of the Devil. And, as Mary Beth Norton has shown, Indian wars cemented English views of Native Americans as combatants in ways that played a fundamental role in the development of the Salem outbreak. The trial records contain little information about Christian Indians, such as those who had lived in the "Praying Towns" that had been established from the 1640s until the 1670s, when King Philip's War suppressed English commitment to native conversions.[6] Despite the suggestive roles of Tituba and John Indian at the very beginning of the outbreak at Salem, English writers about witchcraft-possession were as preoccupied by "Indians" as with actual Indians.[7] And yet, Mather joined the image of the pious Indian with his account of Rule's possession because it put the reader in the right frame of mind to benefit from the moral of both episodes. For the sake of New England's future, colonists likewise had to work to overcome their sinful natures and to submit to the leadership of honorable, godly superiors.

Although it is not known how widely Mather distributed the second manuscript, one copy ended up in the hands of Boston merchant Robert

Calef, who had attended the sessions of prayer and fasting at Margaret Rule's bedside with a skeptical eye. Calef subsequently embarked upon a vehement campaign to challenge not only Mather's beliefs about witchcraft-possession but also the minister's claims to represent legitimate Puritan authority. Calef reprinted Mather's manuscript, along with his own account of Rule and both sides of their correspondence (without permission), in a book entitled *More Wonders of the Invisible World*. Calef drew its title from Cotton Mather's previous *The Wonders of the Invisible World* (1693) and had it published covertly in England in 1700. Though many scholars cite Calef's *More Wonders of the Invisible World* for the information it provides about New England witchcraft, few have devoted much attention to Margaret Rule. This may reflect their primary concern with the underlying causes of the Essex County witchcraft trials, which had ended by the time of Rule's affliction. Alongside all of the complicated political and religious implications of the incident, Mather's transcription ably demonstrates how he merged his own patriarchal privileges with those of the courts and New England's elite. He presented Rule's possession as a fearful disruption of order and simultaneously asserted his right to interpret and restore it. More broadly, Mather claimed the right to interpret the afflictions of the Christian Indian man, Mercy Short, Margaret Rule, and those in Essex County who had denounced George Burroughs; in his providential thinking the survival of the colony depended upon the triumph of his own brand of patriarchal order over other men's attempts to claim that right of interpretation.

Cotton Mather's Treatment of Margaret Rule

Cotton Mather's diary entries reveal that Rule's possession appeared at a time when he believed he remained at the forefront of a cosmic battle between godly and demonic forces and keenly wished for redemption in the world as well as in heaven. In September 1693 he recorded a curious conversation with one Mrs. Carver of Salem, who claimed to have been visited by "shining Spirits, which were good Angels, in her opinion of them." In addition to telling him angelic secrets, Mrs. Carver intimated that "a new Storm of Witchcraft would fall upon the Countrey; to chastise the Iniquity that was used in the wilful Smothering and Covering of the Last; and that many fierce Opposites to the Discovery of that Witchcraft would bee thereby convinced."[8] Though Mather refrained from confirming the angelic nature of Mrs. Carver's spectral visitations, her words would have provided a balm to the anxieties of the past year and a half.

As the immediate conditions that had fueled the trials dissipated, Mather and other strong believers must have struggled to cling to the possibility that they had not been mistaken, or at least that their errors had not been unforgivably grave. Mrs. Carver's claims not only supported his original judgment but also suggested that an even greater resurgence of accusations would sweep away all remaining doubts. History shows that despite lingering uncertainties, the Essex County trials were over, but that trajectory was not inevitable in the fall of 1693, and so one can imagine Cotton Mather's amazement to discover a new "possessed young woman" in his congregation. When Margaret Rule confirmed his suspicions that some of his missing notes about the witchcraft at Salem had been stolen by evil spirits, and correctly foretold their return—they appeared, mysteriously, strewn about the streets of Lynn, Massachusetts—she bolstered his sense that her case was but an extension of the witchcraft-possession cases at Salem and involving Mercy Short.[9] By the following day, Cotton Mather believed he had reason to hope that God "would make my Name and the Names of both my Father's also, to become honorable among His People: that Hee will support us, comfort us, and at last, requite us good, for all the Evil wee meet withal."[10] Mather's attempts to use the Rule narrative to bring readers back to a profitable fear allowed him to provide a strong argument about the legitimacy of the New England he envisioned, which bolstered his own position in relation to his detractors.

As in Warboys, arguments about witchcraft-possession were facilitated by invocations of credit, that combination of economic and relational factors that constituted a person's honor and social standing. Credit was gendered because each of those components centered on a man or woman's identity in relation to gendered cultural expectations. It was both individual and communal, since a person's credit could raise or lower his or her associates' credit just as the reputation of the associates reflected back upon the individual. The bind faced by those involved with witchcraft-possession cases was that the credit of the demoniac and the accused witch were central to the process of making meaning out of the experience, but the conditions that constituted credit—particularly gender—were unstable, inconsistent, and subject to interpretation. Nonetheless, Mather's principal approach was to reinforce the possession of Margaret Rule by comparing it to previous witchcraft-possession episodes upon which the magistrates had already pronounced judgment. As much as it pained Mather that the trials had prompted criticism, he had no choice but to continue to invoke the deference due to the magistrates who sat in authority; he hoped both to defend their collective actions and to remind his readers of the long-standing cultural tradition that accorded honor and respect to those elevated to positions of leadership.

From the start of his narrative, Mather shored up Margaret Rule's possession by representing it as an extension of the demonic troubles previously seen in Essex County, with similar pinching, bruising, distortion of the joints, visions of a "Black Man," and "exorbitant Convulsions."[11] When he named the manuscript about Mercy Short "A Brand pluck'd out of the Burning," Mather referenced the text from Zechariah 3:2 that evoked the salvation of a soul removed from hellfire and symbolized her struggle and eventual deliverance from the Devil's torments. Accordingly, Mather named his manuscript about Margaret Rule "Another Brand pluckt out of the Burning" to link it unmistakably to the case that preceded it. Lest the reader fail to grasp the connection, he wrote that "in almost all the circumstances of it, indeed the Afflictions were so much alike, that the relation I have given of the one, would almost serve as the full History of the other, this was to that, little more than the second part to the same Tune."[12] Because Rule's family attended Mather's Boston church, and given his penchant for using remarkable providences to instruct, Rule may have learned from Mather himself what made Short's possession credible. Rule's affliction resembled the customary witchcraft-possession script enough to convince crowds of observers, but Mather knew he needed to anticipate skepticism, which entailed careful attention to credit.

Like John Darrell, Cotton Mather had to bolster the reputation of those he dispossessed to offset accusations that their suffering was caused by fraud, illness, or their own degradation. At the same time, however, demoniacs became recognizable as such because they acted out, resisted the word of God, and exhibited blasphemous rather than godly behavior. Mather took great pains to buttress Rule's credit by stressing that her behavior resulted from efforts to *resist* the Devil. The obvious place to start a defense of a demoniac's credit was with her family. Like Mercy Short, Margaret Rule's family had been driven away from Maine by Indian war, but unlike Short, Rule had not been a captive herself, and her family remained intact.[13] In this case, Mather wrote that Rule was a "Young Woman . . . born of sober and honest Parents," but added, "what her own Character was before her Visitation, I can speak with the less confidence of exactness, because I observe that wherever the *Devils* have been let loose to worry any Poor Creature amongst us, the great part of the Neighbourhood presently set themselves to inquire and relate all the little Vanities of their Childhood. . . . But it is affirm'd, that for about half a year before her Visitation, she was observably improved . . . [,] furiously concern'd for the everlasting *Salvation* of her Soul, and careful to avoid the snares of *Evil Company*."[14] It is possible that Mather emphasized Rule's increasing concern for her salvation because it signaled her entry into the period of crisis that heralded a spiritual conversion, something that often preceded—or even replaced—witchcraft-possession cases depending upon the views of attending ministers.[15] Mather's last sentence supports this view, but his more circumspect comment about her "Character" suggests that her neighbors—many of whom likely also attended Mather's Boston congregation—may not always have approved. Surprisingly, Mather did not fill in the gaps about Rule's credit by emphasizing her family, beyond noting that her parents were "sober and honest." Given the importance of gossip as a medium for the exchange of information in witchcraft-possession cases, and the unusual extent to which Mather labored to anticipate backlash, the relative subtlety of his account of Rule's family and piety might suggest their shortcomings, or it could suggest his expectation that he would be taken at his word— though the later controversy proved otherwise.

Mather directed the reader's suspicion away from Margaret Rule's credit and toward that of a woman whom "pious People in the Vicinity" suspected of causing the torment. Mather clearly suspected this "Miserable woman, who had been formerly Imprisoned on the suspicion of Witchcraft," but he refrained from naming her because of "the hazard of hurting a poor Woman that might be innocent."[16] As in his previous publications, however, Mather expressed reluctance to draw conclusions about which he hinted there were no real doubts. He went on to describe Rule's suffering at the hands of eight specters:

> Whereof she imagin'd that she knew three or four, but the rest came still with their Faces cover'd . . . she was very careful of my reitterated charges to forbear blazing the Names, lest any good Person should come to suffer any blast of Reputation thro' the cunning Malice of the great Accuser; nevertheless having since privately named them to my self, I will venture to say this of them, that they are the sort of Wretches who for these many years have gone under. . . . Violent Presumptions of Witchcraft . . . altho' I am farr from thinking that the Visions of this Young Woman were Evidence enough to prove them so.[17]

Scholars interested in ascertaining Mather's responsibility for encouraging witchcraft persecution could find evidence for more than one judgment here. He was sincere in wanting to prevent the suffering of innocents, but his expositional choices were calculated; he needed the faulty credit of the accused to bolster the claims of the demoniac. As with those who acted as if they were possessed, Mather's sincerity was not necessarily incompatible with acting or writing in calculated ways. And by the time the reader reached Mather's caveat about the insufficiencies of spectral evidence as proof, the point was overshadowed by the sensational details of Rule's suffering.

Even though Cotton Mather did not know in 1693 how controversial the Rule episode would ultimately become, he anticipated critical readers as soon as he first received Robert Calef's challenging letters. Having defended Rule's credit and denounced that of the accused witch, though anonymously, Mather sought next to tarnish the credit of his detractors. He asserted: "It were a most Unchristian and uncivil, yea a most unreasonable thing to imagine that the Fitt's of the Young Woman were but meer Impostures: And I believe scarce any, but People of a particular Dirtiness, will harbour such an Uncharitable Censure." Having established that skepticism would render one both unreasonable and dirty, Mather averred that it constituted an affront to the good people of Boston. Rule's nine-day fast, for example, "was impossible to be dissembled without a Combination of . . . People unacquainted with one another to support the Juggle. . . . [H]e that can imagine such a thing of a Neighbourhood, so fill'd with Vertuous People is a base Man, I cannot call him any other."[18] Mather relied upon these same credible witnesses from the community to attest to the sensory evidence that established the preternatural origins of Rule's symptoms. Many of those gathered in Rule's bedchamber saw her forced to swallow an invisible liquid, smelled brimstone, and saw the white powder she said was thrown into her eyes. They observed her contortions, saw burns on her skin that appeared to heal at an accelerated rate, and heard her foretell events taking place at a distance. Many also saw Rule float up toward the ceiling; some perceived, and one man actually felt, the invisible form of a "living Creature, not altogether unlike a Rat" at her bedside.[19] The extent to which these events were seen, heard, and felt reveals that Bostonians' fear of demonic malice remained palpable. While relating these shocking details, Mather emphasized reason, cleanliness of mind and spirit, and the collective credibility of the girls' family and neighbors in ways that call to mind Darrell and Harsnett's struggle over the legitimacy of dispossession a century earlier. And as in Darrell's case, Mather's ability to command his readers' trust—to the extent that they would believe his account of such ephemeral phenomena—depended in part upon his maintenance of his credit as an honorable man.

It was important to Cotton Mather's credit that he expressed hesitance to base his confidence in the veracity of Rule's affliction on spectral evidence alone. This was imperative not only because such evidence had become the primary target for criticism of the Essex County trials, by no less an authority than his esteemed father, but also because he harbored his own deep-seated misgivings about signs from beyond the natural realm. Nonetheless, given his providential thinking, he could not resist taking closely to heart any signs of approbation from heaven or censure from devils. Although ministers cautioned against apparent "good spirits," since devils might impersonate their heavenly counterparts, the appearance of angels in Rule's possession struck a chord with Mather. Back in 1684, after extensive fasting and prayer, he had received a visit from an angelic spirit that prophesied Mather's future greatness in terms drawn from Ezekiel 31:3–9. In that vision, Mather learned that he would be like a great cedar in Lebanon, of particularly high stature and with long branches that symbolized the reach of his publications throughout America and Europe. As much as Mather was aching for some degree of assurance that he was among God's elect, he responded to this angelic vision by recording a cautious prayer that Christ would deliver him from the delusions of the Devil. Though he knew he could not trust this good spirit unreservedly, Mather believed there were signs that God had made use of him to combat His enemies, and that the recriminations of his foes likely symbolized the Devil's desire to bring him to harm.[20] Consequently, it is not surprising that he was receptive to Margaret Rule's reports of a benevolent spirit, clothed in bright white garments, which instructed her to pray and resist the Devil. Mather noted that good spirits had been recorded not only "in the Swedish, but also in the Salem Witchcraft" and that Mercy Short also had "the Communications of such a Spirit."[21] He strove to establish the legitimate precedent for angelic spirits as part of his broader goal to use these episodes not only to vanquish the Devil but also to capitalize upon their inherent drama to bring more worldly souls to God. This helps to explain why he would have seen a clear line from the outbreak in Essex County to Mercy Short, and from there to Mrs. Carver and Margaret Rule. By emphasizing the extent to which Rule's case resembled prior instances of witchcraft-possession, Mather strove to use new evidence to defend simultaneously his current and prior actions.

Mather wanted to ensure that readers drew the correct conclusions from these remarkable events, and he therefore tried to differentiate spectral messages that ought to be heeded from those that should not. Naturally, what made Rule's good spirits reliable was their articulation of a familiar vision of godly patriarchy. Rule told Mather that "the white Spirit" instructed her: "Margaret, you now are to take notice that (such a Man) is your Father, God has given you to him, do you from this time look upon him as your Father, obey him, regard him as your Father, follow his Counsels and you shall do well." The man in question is plainly Mather himself, and the message from the white Spirit perfectly matched what Mather advocated not only for Rule but also for all of New England.[22] The ultimate message was to obey the wisdom of godly fathers and thereby please God; to disregard their authority was to do the Devil's work. In this instance, Mather had not only scriptural weight behind his claims to authority—veiled though they were by a sort of attempted anonymity—but direct approbation from what might well be an angel from heaven. Thus Margaret Rule's good spirit created the soundest patriarchal foundation for her claims of being an innocent sufferer of diabolic malice, which happened also to be the version most likely to resonate with Mather.

There were many reasons for Mather to keep his personal angelic visitation private and to obscure its meaning in his diary; not only might devils masquerade as good spirits in order to delude Christians, but to claim to have received angelic visits smacked of hubris. And because Protestants held that miracles had ended with the apostolic age, there was an undercurrent of skepticism surrounding such instances of direct contact with the preternatural. Witchcraft-possession cases, however, offered dramatic contests between good and evil that fit Mather's millennial worldview without appearing to be about him; this perceived distance rendered them more readily suitable for the conversion of unbelievers. His caveat, "I am not so well satisfied about the true nature of this white Spirit, as to count that I can do a Friend much Honour by reporting what notice this white Spirit may have taken of him," did little to overshadow the fact that he differentiated this apparition from the ones that caused the girl's torment.[23] Rule's white spirit so aptly articulated Mather's sense of mission that he simply reported the incident and led readers toward the appropriate conclusions. Mather used his account of Rule's benevolent spirit to model a proper regard for hierarchical authority; the girl should look to her spiritual Father (Mather) as a way to repudiate sinful disorder and to accept her proper place within her family, congregation, and community.

Because Mather believed that he was acting on God's behalf, he knew to expect resistance to this new possession from both demonic and worldly detractors. And because he knew that he was a soldier for Christ, he understood his critics as the opposite: agents of Satan. Mather stated that he was compelled to write the manuscript despite "the hard representations where with some Ill Men have reviled my conduct." He added, "No Christian can, I say none but evil workers can criminate my visiting such of my poor flock as have at any time fallen under the terrible and sensible molestations of Evil-Angels. . . . I have been but a Servant of Mankind in doing so; yea no less a Person than the Venerable Baxter, has . . . in the most Publick manner invited Mankind to thank me for that Service."[24] By invoking Richard Baxter, Mather reminded his reader of his transatlantic links to Puritan divines who shared his view of remarkable providences. This allowed him to present himself as a messenger of God's will despite the recrimination of "ill men" who persecuted him for offering assistance to those in need. As noted above, John Darrell's acquaintance with esteemed men such as Master Ireton forestalled, but ultimately failed to prevent, his unmaking because of the greater power of the bishop and Church of England. Mather wrote from a position of greater security than Darrell, as his family and allies held influence with New England's press and religious and governing institutions.[25] But, like Darrell, Mather had enemies who undermined this support by extending to fervent Puritans the irrationality and immoderation customarily attributed to Catholic priests and demoniacs.

Because witchcraft-possession cases had so recently resulted in the conviction and execution of accused witches, Mather's battle to defend his credit in the wake of Margaret Rule's affliction necessarily involved the justification of those verdicts. He attempted to shape this legacy by emphasizing that "the Name of No one good Person in the World ever [came] under any blemish by means of any Afflicted, Person that fell under my particular cognisance, yea no one Man, Woman or Child ever came into any trouble for the sake of any that were Afflicted after I had once begun to look after 'em."[26] Mather insisted that he had protected innocents and encouraged the recommitment of lapsed Christians by recognizing witches as a serious threat. After Salem, he wrote, these results had profound implications: "The Devil got just nothing; but God got praise; Christ got Subjects, the Holy Spirit got Temples, the Church got Addition; and the Souls of Men got everlasting Benefits; I am not so vain as to say that any Wisdome or Vertue of mine did contribute unto this good order of things: But I am so just, as to say I did not hinder this Good."[27] Announcing this victory over some of New England's witches allowed Mather to prove his dedication to God's service, but his insistence served a psychological need, as well. That some questioned the symptoms of the afflicted and might possibly challenge earlier guilty verdicts was utterly incompatible with his conviction that his actions had served a godly purpose.[28] He thus worked to shore up the legacy of the colony's response to remarkable providences as he sought proactively to control the legacy of his involvement with Margaret Rule. Mather's post-Salem witchcraft-possession narratives constituted propaganda on behalf of patriarchal authority, and like Darrell's earlier publications, they emphasized honorable manhood, reason, and support of established hierarchical relations on the one hand, and compromised credit, excessive passions, and the subversion of proper authority on the other.

Contesting Manhood: Debating Margaret Rule's Possession

If Robert Calef's relation of Burroughs's gallows speech provided a succinct example of his determination to undermine Cotton Mather's authority, his energetic campaign to contradict Mather's account of Margaret Rule's possession demonstrates the scope and intensity of his critique. Capitalizing on the more overtly skeptical climate of the late 1690s, Calef sought to unmake Mather by citing many of the same elements of honorable manhood so central to the debates between John Darrell and Samuel Harsnett a century earlier: he questioned Mather's credit and honorable associations, suggested that excessive passion had overtaken reason, and claimed that Mather's interaction with Rule had endangered proper social hierarchies. Not long after the text appeared, both Mathers instigated a libel case against Calef, who answered their warrant by appearing before a justice of the peace. The case was dismissed, however, after the plaintiffs failed to appear.[29] Cotton Mather felt compelled to address his annoying detractor, however, to the extent that he marshaled some of his peers to publish a rebuttal that challenged Calef's credit along the same lines.[30] Ultimately, the war of words between Calef, the Mathers, and their supporters reveals considerable continuity in the ways writers who contended the implications of witchcraft-possession invoked components of honorable manhood to justify their claims to patriarchal authority.

Few scholars have credited Calef with making much of an intellectual contribution in comparison to those he attacked, although those who blamed the Mathers for the persecution of witches saw Calef as a voice of reason that suggested a broader rationalist sensibility.[31] Calef's acerbic wit and nimble manipulation of the vagaries of witchcraft-possession demonstrated more than persistence, however, and the clarity of his prose occasionally surpassed that of his extraordinarily literate opponent. Furthermore, the published rebuttal to Calef's book demonstrates the efficacy of his arguments, since it would not have been necessary to gather a group of esteemed gentlemen in the Mathers' defense if Calef's book were as ridiculous and marginalized as they claimed. Because Calef placed Margaret Rule's possession at the center of a much broader critique of Cotton Mather and his sort of Puritanism, his challenge demonstrates that witchcraft-possession retained its particular power to spark controversies that began at the bedside of a putative demoniac and rippled outward with potentially devastating implications for the credit of the participants.

Though Robert Calef made myriad challenges to Mather's claims about preternatural phenomena, his retelling of Margaret Rule's possession was the most sensational and effective element of his book. Overall, there were three central ways in which Calef used this episode to challenge Mather, each of which was fundamentally gendered and evoked the debates over John Darrell's dispossessions. First, Calef used claims about Margaret Rule's degraded nature to taint Mather by association. It was a relatively simple matter to question her character and reputation, and there was no easier way to discredit Mather's arguments than to suggest that he had been duped by a whorish dissembler. The second gendered strategy was to unmake Mather as an honorable man in his own right. Given Mather's pedigree and prestige, this was a delicate proposition, but even an elite minister could be compromised by suggestions that his reason had been overwhelmed by passions, or that he had failed to maintain mastery of himself and subordinates. Finally, Calef used the episode with Margaret Rule as a jumping-off point from which to attack Mather on theological grounds. Despite Mather's clear authority in this area, Calef was able to turn Mather's expertise and prolixity into weakness. He also managed to tar Mather with the brush of popish excess and to suggest that Mather, of all people, had failed to use sanctioned scriptural methods. Even when these strategies were accompanied by or subsumed in political and religious strategies, they invoked gender through overlapping claims about credit, reason versus excess, and disruption of social order that struck at the heart of manhood, honor, and legitimate authority.

It made sense that Calef used Margaret Rule as his initial target, as she was the most vulnerable due to her sex, age, and status as a demoniac; these vulnerabilities had the added benefit of facilitating Mather's compromise by association. In *More Wonders of the Invisible World*, Calef claimed to have joined the crowd in Rule's bedchamber—where he said as many as thirty or forty people gathered—and described it in a way that discredited Rule and Mather both. Although both Increase and Cotton Mather had attended, Cotton Mather was the particular target. In a tone both self-righteous and poisonous, Calef depicted Cotton Mather as a fool, at best, and as a lecherous witch-hunter at worst. He wrote that Mather, while laying on hands in an attempt to free Rule from her spectral tormenters, "rubb'd her Stomach (her Breast not covered with the Bed-cloaths) and bid others do so too, and said it eased her, then she revived."[32] Calef reported, as it was not clear at first which part of her body was cursed, that Mather and many of the bystanders placed their hands all over her. She "said that when they did it in the right place she could fetch her Breath, and by that they knew."[33] Calef claimed that Mather not only participated in this charade but also encouraged Rule's concupiscence through his questioning. Calef recorded Mather's interrogation of Rule as follows:

> Q. Do you believe? Then again she was in a Fit, and [Mather] again rub'd her Breast, &c (about this time . . . an attendant assisted him in rubbing of her. The afflicted spake angrily to her saying don't you meddle with me, and hastily put away her hand). . . . Q. The brushing of you gives you ease, don't it? A. Yes. She turn'd her selfe and a little Groan'd. Q. Now the Witches Scratch you and Pinch you, and Bite you, don't they? A. Yes, then he put his Hand upon her Breast and Belly, *viz.* on the Cloaths over her, and felt a Living thing, as he said, which moved the Father [Increase Mather] also to feel, and some others.[34]

This exchange, among others, ably invoked the image of a lustful pretender. And by rejecting the ministrations of the female attendant in favor of those of the men, Rule, rather than the ministers, appeared to orchestrate the spectacle. Even the setting allowed Calef to cast aspersions about the proceedings, because he invoked tropes from misogynist satire about the "boudoir," a woman's private chamber from which she could plan how to deceive and entrap men. There, ballads and pamphlets had long claimed, women carried out excretory functions and slyly disguised their bodies with clothes and cosmetics that tricked men into believing they were beautiful and virtuous.[35] By presenting a lascivious Rule, lounging in a crowded bedchamber, Calef suggested an entirely different scene than the one Mather hoped the reader would see.

After presenting Rule as soliciting the touch of particular bystanders, Calef went on to claim that she used her affliction to arrange assignations with men. Soon after the ministers left, he reported, "the Afflicted desired the Women to be gone, saying, that the Company of the Men was not offensive to her," and "having hold of the hand of a Young-Man, said to have been her Sweet-heart formerly, who was withdrawing; she pull'd him again into his Seat, saying he should not go to Night."[36] The Mathers' absence during this scene did not serve to clear them of responsibility for it, because Calef made the event they took seriously as witchcraft-possession appear threatening not because of what it portended about sin or salvation but because it was so disorderly. This household was no little commonwealth, in which parents monitored Rule's spiritual and physical state. Instead, there was a promiscuous crowd and a scheming young woman whose resemblance to a demoniac allowed her to flout standard rules of decorum. Calef showed the reader that the attribution of Rule's behavior to a demonic affliction made this disruption of hierarchy, sexuality, and sense possible. In this way, Calef managed to use Margaret Rule to challenge in one stroke the notion of witchcraft-possession, the trials in Essex County, and the Mathers' defense of them. Calef disparaged Margaret Rule more effectively by evoking women's seductiveness and susceptibility to seduction, both of which drew their strength from a cultural tradition that linked women's fluid natures to a predilection for vices associated with witchcraft and possession. The question of women's willingness to be possessed, whether sexually by men or spiritually by devils, remained a subject of titillating uncertainty.

Calef's unmaking of Margaret Rule's credit relied upon gendered concepts of womanly weakness, and he invoked her sex, age, and demeanor to support his depiction of her as a licentious fraud. But other notions of womanly weakness simultaneously bolstered Mather's account by reinforcing traditional assumptions about women's susceptibility to witchcraft and demonic possession. Mather explained the connection between witchcraft and women in terms reminiscent of the Bible, literary misogyny, and humoral theory: "I do believe that the *Evil Angels* do often take Advantage from *Natural Distempers*. . . . [T]he Malignant *Vapours* and *Humours* of our Diseased Bodies may be used by *Devils*, therinto insinuating as engine of the Execution of their Malice upon those *Bodies*; and perhaps for this reason one Sex may suffer more Troubles of some kinds from the *Invisible World* than the other, as well as for *that reason* for which the old *serpent* made where he did his first *Address*."[37] In addition to providing an embodied explanation for the phenomena, Mather's words reflected the association between material conceptions of women and cultural images of witches and demoniacs. Such associations triggered implicit disgust and suspicion of female bodies that, while operating below explicit cultural messages, reinforced ideas about womanly weaknesses as a kind of internal threat to the godly community. Because cultural assumptions about women factored significantly in men's arguments for or against witchcraft and possession, gendered language, whether in sermons or satirical pamphlets, could support both Mather's and Calef's claims about Margaret Rule. Furthermore, the ambiguities of the possession script left important questions, such as the innocence of those who acted as if they were possessed, only partially addressed. Calef capitalized upon these inconsistencies, as Samuel Harsnett had, and thus found a way to challenge Mather despite the difference in their social standing.

Calef's second gendered strategy involved targeting Mather's honorable manhood in the more explicit arguments that played out in their correspondence, which Calef reprinted in full. Mather's fevered attempts to invoke notions of honor and manly credit in his own defense reveal the effectiveness of Calef's strategy, because even his language of self-defense was leveraged against him. In his attempts to contradict Calef's charges, Mather invoked the aspects of witchcraft-possession controversy that hinged on reason, self-mastery, and other qualities constitutive of honorable manhood. He complained that Calef's charges were false, and likely malicious, and invoked his own superior breeding to remind the reader that his association with influential and reputable people signaled his greater eligibility to serve as interpreter of this event. These arguments allowed Cotton Mather to paint Calef as an outsider and threat to the established order, but they also created openings from which Calef was able launch additional assaults upon Mather's reason, learning, and motives.

In letters refuting Calef's charges, Mather accused him of partiality, duplicity, and malice right from the moment when both Mathers entered Margaret Rule's bedchamber. Calef's account, Mather complained, contained "a number of Mistakes and Falshoods; which were they willful and design'd might justly be termed gross Lies. The representations are far from true, when 'tis affirmed my Father and self being come into the Room, began the Discourse; I hope I understand breeding a little better than so[.] For proof of this . . . sundry can depose the contrary."[38] Mather particularly resented Calef's accusations that he, along with his father and others, "rubbed" Rule while she lay in some state of undress.

As befitted a son who honored such an august father, Mather claimed to be angrier on his father's behalf than his own. He marveled, "that a Gentleman that from 18 to 54 hath been an Exemplary Minister of the Gospel; and that besides a station in the Church of God, as considerable as any that his own Country can afford, hath for divers years come off with Honour . . . Knows not yet how to make one short Prayer of a quarter of an hour, but in New-England he must be Libell'd for it."[39] He insisted that "Oath" would sufficiently vindicate his father, and moved— with equal vehemence but at greater length—to defend himself. Mather contradicted Calef's claims about the manner in which he touched Rule, precisely where the invisible Imp had been perceived, and other matters both material and immaterial.

Building off of his defense of his father, Mather emphasized his own reputation as a reasonable and learned man. In addition to having studied at Harvard College, Mather wrote and preached prolifically, served as a minister along with his father at Boston's North Church and maintained a famously extensive library. Mather accordingly stressed the preeminence of reason in his account of Rule's possession, and the malice in Calef's, as an outgrowth of his superior status. Mather complained to Calef of the "divers and down-right mistakes, which you have permitted your self, I would hope, not knowingly, and with a Malicious design, to be receiver or Compiler of."[40] As a contrast, Mather offered the reader the benefit of his judgment, learning, and knowledge. To avoid charges that the girl's fits were the result of natural illness, Mather stated that only Sadducees would believe such a thing about a body stuck full of pins. He added, "I think I may without Vanity pretend to have read not a few of the best System's of Physick that have been yet seen in these American Regions."[41] By claiming expertise in preternatural matters based on his knowledge of important religious and medical texts, Mather countered the key elements of Calef's attack on his credit by drawing on his strengths. But these claims also left him vulnerable to Calef's subsequent accusations of immoderation, arrogance, and ambition.

In fact, Calef found several ways to use Mather's extensive claims to manly credit against him. Calef's relative obscurity allowed him to present himself as the one struggling valiantly against a powerful and self-interested opponent. He fashioned himself as an earnest man who recorded only the scenes he witnessed and "writ them down the same Nights in order to attain the certainty of them." By emphasizing his sincerity, Calef laid a foundation for his complaints that Mather's cries of slander and libel against him were unjust.[42] Calef also pointedly complained that Mather made "Pulpit-news" out of their disagreement, thereby abusing his position as minister in pursuit of his own interests. Claiming to maintain a more proper sense of authority and responsibility allowed Calef to appear orderly and temperate. Thus he was able to use Mather's position against him and to separate him from customary sources of respectable manly credit. These strategic accusations allowed Calef to cast doubt upon the word of a man unaccustomed to having to answer to such libelous and degrading charges.

Calef's tactical use of gendered strategies was often ingenious, as when he cultivated a measured tone to make Mather out to be the unruly slanderer. By purporting to desire reconciliation, Calef suggested that Mather's unwillingness to answer him was the result of arrogance. Calef complained, not without cause, that in Mather's formulation any people who "see not with the Authors Eyes, [are] rendered *Sadducees and Witlin[g]s, &c.* and the Arguments that square not with the Sentiments therein contain'd, Buffoonary." Therefore, Calef claimed to write to "vindicate my self therefore from such false Imputations . . . and to vindicate your self, Sir, as much as is in my Power from those Suggestions, said to be Insinuated, as if you wore not the Modesty, and Gravity, that becomes a Minister of the *Gospel*."[43] Calef's cunning formulations demonstrate that his wit, if less refined than Mather's, made him more threatening than a standard coffeehouse witling. His pen turned Mather's dismissal of his critics into arrogance, implying that the minister had overreacted and misinterpreted what was "said to be" insinuated. What Mather called slander, Calef transformed into the justified correction of a minister who had failed to uphold the duties of his calling. In this configuration, it was Calef who respected the honor of the ministry and its role in proper social order.

To bolster the impression of his sincerity, Calef expressed wounded surprise at Mather's defensiveness. In an extension of his bid to avoid the "Inconvenience of Passion," Calef made Mather appear to be the aggressor, writing: "You seem to intimate as if I were giving Characters, Reflections, and Libell's &c. concerning your self and Relations; all of which were as far from my thoughts, as ever they were in writing after either your self, or any other Minister."[44] Calef's expression of surprise at finding his attack on Mather interpreted as such, because of his purported respect for authority, served to perpetuate the gendered contest in which these men were engaged. Calef's success at depicting Mather's haughtiness as evidence of hubris and excessive self-regard allowed him to translate Mather's well-grounded claims to superior reputation, learning, and authority against him.

In response to Mather's invocation of his "breeding," which would have prevented him from instigating conversation at Rule's bedside ahead of his father, Calef was cleverly gracious even as he refused to legitimate Mather's version of events: "As to that which is said of mentioning your self first . . . and your hopes that your breeding was better (I doubt it not) nor do *I* doubt your Father might first apply himself to others; but my intelligence is, that you first spake of the Afflicted or Possessed, for which you had the advantage of a nearer approach."[45] Though not the most dire of Calef's accusations, this did constitute a direct contradiction of Mather's claims about events at Rule's bedside. Furthermore, it suggested both ambition and disorderliness—not to mention a disregard for deference—on Cotton Mather's part. Calef also found it convenient to use nice distinctions in his own defense, such as pointing out that he had written that Rule's breast was not covered "with the Bed-Cloths," as opposed to claiming that they were uncovered entirely. By downplaying his insinuations, Calef made Mather appear oversensitive and inconsistent. Calef also invoked his own adherents to support his contradictory claims about the extent to which Rule had been clothed. When Mather complained that Calef misrepresented and slandered him through his lascivious characterizations, Calef replied: "I am not willing to retort here your own Language upon you; but can tell you, that your own discourse of it publickly, at Sir *W.P*'s [William Phips's] Table, has much more contributed to" assumptions of Rule's undress.[46] Once again, Calef asserted that the inconsistencies were all on Mather's part and that Calef was aware of what passed for conversation at Governor Phips's table. This comment suggested both Calef's close association with people of Mather's own circle and also obliquely implied that he was not alone in questioning Mather's veracity and reasoning.

The third way that Calef targeted Mather was by suggesting that he had failed to follow the established godly practice of using only Scripture, prayer, and fasting to respond to witchcraft-possession. This approach provided Calef with a way to twist Cotton Mather's sophistication into a liability. For example, Calef wrote: "I do request and pray, that if I err, I may be shewed it from *Scripture* or sound *Reason*, and not by quotations out of *Virgil*, nor *Spanish Rhetorick*. For I find the Witlings mentioned, are . . . far from answering your profound questions . . . Sir, (ye being the Salt of the Earth, &c.) I have reason to hope for a Satisfactory Answer to him, who is one that reverences your Person and Office."[47] Here Calef separated himself from ignorant witlings Mather dismissed out of hand. In Calef's formulation, Mather was the one relying upon ungodly literature to cover up the lapses in his own reasoning, and whose failure to satisfy Calef's requests for clarification held a whiff of evasion. Thus Calef fashioned himself as a potential equal to Mather, not in social standing or clerical office but rather as a gentleman requesting guidance in a matter of scriptural importance. In their battle to play up the strengths and downplay the weaknesses of their comparative positions, Calef and Mather both relied upon notions of manly credit to bolster the wide-ranging nature of their dispute.

Beneath Calef's challenges to manly credit lay demonological questions that held serious implications for the cases' potential as propaganda. Therefore Calef capitalized, both explicitly and implicitly, on familiar arguments about the extent of witches' and devils' powers. Calef echoed the long history of skeptical writing on the subject by stating: "That there are witches is not the doubt. . . . But what this Witchcraft is, or wherein it does consist, seems to be the whole difficulty."[48] Calef's preoccupation with the scriptural basis for popular tests of witches and demoniacs led him to accept the writings of some experts, such as John Gaule, as "Truth" but to reject others. For example, Calef criticized Mather's references to William Perkins and Richard Bernard,[49] taking the unexpected approach of criticizing them for failing to ground their points sufficiently in Scripture. He softened his criticism of these men, to an extent: "It were to be unjust to the Memory of these otherwise Wise Men, to suppose them to have any Sinister design; But perhaps the force of a prevailing opinion together with an Education thereto Suited, might overshadow their [J]udgments, as being wont to be but too prevalent in many other cases."[50] In this way, Calef drew an unflattering connection between Mather and the writers on whom he relied, suggesting their credulity and insufficient godliness—a particularly bold accusation coming from the purported merchant to the esteemed minister. Thus Mather and his experts were collectively unmade as men, quite as Darrell's supporters had been, in a way that allowed Calef to claim temperance and rationality at their expense.

Rather than engage substantively with Perkins's or Bernard's texts, Calef emphasized his dissatisfaction with Mather's failure to address the central points on which he had been challenged. Calef parried Mather's dismissive offer of the use of his library as a replacement for argumentation, surely recognizing that Mather's epistolary participation elevated and perpetuated their debate. Calef worked to goad Mather into further correspondence by suggesting that "a little Writing certainly might be of more use, to clear up the controverted points, than either looking over

many Books in a well furnish'd Library, or than a dispute, if I were quali-
fied for it; the Inconveniences of Passion being this way best avoided."
And, he added he was "not without hopes that you will yet oblige me
so far, as to consider the Letter, and if I Err, to let me see it by Scripture, &c."[51] In characteristic form, Calef merged several key arguments
at once, weaving implicit and explicit social conventions into a gendered
trap. He managed to turn Mather's extensive library, which ought to
have sustained his credit as a learned and reasonable man, into a sign of
excess. As with his undue wordiness, Mather's "well-furnish'd Library"
denoted Mather's wealth and connoted his ambition. Calef then offered
a slight self-deprecation to model modesty and deference. Ultimately, he
suggested that profane learning, inattention to Scripture, and excessive
airs and words had tainted Mather's responses. By expressing a desire
to avoid the "Inconveniences of passion" likely to be raised in a meeting, Calef inverted customary understandings of honorable manhood to
establish himself as the more reasonable and principled man.

Calef found other ways to use the inherent inconsistencies and disorder
of the possession script to his advantage, especially as an entry point for
quasi-demonological debate. First and foremost, he attributed the worst
faults to Rule, which made it easier to attack Mather by extension. When
Mather complained about the slanders Calef attributed to Margaret Rule,
Calef wrote that he was hardly to blame: "If you be by the possessed belyed
(as being half an hour with her alone (excluding her own Mother . . .) *I* can
see no Wonder in it . . . what can be expected less from the Father of Lies,
by whom, you Judge, she was possest."[52] In this way Calef made plain the
dangerous tendency of witchcraft-possession cases to grant disproportion-
ate power to low-status, and frequently female, individuals on the basis of
their affliction. Furthermore, Calef drew an explicit connection between
the particular dangers of believing Margaret Rule and broader dangers
for a society that allowed such individuals that degree of authority. The
salacious image of Mather designing to be left alone with the girl evoked
not only the accusations made against John Darrell for having allegedly
seduced William Somers and Katherine Wright into false possession performances, and Darrell's answering charges that his opponents had pres-
sured them to recant, but also a century's worth of anti-Catholic tracts.
This enabled Calef to raise the specter of Catholic excess and carnality,
which still held powerful significance in New England at the turn of the
eighteenth century, without having to do so directly.

Elsewhere, Calef explicitly aligned Mather with base, popish influences. For example, he wrote that if Mather expected him to believe

extraordinary stories about Rule floating toward the ceiling despite witnesses' efforts to pull her down, "the only advantage gain'd, is that which has been so long controverted between Protestants and Papists, whether Miracles are ceast, will hereby seem to be decided for the latter; it being, for ought I can see, if so, as true a Miracle as for Iron to swim, and that the Devil can work such Miracles."[53] By linking Mather's theology to the kind of popish delusions that Protestants believed priests used to seduce witnesses, Calef managed to capitalize on the doctrinal uncertainties that had plagued John Darrell a century before. Darrell and his supporters had been forced to address the difference between miracles and wonders, and to account for the extent of the agency God granted to the Devil;[54] despite his position of relative security, Mather was unable to sidestep these thorny issues. Even if Cotton Mather was never in the same degree of danger as John Darrell, involvement with dispossession in New England in the 1690s entailed risk and invited censure. It is clear that Calef's motives were complex, and included political and anticlerical objectives.[55] Calef shielded his derision of Mather with obsequiousness, but for all of his performative servility Calef ably interwove mocking gendered language into his challenge to witchcraft-possession, even when explicitly addressing politics and religion.

The Margaret Rule controversy forced Mather to confront the fact anew that the same conventions that made witchcraft-possession cases good propaganda also made them dangerous. By reprinting in 1700 excerpts from Mather's witchcraft writing from 1693, Calef capitalized upon the less hospitable climate for witchcraft-possession. The marvelous events that Mather had seen as incontrovertible proof of preternatural interference now sounded implausible, even ridiculous, as when Mather had claimed to knock away a set of invisible chains that bound Mercy Short. Calef inquired whether this feat "were done by the Power or Vertue of any ord'nance of Divine Institution," or if Mather was suggesting it happened on account of "any Physical Vertue in that particular Hand." Calef then added, sarcastically, "but supposing that neither of these will be asserted by the Author, I do think it very requisite, that the World may be acquainted with the Operation, and to what Art or Craft to refer their Power of Knocking off of *Invisible Chains*."[56] The possession script was generally flexible on such points, as inconsistencies could always be attributed to the Devil's tricks, but Calef's invocation of the long-contested question of the possibility of miracles in a postapostolic age constituted a serious challenge. Calef argued that if Mather could not adequately base his practices in Scripture his methods could not be correct, and he must have been deluded by the devils he sought to expel. Given the sense by 1700 that the trials of 1692–93 had been a delusion, it was likely that readers would be receptive to Calef's arguments. His references to Mather's earlier work facilitated a critique sharpened by direct comparisons to the popish and fraudulent narratives on which Protestant critics had long heaped scorn. Thus the very drama that served Mather's interests at first—to startle readers back to God—undermined his interests at the last.

By posing as a kind of martyr, Calef defended himself more effectively against the expected charges of malice and slander. Emphasizing the broader theological issues of witchcraft-possession enabled him to appear reasonable, and in pursuit of an orthodox truth, and so he stressed his determination to persevere despite his opponents' censure. As for his initial reasons for writing, he explained, "I thought it my duty to be no longer an Idle Spectator; And can, and do say, to the Glory of God, in this whole Affair, I have endeavoured a Conscience voide of offence, both towards God and towards Man."[57] Even given the mocking and manipulative nature of Calef's challenge to Mather's authority, and his probable invention or at least exaggeration of the more salacious details, there is no reason to doubt his sincere intent to take Mather to task for the excesses of the Essex County trials after new witchcraft-possession cases arose in their wake. In Calef's view, Mather's actions had resulted in delusion, disorder, and alienation from the true wishes of God, a formulation that depicted Mather as a socially destructive force not unlike the witches he pursued. By linking these accusations to representations of Mather as deluded and self-aggrandizing, the relatively common Calef could invoke the language of honorable manhood to disparage the credit of one of New England's most influential men. Mather clearly saw himself as the martyr for God, soldiering for justice despite the recriminations of profane, worldly enemies. But Calef's unmaking of Mather allowed him to suggest that their roles were actually reversed. Mather's reputation and influence, which ought to have protected him from these challenges, ultimately supported Calef's complaints that Mather's arrogance, ambition, and power had allowed him to manipulate proper social order in the service of his own interests over those of the godly community.

Defending the Mathers

In 1701, in response to the appearance of Calef's book, "several Persons belonging to the Flock of some of the Injured Pastors" published a rebuttal entitled *Some Few Remarks upon a Scandalous Book, against the Government and Ministry of New-England, Written, by one Robert Calef*.[58] The text has not received prolonged scholarly attention, but it demonstrates that one of the authors' primary concerns was the damage that could be done by an upstart who threatened to use controversy over witchcraft-possession to challenge the colonial leadership. Though both Mathers contributed additional writing to the book, the preface authors declared that the two were "neither of them the Authors, of this Composure," lest it appear that the ministers had taken it upon themselves to solicit support.[59] The authors closed rank against Calef and defused him as a threat by unmaking him as an honorable man using many of the strategies Harsnett and Darrell employed a century before. *Some Few Remarks* merged several gendered attacks upon Calef's credit by depicting him as an unruly outlier of questionable occupation, as a man motivated by excessive malice and passions, as lacking both reason and credit, and as a disorderly enemy of God and authority. These charges enabled the authors to set up a binary contrast between a devilish and divisive Calef on the one hand, and the godly Mathers, who embodied the manly virtues of credit, reason, and orderliness on the other. Even though Calef had used gendered language effectively to malign him, Mather also benefited from its use because it provided ways to refute Calef without having to engage substantively with his challenges that held difficult theological implications. It was risky to navigate divisive episodes of witchcraft-possession by unmaking one's enemies as men, however, because the more Mather challenged Calef's legitimacy in those terms, the more he left himself vulnerable to related charges.

The Margaret Rule incident, which had served as a centerpiece of Calef's challenge, provided the kind of drama and controversy that fueled propaganda. Even though by 1700 relations had soured between the Mathers and some of their former allies, the power of the critique pushed this group of supportive Boston gentlemen to demonstrate that they would not easily abdicate authority to a troublemaker. In their attack on Calef, the authors defended all that he had impugned. They reinforced the credit of judges, magistrates, and ministers, particularly the Mathers, as men of piety, reason, and moderation. This entailed a defense of witchcraft-possession itself but also of the other targets of Calef's criticism such as the renewed charter for colonial governance for which Increase Mather had advocated in London, and Cotton Mather's laudatory book about the life of Sir William Phips.[60] Calef had claimed that Cotton Mather inappropriately handled Margaret Rule's possession, and he used those charges as a starting point through which to challenge not only the Mathers but also the government they supported. The authors in turn wrote that "Good men" thought the book was full of "Scurrilous Reflections on the Government, as well as the Ministers of the Countrey," and that "the Book is to perswade the People, that the Judges of the Land; are the Unjustest, Cruellest and most Blood-thirsty men." In addition to this injustice, the authors also complained that Calef was attempting a fundamental reversal of order: "Our Wise men (sayes he) becoming Fools."[61] The authors shrewdly rested their defense of patriarchal order not on the demoniac Margaret Rule but on important and influential men. Calef's challenge, they argued, was just the sort of threat to the established order that angry, ambitious men recurrently made. To represent New England's wise men as fools, they argued, revealed that Calef—like the Devil himself—sought to turn the godly world upside down.

Many of the same strategies that Samuel Harsnett had employed during his possession propaganda war with John Darrell remained in play. For example, the authors of *Some Few Remarks* echoed some of Harsnett's barbs about trade and occupation as a way to minimize Calef's status. They dismissed him as a "Weaver" and emphasized whenever possible that he was lowly and unlearned in comparison to Cotton Mather. They wrote that Calef's book had been written, "(with what help we know not) by one Robert Calef, who presumes to call himself Merchant of Boston; but we wish, Better Wares were vended, by this Merchant."[62] Later, they added that it was doubtless "this Weaver wants work, or he would not have troubled the world with such Trifles."[63] Mather added that "the Weaver (though he presumes to call himself a Merchant) was a stranger to all the Rules of Civility" and that Calef's strongest argument in his book was not that Mather had mishandled an instance of witchcraft-possession but simply that "a certain Weaver . . . won't Believe it."[64] Despite the prevalence of trade-related accusations in *Some Few Remarks*, historians have only been able to draw tentative conclusions about the details of Robert Calef's life. Kenneth Silverman calls Calef "the otherwise obscure . . . merchant, clothier, or dyer with whom Mather had some earlier acquaintance" and suggests that the enmity between the men was due in part to "class antagonism."[65] Although questions of trade and occupation did not dominate the dispute between Calef, Cotton Mather, and the Mathers' supporters, there is no doubt that social and gentlemanly status, as demonstrated in the aforementioned remarks about Mather's extensive library, played a role in their struggle over manly legitimacy.

The defending authors further attacked Calef's credibility on individual and relational levels; they disparaged him as disorderly and malicious and cast aspersions on the motives and character of his supporters. They depicted any who believed Calef's charges as an "unguided multitude," so infected with the book's "venome" that neither reason nor counter-argument could sway them from error. They portrayed Calef as one of New England's internal enemies, with "Abettors" content to "whisper" slanders about their betters, an anxiety heightened by witchcraft and Indian wars. In contrast, the authors presented their book as a defense of unity; they wrote so "that there may be no more Slandering, and Reviling, and Reproaching one another, but that we may be all bound in the Bands of Unity, Singing the Song of the Glorious Angels above."[66] Echoing Cotton Mather, they claimed to write as servants of God chastising an enemy whose discord served the Devil. "New England," they wrote, "was once a place, in which the Feet of them that brought the Good Tidings of the Gospel were beautiful. But there is now sprung up a Number, who seem to be of another Spirit: No wonder then if those who are Faithful to Christ and His Interest, are Reproached and Maligned by them that serve His greatest Enemy."[67] Thus they transformed Calef from a man requesting clarification on scriptural matters to an instrument of worldly and spiritual dissolution. Like the witches whose trials he questioned, Calef's unwarranted publication marked him as the antithesis of proper, patriarchal order.

One of the authors' strongest arguments against Calef was the contrast they drew between him and the honorable men he challenged, as when by invoking the language of manly community they described Cotton and Increase Mather as joined in God's service against Calef's "Malignent Calumnies and Reproaches." All who knew Cotton Mather, they wrote, "look upon him to be a worthy Good man, as a Scholar, and a Gentleman, who would not willingly write a thing that is False . . . and that he spends his life in Studies, that he might do Good to all sorts of men." They further stated that Calef had practically admitted as much and that "others that are displeased at Mr. Mather for his being so significant in the Service of the Churches, yet when they are out of their angry fits, will confess the same."[68] Whereas Calef and his sort wrote out of malice, Mather was a scholar, preacher, and gentleman whose publications were beneficent. They also suggested that Mather's "significance" explained his critics' resentment. These bitter men, unable to produce legitimate challenges to Mather's name, instead had "angry fits" in which they—like children—temporarily surrendered their reason.

Later, the authors claimed that because Calef was unable to challenge the reputations of Mather's supporters, he similarly "gives a Kick at these great men"[69] as if struggling against the elders who sought to restrain his intemperate fits. The authors depicted Calef's adherents as petulant children and linked their lack of self-moderation to their lower status. They were "little men" who did not know, as Increase Mather did, "what it is to attend in the Court of Kings." The Mathers called them "Infatuated men" who "have only laid themselves open to the Resentments of Good men . . . and (while we were far from doing or wishing them any Hurt) they have Hurt themselves a Thousand Times more than either of us."[70] Like children having tantrums, Calef and his supporters lashed out against the restraining hands of men whose wisdom better suited them for leadership.

The reference to the "Court of Kings" constituted a response to one of Calef's explicitly political barbs—his criticism of the new charter attained for Massachusetts by Increase Mather in 1692. Although Margaret Rule's possession served as the centerpiece around which Calef structured his challenge to Cotton Mather, his invocation of the charter marked him as a critic of both Mathers. The main thrust of his criticism was that Increase Mather had capitulated too readily to the new monarchs' terms—despite four agonizing years attempting to secure Massachusetts's traditional privileges. In response to Calef's claim that Increase had "procured a Charter for Sir William to be Governour, and himself Established Praesident of the Collidge," the elder Mather replied in *Some Few Remarks*, "Can there be greater Nonsense mixed with Malice!" He added, "I suppose that all Reasonable Men will own, That Reproaches cast on me, for my Expensiveness in the Publick Service, are most Ungrateful and Unworthy."[71] There were known critics of the charter, especially Elisha Cooke and others who disparaged the concessions of Massachusetts's independence to royal oversight.[72] But in the text Increase Mather sidestepped the controversy by ascribing the true failure to Calef. He first claimed that not "so much as one Vertuous or Sensible man" failed to recognize the depravity of Calef's book, and he went on to suggest, more darkly, that "the absurd man be one of such Extream Unreasonableness, that some of his best Friends have told me, that they have long ago signified unto him, that . . . they did not wonder, that no Minister did care to be concerned with him."[73] This disparagement of Calef's spiritual position handily placed Calef not only outside of the community of honorable men but also far enough beyond it to suggest a desired banishment.

The authors depicted Calef as immoderate and unwilling to recognize his betters, which revealed his character to be thoroughly incompatible with honorable manhood. Just as complaints about Calef's unreasonableness had encouraged readers to see him as an unruly child, complaints about his malice also conjured an image of a youth in thrall to excessive passions. Invocations of malice played such a central role in *Some Few Remarks*, particularly in Cotton Mather's contributions, that they appear obsessive to the point of tedium. At the same time, this repetition established their importance. The authors challenged Calef to "vent thy malice; speak what thou hast to Accuse them of; they shall come off with flying Colours"; "It must needs be Malice that has invented such a Ridiculous Story"; "What reason then, has this man to speak so Falsely, and Maliciously, of him?" Cotton Mather claimed Calef's book primarily served to reveal "a few persons in the Land that will distinguish themselves by an Exalted Malignity," and that Calef's "Malice (like that of Him, whose Instrument he has herein made himself) has here gone beyond his Wit." And lastly, "to see such a Man and such a Book treat me with such Brutish Malignity" led Mather to pray that "Malice it self may never hiss with the least Colour of Reason any more."[74]

Cotton Mather took a great deal of comfort in the idea that his persecution, which he felt so pointedly, demonstrated his worth. His confidence in the imminence of the millennium led him to believe that Satan would increase assaults against the most ardent servants of God. Thus he wrote, perhaps in an attempt to convince himself, that "(through the Grace of Christ) we can Desire all the Malice of all our Enemies." The authors reinforced this notion by depicting Calef as a serpent. "Spit on, Calef; thou shalt be like the Viper on Paul's hand, easily shaken off, and without any damage to the Servant of the Lord."[75] Mather believed that godly New England stood poised at the end of history, and any who attempted to thwart its mission must ultimately face God's wrath. The authors of *Some Few Remarks* reinforced his view of Calef's demonic allegiance, writing that the arguments in his book were "inhumane, and fit for none but a Servant of the worst Master. . . . One would have thought, that the Fear of God (if he has any) should have darted that Scripture into his mind . . . Exod. 22. 28. *Thou shalt not speak Evil of the Ruler of thy People*."[76] Unlike the Mathers' righteous anger, Calef's "venome" resulted from excessive rage and hate. Such constitutional weakness differentiated him from honorable men and marked him as lacking the self-mastery and reason necessary to command authority. These characterizations show Calef as a devilish force, and although it would not have helped their case to suggest that Calef resembled a witch, the images resonated. Calef's comparison of Margaret Rule's symptoms to those of Quakers and fraudulent demoniacs was, according to Cotton Mather, "as Dangerous and as Damnable a position, as ever dropt from the Pen of man: 'tis fit only to be written with a Quill of an Harpy."[77] Quite like a witch or scold, Calef's malicious and blasphemous words gave proof of his discontent and evil designs on others, especially those who represented godly and ordered government. Thus Calef's most unwelcome attack nonetheless reinforced Cotton Mather's certainty that he was a legitimate ruler of his people.

The Mathers' ability to summon the honorable manly community to their defense was a crucial factor in their ability to weather not only Calef's book but also the dissatisfied mutterings in Boston for which it provided a forum. For this reason, the authors of *Some Few Remarks* took care to differentiate Calef from those he critiqued. This strategy, to the extent that it established Calef as an inversion of his worthy targets, was central to their argument that Calef advocated the destruction of all they represented. His goal, they wrote, was "to render the Land, and the Judges obnoxious (tho' all the Learning that he and wiser men than he, pretends unto, is insufficient to dive to the Bottom of the matter."[78] Increase Mather defended his handling of the new charter along similar lines. He emphasized its gains, "for which better men than Robert Calef are of Opinion, that the Countrey owes me Thanks." He added, "after the Charter was finished, several Right, Honourable Persons said to me, they were glad of what was gained."[79] Cotton Mather used the same strategy in response to Calef's criticism of his witchcraft publications. He highlighted the support his works received from eminent divines as Richard Baxter, whose preface to *Memorable Providences* bespoke its correctness. Mather further defended that volume by asserting it was "not only ordered by the Governour, to be Published, with Terms of the highest Respect, but also was Perused and Approved by as Eminent persons as any in the Countrey."[80] These examples demonstrate the powerful customary link between honorable manhood and standing in a creditable community. The contributors to *Some Few Remarks* asserted their legitimacy by gathering the names of honorable men who recognized them and used those names to buttress themselves against assaults from an outsider.

Just as Calef had compared the Mathers' work with Margaret Rule to fraudulent Quakers and Catholic possessions, Cotton Mather and his defenders depicted Calef as an unsettling force whose attacks on New

England's judges and patriarchs aligned him not only with worldly enemies but even with Satan himself.[81] As a result, each accusation that Mather and his defenders levied at Calef simultaneously served to shore up the Mathers as the positive end of the binary. When Cotton Mather wrote in defense of his behavior after the "Storm was raised at Salem," he emphasized his selfless generosity that emerged from a desire to be of service to God and all those who suffered for Christ's sake. Despite this generosity, though, Mather asks, "How came it then to pass, that many people took up another Notion of me? Truely, Satan knows. Perhaps 'twas because I thought it my Duty always to speak of the Honourable Judges with as much Honour as I could. . . . Perhaps also my Disposition to avoid Extreams . . . causeth me generally to be obnoxious unto the Violent in all parties. Or, perhaps my great Adversary always had certain people full of Robert Calef's Malignity, to serve him with Calumnies and Reproaches."[82] This brief passage simultaneously established Robert Calef as an agent of Satan and reinforced Mather's own position as a respectful member of godly society who was as willing to offer appropriate deference as to expect it from others. The qualities of honorable manhood Mather exemplified were especially clearly articulated in his claim to be by nature a man who embraced duty and shunned extremes. These arguments took on additional power because they linked components of legitimate manhood to the religion and politics of New England. Mather's self-fashioning in the quotation above made use of readers' customary association of the positive qualities as constitutive of honorable manhood, whereas the passions, excess, malice, and discontent of his enemies were believed to be rampant among youths, women, children, and Catholic, Quaker, and Indian enemies.[83]

Perhaps to reassure himself as well as the reader, Mather asserted that Calef's efforts had amounted to nothing and that whatever stir the book made upon its appearance had passed. Mather claimed that readers "at first were a little eager to see the Book, as they would be to see a Prodigy for they generally reckoned it to be a very Prodigy of wickedness. But they are now satisfied, That if he should go on to write never so many more such Volumns, they would lye upon his hands; no sober people would vouchsafe to look upon them."[84] Mather's prediction disclosed his own hopes for the future, in which he, and not Calef, authored books that would attract the attention and appreciation of people of substance. This wish harkened back to his angelic visitation of 1684, when he received confirmation that he was special to God and would have unusual importance and influence. Mather thirsted for this vindication, but despite having all the privileges of elite patriarchal status, his defense of the judges and the witchcraft trials constituted the kind of blot on his credit that Calef intended.

Mather's frustration with this state of affairs led him to vacillate between dispassionate reason and profound resentment. At times his expression of moral superiority coexisted uneasily with his desire for revenge. "All we have to add," he wrote, "is That we would Bless and not Curse those who Persecute us, and fervently Pray to God, for His Best Blessings on the very Worst of all our Persecutors . . . That though they may oblige us to Defend our selves, we hope, they shall not provoke us to Revenge any wrongs they may do unto us." But having arrived at this dark suggestion, Mather then quickly recast himself as the victim rather than harasser: "And if any by their Envious Vexing and Carping . . . do . . . make New-England, the only Countrey where it is a Crime for Innocency to have a Vindication, we Forgive these also, and Pray, That they may be forgiven."[85] When Mather encouraged readers to lift their eyes from the messy realm of New England to heaven, he modeled a self-abnegating charity for his detractors. When he made semi-veiled threats, as when he wrote, "I am veryily perswaded, that the Holy Lord, whose we are, and whom we serve, will at some time or other [punish him] for this his deliberate wickedness,"[86] Mather invoked God's likely judgment upon those who sought to ruin His most beloved servants.

Overall, *Some Few Remarks upon a Scandalous Book* provided a platform from which Mather could reiterate his self-concept as part of God's plan for New England and characterize his detractors as Satan's instruments. He attempted to remain humble despite the grandeur of this formulation, and his struggle to sustain his vision of New England against escalating change echoed within his frustrated rhetoric. *Some Few Remarks* is filled with references to the religious and political disputes that marked the age, from the charter to the record of the governor, and from the threats of Quakers and Indians to the missteps taken at Salem. But in attempting to discredit Calef, the authors relied on gendered strategies that transcended the specific conditions of New England and that had successfully cast aspersions on the Mathers in the first place. When the authors addressed Calef, saying, "We wonder Friend, what made you to wander so far from the design of your Book, (which you tell us, p. 3 of your preface, is *to prevent any more such Bloody Victims or Sacrafices, and the Vindication of the Truth*)," they claimed to "gladly suppose, it was not to raise your . . . own Credit upon the fall of Theirs, was it? If so, the stone rolls upon your self."[87] Their assertion sounds hollow because despite having the last word, and all earthly advantages, Cotton Mather did not emerge from these documents as the victor. Historians know little about Robert Calef outside of his book and the likely location of his grave,[88] but no matter how dastardly or prescient a figure he was, Mather failed to answer him on the scriptural points central to witchcraft and possession and fell prey to some of the very weaknesses to which Calef referred. In time, Mather's defense of witchcraft and possession marked him as one brand of Puritan father: honorable and venerated, but no longer a political force who shaped what constituted orthodoxy in New England. While operating both above and below the surface, gendered conceptions of credit, trade, and honor among gentlemanly peers provided both sides with a language through which to bolster their own claims while unmaking their opponents.

Witchcraft-Possession and Patriarchal Continuity

In *Memorable Providences* (1689), Mather had acknowledged his impatience with Sadducees and wits who refused to see that preternatural wonders proved his providential understanding of God's plan. Those same sentiments appear in Mather's 1693 manuscript about Margaret Rule, but by that time he faced a kind and degree of criticism he never anticipated. His resentment of this treatment led him to take a much more defensive stance in comparison to the assured tone of the earlier account. In anticipation of his critics, Mather asserted that his response had been cautious and sober and had resulted in order, justice, and godliness, noting: "I have also checked and quell'd those forbidden curiosities . . . when I have seen wonderful *Snares* laid for *Curious* People, by the secret and future things discovered from the *Mouths of Damsels possest with a Spirit of divination* . . . the Reputation of *no one* good Person in the World has been damaged, but instead thereof the Souls of many, especially of the rising Generation . . . who were strangers to real Piety, were now struck with the lively demonstrations of *Hell* evidently set forth before their Eyes." And despite the fact that Mather's labors had robbed the Devil and swelled the churches, Mather decried

> those that pick up little incoherent scraps and bits of my *Discourses* in this fruitful discharge of my Ministry, and so traversted 'em in their abusive *Pamphlets*, as to perswade the Town that I was their *common Enemy* in those very points. . . . Yea to do like *Satan* himself, by sly, base, unpretending *Insinuations* as if I wore not the

Modesty and Gravity which became a Minister of the Gospel, I could not but think my self unkindly dealt withal, and the neglects of *others* to do me *justice* in this affair has caused me to conclude this Narrative with complaints in *another hearing* of such Monstrous Injuries.[89]

Mather could not refrain from addressing the context of Salem while he tried to make space for Rule's new affliction. The crux of his argument was that rather than acting rashly he had counseled moderation and prudence, by suppressing the names of suspected witches and by discouraging foolish superstitions, and that those who debased his reputation in scurrilous pamphlets resembled the Devil. Once again, however, what appears to represent change—his increasingly cautious and aggrieved tone—actually reflected the continuity of his attempts to marshal the gendered language of authority and order to bolster his claims. To a remarkable degree, the passage calls to mind John Darrell's wounded self-defense a century earlier, when that godly minister protested that Harsnett slandered him with "sluttish" false accusations, "thinking thereby utterly to shame me, and disgrace me forever viz. to make the world believe that I am a vicious and unclean person."[90] The immediate context of the various witchcraft-possession cases changed, and the men who succeeded in accessing and maintaining power changed, but beneath it all was a common cultural foundation in patriarchal hierarchy, which provided the language that both winners and losers wielded on behalf of themselves and against their opponents.

As we saw above, in 1693 Cotton Mather began his narrative of Margaret Rule's possession with a vignette of a Christian Indian man whose spectral affliction substantively matched the experiences of the Goodwin children, the possessed accusers at Salem, Mercy Short, and Margaret Rule. Just as Mather had used that figure of an "Indian" to serve his larger agenda, so did Calef find one to serve his own. Calef concluded his narrative with a purported account of what an "Indian told Captain Hill, at Saco-Fort." Notably, Calef brought the reader back to the ongoing battles on the Maine frontier against allied French and Indian forces, and of Calef's criticism of Sir William Phips's aborted attempt to capture Quebec.[91] He reported: "The Indian told him that the French Ministers were better than the English, for before the French came among them there were a great many Witches among the Indians, but now where were none, and there were much Witches among the English Ministers, as Burroughs, who was Hang'd for it. . . . Were

I disposed to make reflections upon it, I suppose you will Judge the Field large, enough, but I forbear, as above."[92] Calef used this account to merge his condemnation of witchcraft trails and dispossessions with censure of the established hierarchy in Massachusetts and its troubled military campaign against French and Indian enemies. It allowed him to construct a stronger critique of Mather's laudatory biography of Phips and to link his disparagement of the minister and the witchcraft trials to a general incompetence. It was particularly assertive to suggest that the witchcraft trials Mather defended had contributed to Indians' preference of French Catholics over English Protestants. If Reverend George Burroughs truly had been a witch, as Mather maintained, then it became difficult to answer this "Indian." More than a criticism of the governing body's military campaign—though it was—Calef suggested that rather than carry out Mather's millennial purpose, the trials had in effect served the Devil's interests. It is telling that both men found an image of an Indian man to suit their objectives. Calef might simply have been following Mather's form, to provide a kind of bookend for their debate. Still, Mather's representation of the "Pious Indian" was pedagogical precisely because it would strike English readers as an anomaly. Despite Mather's use of the image as a reminder of the universality of sin and the importance of a "good death,"[93] Calef's Indian would have sounded more familiar, real, and threatening.

From 1620 to 1700 in the Anglo-Atlantic, profound political and religious upheaval, a climate increasingly skeptical of preternatural phenomena, and the eventual institution of official tolerance for Anglicans all made their mark upon published possession narratives. But despite these changes, and New England Puritans' stronger claims to institutional power in comparison to their English counterparts, many of the unique characteristics of the outbreak in Salem and Essex County dissolved into the greater continuity in patriarchal principles and language. And even when authors submerged explicit gendered arguments while describing demoniacs, they nonetheless invoked bodies and conceptions of sin in ways that drew upon long-standing cultural scripts in which gender provided a foundation. Those who acted as if they were possessed tried both to claim and externalize their sinful natures and struggled through their fits in hopes of deliverance from the assaults of devils and men. Despite the myriad differences across a century and an ocean, what remained constant was the way that both believing and skeptical parties attempted to bolster their position by aligning themselves as representatives of proper patriarchal order in contrast to their debased opponents.

By 1700 the witchcraft trials at Salem and Essex County had been over for seven years, and there had been no subsequent outbreak to fulfill Mrs. Carver's prediction. Rather than dramatic wars between angels and devils and an impending millennium, New England was left with factionalism and bickering over church policies. The raids on New England settlements by the French and their Indian allies remained a terrifying and puzzling manifestation of the mysteries of God's will. How could Cotton Mather square the outcomes of the Essex County outbreak against his predictions? What did it mean for his credit if his community no longer looked to him to interpret the providential significance of supernatural signs? The aborted libel suit against Robert Calef left a notable silence, because for all the talk of God's terrible judgment, Calef and his sort lived on in a Boston that became more their city than Mather's. While neither Mather nor Calef was irreparably unmade by their published debate, both suffered slights as a result. Gender had informed their language of attack, and it surely contributed to their ongoing efforts to advocate for themselves and their interests. Cotton Mather continued to publish prolifically, and Calef retreated into silence. Each man, by behaving as he had before the controversy, completed his own argument in favor of his commitment to order, reason, and deference. The gendered language of manhood was flexible enough to support Mather and Calef's opposing arguments about witchcraft-possession, and also their opposing reactions to its decline.

The continuity between Cotton Mather's war with Calef and the Darrell-Harsnett debates a century earlier demonstrates that gendered language still permeated witchcraft-possession accounts at the turn of the eighteenth century. Like their forebears, Calef and Mather each worked to unmake the other by highlighting his opponent's excessive passions, ambition, insufficient reason, and reliance upon degraded adherents. The problem for New England's Puritan leadership, at least those who favored Increase Mather's new charter but opposed the liberal church reforms of the Brattle Street Church,[94] was that witchcraft-possession retained its use as a tool for conversions but also made participants vulnerable to accusations that they had fallen victim to the very sins the dispossession sought to purge. Because Cotton Mather saw himself as fighting a war against Satan, he cast critics like Robert Calef as dark inversions of himself—much as the witch image inverted honorable womanhood and manhood. Mather's sense of demonic opposition was strengthened by the sense that even his recent victories over the enemy were far from complete. As David Levin explains: "Society was moving beyond the control of the people who called themselves the Lord's. Yet the central fact that marks 1692–93 as the end of Cotton Mather's most effective political action is the separation of the political world from the world of spirits"[95] that took place when Governor Phips overruled the Special Court of Oyer and Terminer. Bostonians did not move toward skepticism as a result of a more "modern" or scientific mind-set, but the institutionalization of religious tolerance in 1692–93 ushered in a period of increasingly secular political language that served to shift power away from the Mathers and their peers.[96] Gendered language was one of the tools men used in the struggle to preserve themselves amid change—to lay claims to appropriate patriarchal order, mastery of subordinates, and the reason and self-moderation necessary for leadership.

Elizabeth Foyster writes that manhood in the seventeenth century "was characterised by neither sudden transformation caused by crisis, nor by stasis. Rather, it was a history marked by the endurance of patriarchal ideology, which overlay the constantly shifting daily practice of gender relations."[97] This endurance helps to explain why demoniacs, accused witches, and possession propagandists in England and New England continued to rely upon the gendered strategies imbued in witchcraft-possession. Even as these phenomena remained associated with female weaknesses and proclivities, men became involved alongside women and, like them, invoked gendered aspects of the possession script in an attempt to maintain their innocence. Although political and religious turmoil created uncertainty about who could rightfully claim authority, the patriarchal nature of that authority was never in question. The dawning of the eighteenth century ushered in a period of growth, in which the constantly shifting gender relations of everyday life would come to reflect broader fluctuations in the meanings of manhood and womanhood based on religion, race, and social status. But for as long as representatives of authority—as well as middling and common folk—valued the explanatory powers of the preternatural realm, these incidents continued to reverberate across the Anglo-Atlantic. Therefore possession narratives demonstrate that despite profound change, and important local variations in the articulation of possession and witchcraft-possession in England and New England, these phenomena retained their foundation in gendered cultural understandings of bodies, sin, and proper patriarchal order.

Epilogue: Continuity and Patriarchy at the Turn of the Eighteenth Century

The witchcraft-possession outbreak in Salem and Essex County, Massachusetts, ended abruptly, and fostered a climate that suppressed officials' willingness to respond to witchcraft accusations that emerged from the spectral realm. Its end marked colonial America's last official executions for witchcraft, but popular belief in the realities of witchcraft and possession persisted on both sides of the Atlantic.[1] Indeed, while the Mathers were struggling to negotiate the evolving political situation in Boston throughout the 1690s, published accounts and treatises about demonic possession and witchcraft-possession continued to appear in England.[2] These new cases sparked fresh propaganda wars between Anglicans, Puritans, and Catholics, and despite their variation, to a great extent they, and printed debates about them, highlighted the symptoms, treatments, and controversies that had emerged over the long seventeenth century. The considerable transatlantic continuity in possession phenomena, and the ways writers used them to address contentious religious and political questions, centered on the sustained cultural reliance upon patriarchal models of power and authority.

Practically on the heels of Salem, Catholic priests exorcized the twelve-year-old son of one Mr. Crook in Lancashire, England, a stronghold for nonconformists over which Anglican officials sought to gain greater control. The Anglican clergyman of the parish, Zachary Taylor, published a scathing review of the case based upon material sent him by his colleague

Thomas Marsden. The text of *The Devil Turn'd Casuist* (1696) reflected nearly the same approach of attributing supposed possessions to natural illness, fraud, and popery that Samuel Harsnett and others had taken a century before. The narrative presented the case of the twelve-year-old as "such a Medley of Fopperies, as will be hard to believe that any who call themselves Christians should be Guilty of; for the Priests have so far over-acted each part of the Play, that the plain Relation of it will appear more like Burlesque than Narrative."[3] As Harsnett had so clearly grasped, the performative aspects of possessions lent themselves to unsavory comparisons with stage plays and stunts that gulled onlookers. At the crux of this case was the Anglican position that the priests took advantage of the boy's illness, which was actually a "curable epilepsy," to declare "him to be Possest by an Evil Spirit, which too easily catch't the belief of most of his Protestant Neighbours; Some concluded him to be hurt by an Evil Tongue; others thought, because his Stepmother was a Papist, that the whole was a Counterfeit, acted to gain advantage to the Roman Interest in those parts."[4] After demonstrating the ongoing power that possessions had as propaganda and evangelism, Marsden presented the boy's condition as a natural illness despite the fact he had seemed to speak with another voice "mistaken by some present for the voice of the Devil." The boy does appear to have attempted a possession performance, since he strove to tell secrets and name strangers in his unusual voice. He apparently had had some success in this until Marsden arrived and asked the boy to identify him, at which point the boy incorrectly named a different clergyman. Marsden added smartly, "Upon this I said to the Company, Gentlemen, this is a dull Devil that cannot distinguish the Vicar of Walton from the Curate of Rufford,"[5] after which he moved on to describe the natural means by which he affected the cure.

The narrative reached its desired conclusion not only through boy's restoration to health, and the narrator's triumph over credulous relatives and scheming priests, but also by Marsden's addendum that "From that time till a few years ago, I never saw young Mr. Crook; when riding near his house towards Preston, he call'd to me, treated me courteously, and gave me thanks for my past care of him. I was glad to see him a proper man, in good health, the Husband of a good Wife, the Father of pretty Children. And I am glad to hear he has the General Character of an ingenious, honest, well-bred person."[6] The attribution of the case to illness, rather than fraud, allowed Marsden and Taylor to show a former supposed demoniac restored to health and order. By leaving the reader with a sense of how proper a man the young Mr. Crook had become, this skeptical tract provided the kind of satisfying ending that Puritan texts usually supplied through godly redemption and conversion. The great flexibility of the possession script allowed opponents to maneuver around the risks and opportunities of possession propaganda in pursuit of the strongest argument. If the cautious near-skepticism of Anglican writers usually cast them in the roles of decrying fraud, popery, and delusion, in this case the authors could also claim to have brought about a happy ending in which they restored health, moderation, reason, and patriarchal order not only to the boy but also to his community.

In the case of Richard Dugdale, who became possessed in the same region in 1689 and was dubbed the "Surrey Demoniac" in publications that appeared in 1697, there was no such storybook ending. Dugdale's dispossession offered a particularly tempting target for Anglican leadership wishing to suppress nonconformist activity in the region, especially once godly pamphlets by ministers Thomas Jollie and John Carrington appeared to promulgate it. Zachary Taylor became more widely known for his role in this contentious witchcraft-possession pamphlet war, which began with possession and ended with myriad controverted religious points among Anglicans and dissenters.[7] The controversy addressed many compelling and familiar aspects of possession phenomena: questions of fraud, illness, popish trickery, the difference between possession and obsession, the comparative credit of the men involved, and the question of what effects would result from either side's agenda (that is, popish dissimulation and Presbyterian enthusiasm on Jollie's part, or the despotic promotion of atheism and Sadducism on Taylor's). The Dugdale case resembled John Darrell's disastrous attempts to minister to the apprentice William Somers at the turn of the seventeenth century, and both sides referred to Darrell and Harsnett directly while reifying their arguments and counterarguments.[8] Furthermore, the godly ministers who sought to use Dugdale's delivery as a sign of God's great work were acquainted with the Mathers and wrote in part as a result of the appearance in England of publications about the outbreak at Salem.[9] As a whole, the Dugdale episode shows continuity in the script followed by would-be demoniacs, in the arguments used by believing and skeptical polemicists and in the ways that manhood and invocations of patriarchal authority and order provided a flexible language of disputation in Anglo-American possession phenomena.

The Dugdale case was not the last contentious possession episode to capture the attention of Englishmen on both sides of the Atlantic, but it set the tone for the cases that emerged after the turn of the eighteenth century.[10] It provides an example of the great difficulty godly ministers faced in maintaining the credit of demoniacs once a case attracted the scrutiny of powerful and skeptical authorities. Just as Harsnett had managed to procure William Somers's allegiance and disparage the others whom Darrell had dispossessed, Taylor had little trouble unmaking Richard Dugdale, whose character and behavior had also troubled his godly attendants. Cotton Mather attested to this in *Some Few Remarks upon a Scandalous Book* (1701), when he announced that "my Reverend Friend Mr. Thomas Jolly, one of the most Holy Servants that the Lord Jesus Christ has upon Earth, and an Aged and Famous Minister of the Gospel, Published an Account of a certain Demoniac (one Richard Dugdale)." Despite Jollie's heroic efforts on Dugdale's behalf, Mather wrote:

> After all, the Young man was delivered; but as he was a very Vicious Fellow before his Possession, so he was not much mended after his Deliverance. When the Tragedy was over, one Zachary Tailor, Printed a Virulent Book, (Just like our Calefs) which affirmed unto the Nation, That the whole Business of Dugdale, was a Cheat, and a Sham, and a Combination of the Roman-Catholick and the Non-Conformists, to put a Trick upon the Nation: and Reviled that Reverend man of God, Mr. Jolly, as Guilty of much Falsity, and Forgery, and Blasphemy, and Cursing, and as designing to hurt the Cause of Revealed Religion, and as worthy to have his Tongue bored through with an hot Iron, and other Infamous passages, that can't be Numbred.[11]

Mather took comfort in the fact that the suffering that he and Jollie faced at the hands of devilish detractors marked them as noble sufferers in Christ's name, however the world might treat them. Even given the different level of authority that Robert Calef and Zachary Taylor held in relation to those they criticized, the overlap between their skeptical challenges to godly possessions resonated across the Atlantic and demonstrated that the disparagement of a demoniac remained an effective way to undermine ministers like Mather and Jollie. A sinful life was no bar to making one the subject of a true possession, of course, but the dismantling of these subjects' credit—as seen in Thomas Brattle's turn against the largely female afflicted accusers and confessing witches in Salem—was most easily accomplished. These critiques drew strength from claims of fraud, whether intentional or delusional, Catholic or Puritan, that had been a strong current in witchcraft-possession debates since the late sixteenth century.

Taylor's handling of the Dugdale controversy did a great deal to forward skeptical attitudes toward possession. These gains were reinforced by another important skeptical tract in 1698 that harkened back to the aforementioned fraud case of William Perry, or the Boy of Bilson, that had appeared in 1622 and was widely cited across the seventeenth century. Robert Howson published *The Second Part of the Boy of Bilson: Or, a True and Particular Relation of the Impostor Susanna Fowles* to highlight the continuity in the debate over possession phenomena as popish delusion mingled with degraded immorality.[12] One of the reasons given for why Fowles began the charade was her discontent with her new husband, which immediately followed his discovery that she did not have the fortune she had claimed. In the course of their arguing she vented "unreasonable and extravagant Passions" and "did frequently Imprecate the *Devil to fetch her from him and his Family.*"[13] Fowles later confessed that a Catholic relative had inveigled her to feign possession and to respond to the efforts of Catholic priests to exorcise her. Robert Howson appeared to take vindictive pleasure both in the rough treatment that preceded Fowles's downfall and in her being committed to Bridewell prison for blasphemy. His emphasis on her intractability and intemperate greed calls to mind the words of the godly Richard Baxter, who occupied quite a different point on the devotional spectrum than Taylor and Howson. Baxter wrote in 1691 that fraudulent possessions were generally conducted by two sorts of persons: those trained by "Papists Priests, to honour their Exorcisms" like the Boy of Bilson, or "Lustful, Rank, Girls and young Widows, that plot for some amorous, procacious Design, or have Imaginations conquered by Lust."[14] The paradox for godly writers like Baxter and Jollie was that they had to express their great disdain of Catholic and fraudulent possessions in order to set their own cases apart, but these efforts ultimately reinforced the skeptical discourse that suppressed what they saw as true possession phenomena. The specters of devious priests, lascivious women, and disorderly youths had always shadowed possession cases, but the consolidation of power on the side of skeptics led such images to dominate published representations of demoniacs at the turn of the eighteenth century. Just as the controversies at the end of the sixteenth century had created a climate that suppressed published possession accounts, so too did the propaganda wars of the 1690s. And while the debates ultimately extended into the eighteenth century, 1700 marked the end of the period when Puritans on either side of the Atlantic had sufficiently strong footing to claim to represent the official discourse of witchcraft-possession. In this way, gendered conceptions of discontent and disorder remained at the center of published articulations of possession phenomena despite shifting power relations among the men who claimed that their interpretations represented the true interests of proper patriarchal order.

That witchcraft in the Anglo-American context was a predominantly female phenomenon can be seen, for example, in traditional beliefs about women's susceptibility to supernatural influence and the consistently higher numbers of women accused and executed as witches. The thoroughly gendered nature of the crime, and the methods used to detect and prosecute it, has provided scholars with a lens through which to observe how early modern people reacted to tensions within families and communities. Still, to restrict witchcraft-possession analytically to "something female" obscures some of the ways these cases functioned; for demoniacs, men accused of witchcraft by the possessed, and men who published propaganda about the cases, invocations of honorable manhood and patriarchal order shaped competing claims to power. Even though gender was malleable and intermittently superseded by other concerns, it remained inextricably linked to those who experienced, were implicated by, or interpreted witchcraft-possession.

For demoniacs, gendered assumptions about their bodies and temperaments continued to shape their ability to lay claim to a legitimate possession. In the course of working to determine what made a demoniac or a witch, early modern people grappled with what made a proper woman and man. Demoniacs had always been the focus of intense and critical scrutiny, but by the turn of the eighteenth century a general transference of suspicion from witches onto those who acted as if they were possessed provided men in authority with a way to preserve social order without having to tread the tricky legal and scriptural ground of witchcraft prosecution. Possession cases had not lost their potential to provide the kind of divine authority that aided Catholics and Puritans in their attempts to gain legitimacy and converts.[15] But this potential evaporated when they bred more strife than cohesion,[16] and when powerful men increasingly relegated belief in such phenomena to the realm of silly, foolish old women. The gendering of credulity in opposition to manly reason helped seal the fate of witchcraft-possession. Gender's role in the course of possession cases was far from simple, however, because as much as gendered language permeated these events, its malleability allowed its use by all sides in contradictory ways. Ultimately, authors on both sides of the Atlantic used gendered language in ways that reflected the vicissitudes of power.

Men named as witches by possessed accusers, like John Samuel and George Burroughs, faced neighbors and officials who were open to the idea that they had sought power from the Devil to harm. Their accusers reported spectral torture at their hands, hinted at pressure to covenant with Satan, and exhibited fits and recoveries timed to deepen observers' certainty of their guilt. Men accused of being witches were somewhat better positioned than their female counterparts, given that the weighty cultural tradition that associated witchcraft with women made men less than usual suspects. Still, men were sinners whose temptations or ambitions could get the better of them, and as witches they might take positions of authority among others. Samuel and Burroughs do not provide a representative overview of male witches, nor are their stories meant to supersede the stories of the female witches who greatly outnumbered them. But their experiences demonstrate that in moments of crisis the languages of manhood mattered and provided tools both to free and to condemn the accused. Men who were accused of witchcraft by the possessed walked a line between deficient and excessive manhoods and had to assert their rationality and mastery without appearing too angry, resentful, or presumptuous. In the end, status as a man with good credit among other honorable men had the potential to redeem the accused, but such credit rested uneasily on public opinion, temperament, and shifting power relations.

The men who published propaganda about witchcraft-possession cases were drawn in by the powerful grasp these episodes held with popular imagination and with their power to forward sectarian religious claims. After all, possessions were dramatic enactments of the struggle between God and Satan, and between sinful temptation and godly redemption. Ministers who wanted their congregants to be mindful of these cosmic contests might achieve more at the bedside of a demoniac than through years of preaching. In addition, written accounts of possession sold well, allowing ministers to spread the word more effectively than before; they did not fail to perceive that these narratives could be "profitable" in a doubled sense. Sensationalism was possession's appeal but also its great risk. As Puritan ministers John Darrell and Cotton Mather discovered, even their sober reputations and conviction in the veracity of what they observed was not enough to protect them from accusations of being crass liars, chattering dupes, or lascivious manipulators. Though they operated in different political and religious contexts, their witchcraft-possession tracts relied upon gendered strategies that accounted for many of their central claims to represent order and authority.

A transatlantic cultural history of manhood in witchcraft-possession reveals that even as particular episodes incorporated local pressures, and specific religious and political conflicts, gender and patriarchal order were among the central organizing principles that shaped cases' configuration and outcomes. Possession propaganda relied upon gendered language, invocations of manhood, and strategies for unmaking men and women into witches that indicate gender's ongoing centrality throughout the long seventeenth century. Attention to gender broadly conceived restores dynamics of power to discussions of witchcraft prosecution without insisting that patriarchal interests could be served *only* by the oppression of women by men. That gender operated inconsistently, influencing some men and women more than others, did not compromise its significance. In fact, patriarchy in the early modern Anglo-Atlantic was as complex as the population itself, with all of its shifting alliances and fortunes. Since early modern people had to justify their beliefs and actions in accordance with their own cosmology, they were under no obligation to be explicit when implicit invocations worked just as well. Despite its inconsistencies, the malleability of patriarchal discourse made it a pervasive and resilient organizing principle of preternatural phenomena. Ultimately, published propaganda about demoniacs, witches, and possessions demonstrates that these incidents had at their core deeply held cultural beliefs in which gender was profoundly implicated.

This book has found considerable continuity in the witchcraft-possession script, in the language and strategies used by believers and doubters, and in the patriarchal foundations of the authority to make meaning from the bodies of those who acted possessed. This does not mean that nothing changed or that contextual factors did not matter enormously to those involved. Nor does this continuity suggest that the prevalence of patriarchal power reduced early modern people to hapless victims. But in addition to bringing to light the astonishingly varied and vivid details of preternatural affliction, published accounts of demonic possession and witchcraft-possession demonstrate some of the cultural conventions that spanned the tumultuous long seventeenth century, as well as the Atlantic Ocean. Even rare and unrepresentative episodes such as these reveal an unexpectedly resilient link between men and women, manhood and womanhood, and the uncertain boundaries between the natural and preternatural worlds.

NOTES

Notes to the Introduction

1. I. D., *The most wonderfull and true storie, of a certaine Witch named Alse Gooderige . . . As also a true report of the strange torments of Thomas Darling, a boy of thirteene yeres of age, that was possessed by the Devill, with his horrible fittes and terrible Apparitions. . . .* (London, 1597).

2. Devilish interference was "preternatural" because it operated in ways that were natural but surpassed human understanding, whereas the "supernatural" genuinely originated beyond the natural realm and was reserved for God (Jeremy Schmidt, *Melancholy and the Care of the Soul: Religion, Moral Philosophy and Madness in Early Modern England* [Aldershot, UK: Ashgate, 2007], 134; Stuart Clark, *Thinking with Demons: The Idea of Witchcraft in Early Modern Europe* [New York: Oxford University Press, 1997], esp. chaps. 10 and 11).

3. For interpretation and analysis of these legal developments, see John Newton and Jo Bath, eds., *Witchcraft and the Act of 1604* (Boston: Brill, 2008). Condemned witches in parts of Europe were burned at the stake, but England hanged its witches except in rare cases that overlapped with petty treason, such as when a woman was convicted of having used malefic witchcraft to kill her husband.

4. This state of affairs persisted, despite the restoration of Roman Catholicism during Queen Mary's reign, after Queen Elizabeth reinstituted the second prayer book when she took the throne in 1558.

5. For questions about the suitability of the term "Puritan," see Patrick Collinson, "A Comment: Concerning the Name Puritan," *Journal of Ecclesiastical History* 31, no. 4 (October 1980): 483–88; Michael Winship, "Were There Any Puritans in New England?," *New England Quarterly* 74, no. 1 (March 2001): 118–38; and Dwight Brautigam, "Prelates and Politics: Uses of 'Puritan,' 1625–1640," in *Puritanism and its Discontents,* ed. Laura Lunger Knoppers (Newark: University of Delaware Press, 2003). Scholars have argued that capitalizing "Puritan" suggests too unified a movement and might reinforce the long-standing American investment in seeing Puritanism as providing

the nation's central origin story. On these questions, see David D. Hall, "Narrating Puritanism," in *New Directions in American Religious History*, ed. Harry S. Stout and D. G. Hart (New York: Oxford University Press, 1997), 73–75.

6. Keith Thomas, *Religion and the Decline of Magic* (New York: Oxford University Press, 1971), 477–80.

7. For the final controversies that brought official prosecution of witchcraft trials to an end by the mid-eighteenth century, see Ian Bostridge, *Witchcraft and Its Transformations: 1650–1750* (New York: Oxford University Press, 1997).

8. C. L'Estrange Ewen, *Witch Hunting and Witch Trials: The Indictments for Witchcraft from the Records of the 1373 Assizes Held from the Home Court 1559–1736* (London: K. Paul, Trench, Trubner, 1929), 111–13. James Sharpe explains that the proportion of women among the accused in the active southeast of England was just under 90 percent and "rose to 95 per cent of the forty witches prosecuted after 1660" (Sharpe, *Instruments of Darkness: Witchcraft in Early Modern England* [Philadelphia: University of Pennsylvania Press, 1996], 107–8, 114). For New England, Carol F. Karlsen writes that the "single most salient characteristic of witches was their sex. At least 344 persons were accused of witchcraft in New England between 1620 and 1725. Of the 342 who can be identified by sex, 267 (78 percent) were female" (Karlsen, *The Devil in the Shape of a Woman: Witchcraft in Colonial New England* [New York: Norton, 1987], 47).

9. This has been especially important for areas of Europe, such as Russia, Scandinavia, and the Iberian Peninsula, with witchcraft traditions and patterns of prosecution that differed from those in the parts of western Europe most often covered by historians (see, for example, Valerie Kivelson, *Desperate Magic: The Moral Economy of Witchcraft in Seventeenth-Century Russia* [Ithaca, NY: Cornell University Press, 2013]; and Marko Nenonen and Raisa Maria Toivo, eds., *Writing Witch-Hunt Histories: Challenging the Paradigm* [Leiden: Brill, 2014]). For insight about what made the witchcraft outbreak at Salem and Essex County exceptional and set it apart from witchcraft elsewhere in New England or England, see Mary Beth Norton, *In the Devil's Snare: The Salem Witchcraft Crisis of 1692* (New York: Knopf, 2002), 8–12.

10. During the period under review, patriarchy was the central model for political and social hierarchies, with pervasive influence across early modern society despite the fact that individuals' lived realities did not always function according to the patriarchal ideal. Judith Butler rightly cautions against invoking patriarchy as a "universalizing concept that overrides or reduces distinct articulations of gender asymmetry in different cultural contexts," but its use here refers to the ways the political and legal implications of patriarchalism manifested in social and discursive realms specific to early modern England and colonial New England. It refers to a cultural structuring of power in which men and women of varying sorts participated to shore up their claims to credit and legitimacy (see Butler, *Gender Trouble: Feminism and the Subversion of Identity* [New York: Routledge, 1990], 45–46; and Joan Scott, "Gender: A Useful Category of Historical Analysis," *American Historical Review* 91, no. 5 [December 1986]: esp. 1057–59). For the implications of historicizing patriarchy and investigating continuity as well as change in women's history, see Judith M. Bennett, "Women's History: A Study in Continuity and Change," *Women's History Review* 2, no. 2 (1993): 173–84; Michael McKeon, "Historicizing Patriarchy: The Emergence of Gender Difference in England, 1660–1760," *Eighteenth-Century Studies* 28, no. 3 (Spring 1995): 295–322; Judith M. Bennett, *History Matters: Patriarchy and the Challenges of Feminism*

(Philadelphia: University of Pennsylvania Press, 2006), esp. chap. 4; and Dror Wahrman, "Change and the Corporeal in Seventeenth- and Eighteenth-Century Gender History: Or, Can Cultural History be Rigorous?," in *Gender and Change: Agency, Chronology and Periodisation*, ed. Alexandra Shepard and Garthine Walker (Hoboken, NJ: Wiley-Blackwell, 2009), 166–90; originally published in *Gender & History* 20, no. 3 (November 2008): 584–602.

11. Marion Gibson, *Reading Witchcraft: Stories of Early English Witches* (New York: Routledge, 1999), 186–90.

12. See ibid., 28–29; and David Harley, "Explaining Salem: Calvinist Psychology and the Diagnosis of Possession," *American Historical Review* 101, no. 2 (April 1996): 307–30. Harley cautions historians against eliding these terms, arguing that diagnoses of possession marked the failure of afflicted individuals to convince others that they were blameless victims of witchcraft (311–12). For more about how questions of culpability played out in New England Puritanism, see Karlsen, *The Devil in the Shape of a Woman*, esp. chap. 7; and Richard Godbeer, *The Devil's Dominion: Magic and Religion in Early New England* (Cambridge: Cambridge University Press, 1992), esp. chap. 3.

13. For the former, consider Thomas Cooper's differentiation between Satan's overtures "either by Reall possessing of the soules & bodyes of men, or else by Obsession, and inspiring them with him evill counsels," in *The mystery of witch-craft Discovering, the truth, nature, occasions, growth and power thereof. . . .* (London, 1617), sig. A4v; and, decades later, Thomas Jollie's claim that "If the distinction of Obsession from Possession, be used among the Papists; is every distinction among Papists, a Popish Distinction? The Truth is, both Ancient and Modern Writers only make use of the Term Obsession as more proper," in Jollie, *A vindication of the Surey Demoniack as no Impostor: or, A Reply to a certain Pamphlet Publish'd by Mr. Zach. Taylor, called The Surey Impostor* (1698), 30. Regarding the blurred boundaries, see Robert Burton's comment that "whether by obsession, or possession, or otherwise, I will not determine; 'tis a difficult question," in *Anatomy of Melancholy*, ed. Thomas C. Faulkner, Nicholas K. Kiessling, and Rhonda L. Blair (Oxford: Oxford University Press, 1989), 194. The anonymous narrator of Thomas Sawdie's possession case in 1664 explained: "All acknowledge, that the word . . . signifies such as are afflicted, tormented, or vexed with Devils. Whether this be called an *essential*, or a *virtual Possession*, or whether a *Possession*, or an *Obsession*, I much care not, so it be acknowledged that the Devils acted in those bodies not onely Morally, but Physically, above the reach of humane power" (*A Return of Prayer: or A Faithful Relation of some Remarkable Passages of Providence concerning Thomas Sawdie, a Boy of Twelve Yeares of Age . . . Who was possest with an Unclean Spirit, and through the mercy by Prayer and Fasting, dispossest and delivered. . . .* [1664], 16). When William Drage wrote, "Now here it remains that we make Distinction, *if any is to be made*, betwixt the obsessed or possessed with evil Spirits, and the bewitched by Ceremonies," he worked through the blurred boundaries among the phenomena (Drage, *Daemonomageia: A Small Treatise of Sicknesses and Diseases from Witchcraft and Supernatural Causes* [London, 1665], 10–16, emphasis added). Throughout this book, I have updated the spelling and structure of seventeenth-century sources to improve clarity and readability.

14. Brian P. Levack, *The Devil Within: Possession and Exorcism in the Christian West* (New Haven: Yale University Press, 2013), 16–18.

15. Keith Thomas states, "The epithets 'possessed' and 'bewitched' came very near to being synonymous" (Thomas, *Religion and the Decline of Magic*, 478). D. P. Walker adds that the "distinction of terms . . . was not observed by most sixteenth-century writers, who tend to use the two terms indifferently" (Walker, *Unclean Spirits: Possession and Exorcism in France and England in the Late Sixteenth and Early Seventeenth Centuries* [Philadelphia: University of Pennsylvania Press, 1981], 7).

16. Levack, *The Devil Within*, 18, 73.

17. In his 1684 compendium of wonders, Increase Mather listed six likely signs of possession but also asserted that some "conceive (and that as they suppose upon Scripture grounds:) that Men may possibly be Daemoniacal, when none of those mentioned particulars can be affirmed of them." Furthermore, when he related a tale of an apparent haunting that involved a combination of human and spectral agency, Mather wrote that "whether the afflicted persons were only possessed, or bewitched, or both, may be disputed" (Increase Mather, *An essay for the recording of illustrious providences wherein, an account is given of many remarkable and very memorable events. . . .* [hereafter cited as *Remarkable Providences*] [Boston, 1684], 170–71, 196). There is a similarly intricate approach to discernment and culpability in a diary entry by Increase Mather's son, Cotton Mather, from May 1692. He recorded that "The *Devils*, after a most preternatural Manner, by the dreadful Judgment of Heaven took a *bodily Possession*, of many people, in *Salem*, and the adjacent places; and the Houses of the poor People, began to be filled with the horrid Cries of Persons tormented by *evil Spirits*" (*Diary of Cotton Mather, 1681–1708*, ed. W. C. Ford, 2 vols., in *Massachusetts Historical Society, Collections*, 7th ser., 7–8 [1912]: 150).

18. Some English cases resulted in charges and imprisonment for fraud or blasphemy, but although we might expect those considered possessed to have been excommunicated—if their condition entailed an irredeemable capitulation to Satan— propagandists did not take up this issue in any sustained way. Within strongly Calvinist environments, apparent possessions sometimes marked the crisis of faith that preceded the subject's experience of God's grace, which further complicates the question of culpability for those who performed symptoms associated with possession even if their ministers maintained they were obsessed or only "near" to being truly possessed.

19. Joseph Glanvill, *Saducismus Triumphatus: or, Full and plain evidence concerning witches and apparitions in two parts: The first treating of their possibility, the second of their real existence* (London: 1681), 202.

20. Increase Mather, *Angelographia, or, A discourse concerning the nature and power of the holy angels. . . .* (Boston, 1696), 17. To Catholics, "discernment" meant to determine whether the sufferer's visions of angels, for example, were genuinely holy. Protestants were suspicious of holy possessions and construed most of these apparitions to delusions of the Devil (Levack, *The Devil Within*, 207–11). In the primarily Protestant context explored here, I use "discernment" to refer to witnesses' attempts to determine not only whether specters signified good or evil spirits but whether possession symptoms originated in illness, madness, fraud, or preternatural interference from devils or witches.

21. On questions of embodiment and the humoral system, see Thomas Laqueur, *Making Sex: Body and Gender from the Greeks to Freud* (Cambridge: Harvard University Press, 1992); Karen Harvey, *Reading Sex in the Eighteenth Century: Bodies and*

Gender in English Erotic Culture (Cambridge: Cambridge University Press, 2004); and Helen King, *The One-Sex Body on Trial: The Classical and Early Modern Evidence* (Farnham, Surrey, UK: Ashgate, 2013). For the patriarchal foundations of early modern England and America, see Gerda Lerner, *The Creation of Patriarchy* (New York: Oxford University Press, 1986); Carol Pateman, *The Sexual Contract* (Oxford: Blackwell, 1988); Susan Amussen, *An Ordered Society: Gender and Class in Early Modern England* (Oxford: Blackwell, 1988), esp. chap. 2; Sylvia Walby, *Theorizing Patriarchy* (Oxford: Blackwell, 1990); Kathleen M. Brown, *Good Wives, Nasty Wenches, and Anxious Patriarchs: Gender, Race, and Power in Colonial Virginia* (Chapel Hill: University of North Carolina Press, 1996); Mary Beth Norton, *Founding Mothers and Fathers: Gendered Power and the Forming of American Society* (New York: Knopf, 1997); Sara Mendelson and Patricia Crawford, *Women in Early Modern England, 1550–1720* (Oxford: Oxford University Press, 1998); Bernard Capp, *When Gossips Meet: Women, Family, and Neighbourhood in Early Modern England* (Oxford: Oxford University Press, 2003); and Kelly A. Ryan, *Regulating Passion: Sexuality and Patriarchal Rule in Massachusetts, 1700–1830* (New York: Oxford University Press, 2014).

22. For the ways such beliefs may have contributed to a crisis in gender relations in Tudor and Stuart England, see David Underdown, "The Taming of the Scold: The Enforcement of Patriarchal Authority in Early Modern England," in *Order and Disorder in Early Modern England*, ed. Anthony Fletcher and John Stevenson (Cambridge: Cambridge University Press, 1985); and Martin Ingram, "'Scolding Women Cucked or Washed': A Crisis in Gender Relations in Early Modern England?," in *Women, Crime and the Courts in Early Modern England*, ed. Jenny Kermode and Garthine Walker (Chapel Hill: University of North Carolina Press, 1994). For studies that see the subjugation of women as central to the development of the scientific revolution and capitalism, respectively, see Carolyn Merchant, *The Death of Nature: Women, Ecology and the Scientific Revolution* (New York: HarperCollins, 1980), chap. 5; and Silvia Federici, *Caliban and the Witch: Women, the Body and Primitive Accumulation* (Brooklyn, NY: Autonomedia, 2004), chaps. 4 and 5.

23. On the question of women's participation as accusers, see Diane Purkiss, *The Witch in History: Early Modern and Twentieth-Century Representations* (New York: Routledge, 1996), chap. 4; Malcolm Gaskill, "'Devil in the Shape of a Man': Witchcraft, Conflict and Belief in Jacobean England," *Historical Research* 71, no. 175 (June 1998): 142–71; and Sharpe, *Instruments of Darkness*, chap. 7. On women's participation in the maintenance of patriarchal order, see Laura Gowing, "Ordering the Body: Illegitimacy and Female Authority in Seventeenth-Century England," in *Negotiating Power in Early Modern Society: Order, Hierarchy and Subordination in Britain and Ireland*, ed. Michael J. Braddick and John Walter (Cambridge: Cambridge University Press, 2001), 44–46, 60–62.

24. See, for example, Anthony Fletcher, *Gender, Sex and Subordination in England 1500–1800* (New Haven: Yale University Press, 1995); Elizabeth Foyster, *Manhood in Early Modern England: Honour, Sex and Marriage* (London: Longman, 1999); Tim Hitchcock and Michele Cohen, eds., *English Masculinities, 1660–1800* (New York: Longman, 1999); Alexandra Shepard, *Meanings of Manhood in Early Modern England* (Oxford: Oxford University Press, 2003); Karen Harvey and Alexandra Shepard, "What Have Historians Done with Masculinity? Reflections on Five Centuries of British History, circa 1500–1950," *Journal of British Studies* 44 (April 2005): 274–80; and

Karen Harvey, *The Little Republic: Masculinity and Domestic Authority in Eighteenth-Century Britain* (Oxford: Oxford University Press, 2012). For New England, see Lisa Wilson, *Ye Heart of a Man: The Domestic Life of Men in Colonial New England* (New Haven: Yale University Press, 1999); Anne S. Lombard, *Making Manhood: Growing Up Male in Colonial New England* (Cambridge: Harvard University Press, 2003); Thomas A. Foster, *Sex and the Eighteenth-Century Man: Massachusetts and the History of Sexuality in America* (Boston: Beacon Press, 2006); and Thomas A. Foster, ed., *New Men: Manliness in Early America* (New York: New York University Press, 2011). For broader contexts, see R. W. Connell, *Masculinities* (Berkeley and Los Angeles: University of California Press, 1995); Michael Kimmel, *Manhood in America: A Cultural History* (New York: Free Press, 1996); and Lynne Segal, "Masculinities; Manhood in America: A Cultural History; A New Psychology of Men; Unlocking the Iron Cage; The Men's Movement, Gender Politics, and American Culture," *Signs* 22, no. 4 (Summer 1997): 1057–61. On the need for studies that consider the mutual construction of gender for men and women, and gendered power, see Toby L. Ditz, "The New Men's History and the Peculiar Absence of Gendered Power: Some Remedies from Early American Gender History," *Gender & History* 16, no. 1 (April 2004): 16–26.

25. For gender in European witchcraft and possession, see Lara Apps and Andrew Gow, *Male Witches in Early Modern Europe* (New York: Manchester University Press, 2003); Nancy Caciola, *Discerning Spirits: Divine and Demonic Possession in the Middle Ages* (Ithaca, NY: Cornell University Press, 2003); Sarah Ferber, *Demonic Possession and Exorcism in Early Modern France* (London: Routledge, 2004); Lyndal Roper, *Witch Craze: Terror and Fantasy in Baroque Germany* (New Haven: Yale University Press, 2004); Nicky Hallett, *Witchcraft, Exorcism and the Politics of Possession in a Seventeenth-Century Convent* (Burlington, VT: Ashgate, 2007); Rolf Schulte, *Man as Witch: Male Witches in Central Europe*, trans. Linda Froome-Döring (New York: Palgrave Macmillan, 2009); Alison Rowlands, ed., *Witchcraft and Masculinities in Early Modern Europe* (New York: Palgrave Macmillan, 2009); Laura Kounine, "The Gendering of Witchcraft: Defence Strategies of Men and Women in German Witchcraft Trials," *German History* 31, no. 3 (September 2013): 295–317. For men, magic, and power, see Thomas, *Religion and the Decline of Magic*, chaps. 10–12; Lyndal Roper, "Stealing Manhood: Capitalism and Magic in Early Modern Germany," *Gender & History* 3, no. 1 (Spring 1991): 4–22; and Frances Timbers, *Magic and Masculinity: Ritual Magic and Gender in the Early Modern Era* (New York: Tauris, 2014). On demonic possession, see Philip C. Almond, *Demonic Possession and Exorcism in Early Modern England: Contemporary Texts and their Cultural Contexts* (Cambridge: Cambridge University Press, 2004); H. C. Erik Midelfort, *Exorcism and Enlightenment: Johann Joseph Gassner and the Demons of Eighteenth-Century Germany* (New Haven: Yale University Press, 2005); Nathan Johnstone, *The Devil and Demonism in Early Modern England* (New York: Cambridge University Press, 2006); and Richard Raiswell and Peter Dendle, eds., *The Devil in Society in Premodern Europe* (Toronto: Centre for Reformation and Renaissance Studies, University of Toronto, 2012); and Levack, *The Devil Within*.

26. There is a particular need to look beyond causes in witchcraft studies, which have for some time focused perhaps too closely on determining single or particular explanations for trials and executions. The search for causes has pervaded accounts of the outbreak at Salem, Massachusetts, particularly in studies that emphasize disease models, such as Linnda R. Caporael, "Ergotism: The Satan Loosed in Salem?," *Science*

192, no. 4234 (April 2, 1976): 21–26; Nicholas P. Spanos and Jack Gottlieb, "Ergotism and the Salem Village Witch Trials," *Science*, n.s., 194, no. 4272 (December 24, 1976): 1390–94; Mary K. Matossian, *Poisons of the Past: Molds, Epidemics, and History* (New Haven: Yale University Press, 1989); and Laurie M. Carlson, *A Fever in Salem: A New Interpretation of the New England Witch Trials* (Chicago: Ivan R. Dee, 1999). The search for causes also factors, though in more historically grounded ways, in much of the foundational scholarship about Salem. See, for example, Paul Boyer and Stephen Nissenbaum, *Salem Possessed: The Social Origins of Witchcraft* (Cambridge: Harvard University Press, 1974); John Demos, *Entertaining Satan: Witchcraft and the Culture of Early New England* (Oxford: Oxford University Press, 1982); Karlsen, *The Devil in the Shape of a Woman*; Elizabeth Reis, *Damned Women: Sinners and Witches in Puritan New England* (Ithaca, NY: Cornell University Press, 1997); Godbeer, *The Devil's Dominion*; and Norton, *In the Devil's Snare*. On the meaning of a cultural approach, see Clifford Geertz, "Blurred Genres: The Reconfiguration of Social Thought," *American Scholar* 49, no. 2 (Spring 1980): 165–79; for this approach applied to the history of witchcraft, see Stuart Clark, *Thinking with Demons*, 402.

27. On this question, see Alexandra Shepard and Garthine Walker, "Gender, Change and Periodisation"; and Judith M. Bennett, "Forgetting the Past," both in *Gender and Change*, ed. Shepard and Walker, 1–10; 277; originally published in *Gender & History* 20, no. 3 (November 2008): 453–62, 672.

28. On these tensions, see Elspeth Whitney, "The Witch 'She'/The Historian 'He': Gender and the Historiography of the European Witch-Hunts, *Journal of Women's History* 7, no. 3 (Fall 1995): 77–101; Purkiss, *The Witch in History*, chap. 3; and Willem de Blécourt, "The Making of the Female Witch: Reflections on Witchcraft and Gender in the Early Modern Period," *Gender and History* 12, no. 2 (2000): 287–309.

29. Shepard, *Meanings of Manhood*, 1.

30. Ibid., 6. See also Alexandra Shepard, "From Anxious Patriarchs to Refined Gentlemen? Manhood in Britain, circa 1500–1700," *Journal of British Studies* 44, no. 2 (April 2005): 281–95; E. J. Kent, *Cases of Male Witchcraft in Old and New England, 1592–1692* (Turnhout, Belgium: Brepolis, 2013), 18–20; and Raisa Maria Toivo, "Gender, Sex and Culture of Trouble in Witchcraft Studies: European Historiography with Special Reference to Finland," in *Writing Witch-Hunt Histories*, ed. Nenonen and Toivo, 87–108.

31. For example, Alexandra Shepard argues that between 1560 and 1640, the "distribution of patriarchal dividends became increasingly related to distinctions of social position rather than divisions of age or marital status" (see Shepard, *Meanings of Manhood*, 7).

32. Despite the fact that even "Puritan Massachusetts" was not as homogeneous as the term implies, especially given the ways that diversity placed pressures upon the developing colony as early as the 1640s, this book refers to New England as Puritan because it addresses the predominant channels of power that remained culturally English and Puritan until the end of the seventeenth century. On the diversity of the early New England colonies, see, for example, David D. Hall, *Worlds of Wonder, Days of Judgment: Popular Religious Belief in Early New England* (Cambridge: Harvard University Press, 1989); Richard Archer, *Fissures in the Rock: New England in the Seventeenth Century* (Hanover: University of New Hampshire Press, 2001); Richard Gildrie, *The Prophane, the Civil, and the Godly: The Reformation of Manners in Orthodox New*

England, 1679–1749 (University Park: Pennsylvania State University Press, 1994); and Marsha L. Hamilton, *Social and Economic Networks in Early Massachusetts* (University Park: Pennsylvania State University Press, 2009).

33. Malcolm Gaskill has posited that "when a man was placed in a female category, this category remained essentially female. . . . Perhaps, after all, we might see witchcraft as a uniquely female crime, regardless of the sex of the offender" (Gaskill, "Masculinity and Witchcraft in Seventeenth-Century England," in *Witchcraft and Masculinities*, ed. Rowlands, 172). Lara Apps and Andrew Gow argue that witchcraft theorists may have feminized male witches when, for example, they described them as having teats and suckling imps. Although my reading of Burroughs's "unmaking" does not echo this approach, the two are not necessarily mutually exclusive. On the question of feminization, see Apps and Gow, *Male Witches in Early Modern Europe*; and Kent, *Cases of Male Witchcraft*, 7, 13.

34. On historical approaches to modern witchcraft prosecution, see Malcolm Gaskill, *A Very Short Introduction to Witchcraft* (New York: Oxford University Press, 2010), 119–23; and Ronald Hutton, "Witchcraft and Modernity," in *Writing Witch-Hunt Histories*, ed. Nenonen and Toivo, 191–211.

Notes to Chapter 1

1. *A true and most Dreadfull discourse of a woman possessed with the Deuill: who in the likenesse of a headlesse Beare fetched her out of her Bedd. . . .* (London, 1584), sig. A4v–A5r.

2. Ibid., sig. B2v–B3r.

3. A reference to the Cooper narrative appeared in Samuel Harsnett's *A discovery of the fraudulent practices of John Darrell . . . in his proceedings concerning the pretended possession and dispossession of William Somers at Nottingham. . . .* (London, 1599), 17, in which he grouped it with fraudulent cases that he claimed were staged as proselytizing delusions.

4. On Protestants who mimicked elements of Catholic exorcisms despite denying doing so, see Levack, *The Devil Within*, 109–10.

5. T. I., *A miracle, of miracles As fearefull as euer was seene or heard of in the memorie of man. . . .* (London, 1614), sig. A4r. Based on a reference in the preface to John Hillard's book *Fire from Heaven: Burning the body of one John Hittchell of Holnehurst. . . .* (London, 1613), Percy Simpson argues that the author T. I. was likely John Trundle, the publisher of Hilliard's volume (Simpson, "The 'Headless Bear' in Shakespeare and Burton," reprinted in *Studies in Elizabethan Drama* [Oxford: Clarendon Press, 1955], 90–94, 90n1).

6. See, for example, Margaret Spufford, *Small Books and Pleasant Histories: Popular Fiction and Its Readership in Seventeenth-Century England*, 2nd ed. (Cambridge: Cambridge University Press, 1985); Peter G. Platt, ed., *Wonders, Marvels, and Monsters in Early Modern Culture* (London: Associated University Presses, 1999); and David Cressy, *Travesties and Transgressions in Tudor and Stuart England: Tales of Discord and Dissension* (Oxford: Oxford University Press, 2000).

7. *Most Fearefull and strange Newes from the Bishoppricke of Durham, Being a true Relation of one Margaret Hooper . . . Who was most fearefully possessed and tormented with the Devill. . . .* (London, 1641), 2.

8. Percy Simpson records a later reprinting of the 1641 version by one M. A. R. of Newcastle, in 1843 (Simpson, *Studies in Elizabethan Drama*, 93).

9. Sharpe, *Instruments of Darkness*, 146–47.

10. An early cryptic reference to a headless bear resides in the 1583 edition of John Foxe's influential compendium of Puritan martyrs, *Actes and monuments of matters most speciall and memorable* (London, 1583), 1207, and also in William Shakespeare's *Midsummer Night's Dream* (1600), act 3, scene 1, 111–14. In a similar vein, the poetical preface to the 1632 edition of Robert Burton's *Anatomy of Melancholy* stated: "Me thinks I hear, me thinks I see/Ghosts, goblins, fiends, my phantasy/Presents a thousand ugly shapes,/Headless bears, black men and apes,/Doleful outcries, and fearful sights,/ My sad and dismal soul affrights" (see Burton, *The Anatomy of Melancholy*, ed. Thomas C. Faulkner, Nicholas K. Kiessling, and Ronda L. Blair, vol. 1 [Oxford: Clarendon Press, 1989], lxx). The Puritan divine Richard Baxter made another reference to a spectral headless bear in *The Certainty of the World of Spirits: Proving the immortality of souls, the malice and misery of the devils, and the damned, and the blessedness of the justified* (London, 1691), 58–59. In 1692, Henry Purcell's opera *The Fairy-Queen*, based upon Shakespeare's *Midsummer Night's Dream*, brought the headless bear back into print and view at the Queen's Theater in London (see Purcell, *The Fairy-Queen an Opera: Represented at the Queen's-Theatre by Their Majesties Servants* [London, 1692], 26). See also H. Littledale, "A Headless Bear," in "Miscellaneous Notes," *Modern Language Review*, ed. John G. Robinson, vol. 2 (Cambridge: Cambridge University Press, 1907), 63; and Charles A. Rahter, "Puck's Headless Bear—Revisited," in *Shakespeare: Text, Subtext, and Context*, ed. Ronald Dotterer (Selinsgrove, PA: Susquehanna University Press, 1989), 159. Like the headless bear, a spectral "black man" was "an evil spirit, the devil, as well as a bogeyman invoked to frighten children (see "black man, n.," OED Online, www.oed.com).

11. Stuart Clark, *Thinking with Demons*, 394.

12. The performative nature of possession cases has been profitably explored by a variety of historians and literary scholars. See, for example, Stephen Greenblatt, *Shakespearean Negotiations: The Circulation of Social Energy in Renaissance England* (Berkeley: University of California Press, 1988); Michael MacDonald, ed., *Witchcraft and Hysteria in Elizabethan London* (New York: Tavistock/Routledge, 1991); Sharpe, *Instruments of Darkness*, 195–99; and Levack, *The Devil Within*, esp. 29–30.

13. Stuart Clark, *Thinking with Demons*, 410.

14. [Edward Nyndge], *A Book Declaring the Fearfull Vexasion of one Alexander Nyndge* (1573); Edward Nyndge, *A true and fearfull vexation of one Alexander Nyndge* (1615).

15. George More, *A true Discourse concerning the certaine possession and dispossession of 7 Persons in one familie in Lancashire.* . . . (Middleburg, 1600), 78–82.

16. Letter from Alderman Thomas Heyrick, of Leicester, to his brother Sir William, July 18, 1616, reprinted in G. L. Kittredge, "King James I and 'The Devil Is an Ass,'" *Modern Philology* 9, no. 2 (October 1911): 197–98.

17. Reginald Scot, *Discoverie of Witchcraft: vvherein the lewde dealing of witches and witchmongers is notablie detected.* . . . (London, 1584), 127.

18. A. Ri., *The triall of Maister Dorrell, or A collection of defences against allegations not yet suffered to receiue convenient answere Tending to cleare him from the*

imputation of teaching Sommers and others to counterfeit possession of divells. . . . (Middelburg, 1599), 97.

19. William Hinde, *A faithfull remonstrance of the holy life and happy death of John Bruen of Bruen-Stapleford. . . .* (London, 1641), 149. While some dismissed Harrison as a fraud right away, the case was long heralded as unimpeachable because the bishop granted a license for a private session of prayer and fasting on the boy's behalf. For arguments that Harrison was a fraud, see John Deacon and John Walker, in *A summarie answere to all the material points in any of Master Darel his books. . . .* (London, 1601), 71–78.

20. Hinde, *A faithfull remonstrance*, 150–51.

21. Nyndge, *A Book Declaring the Fearfull Vexasion*, sig. A3r.

22. John Swan, *A true and breife report, of Mary Glouers vexation and of her deliuerance by the meanes of fastinge and prayer. . . .* (London, 1603), 42.

23. Scot, *Discoverie of Witchcraft*, 126–29.

24. I. D., *The most wonderful and true storie, of a certaine Witch named Alse Gooderige*, 34–35.

25. Richard Galis, *A Brief Treatise conteyning the most strange and horrible crueltye of Elizabeth Stile. . . .* (London, 1579). See also Gibson, *Reading Witchcraft*, 113–17.

26. Galis, *A Brief Treatise*, sig. C3r.

27. More, *A true Discourse*, 42.

28. Thomas Potts, *The Wonderfull Discoverie of Witches. . . .* (London, 1613), sig. K3r–N3r; Richard Bernard, *A guide to grand-jury men divided into two books* (London, 1627), 198.

29. *The most strange and admirable discoverie of the three witches of Warboys: arraigned, conuicted, and executed at the last assises at Huntington, for the bewitching of the fiue daughters of Robert Throckmorton esquire. . . .* (London, 1593), sig. C1r.

30. Ibid., sig. B4r–C1v.

31. More, *A true Discourse*, 39–40.

32. Ibid., 44–45.

33. Ibid., 55.

34. Hinde, *A faithfull remonstrance*, 150.

35. John Fisher, *The Copy of a Letter Describing the wonderful woorke of God in delivering a Mayden within the City of Chester, from an horrible kinde of torment and sicknes. . . .* (London, 1564), sig. A4r.

36. John Chrysostom, *Disclosing of a late counterfeyted possession by the deuyl in two maydens within the citie of London* (London, 1574), sig. A4r–A4v.

37. James Sharpe, *The Bewitching of Anne Gunter: A Horrible and True Story of Deception, Witchcraft, Murder, and the King of England* (New York: Routledge, 2001).

38. More, *A true Discourse*, 25. Another demoniac in Lancashire, Eleanor Hurdman, demonstrated her unfailing sense of the time, though she kept her face turned away from the hourglass.

39. Ibid., 25–26, 41.

40. Chrysostom, *Disclosing of a late counterfeyted possession*, sig. B1v.

41. [Michel Marescot], *A True Discourse, upon the matter of Martha Brossier of Romorantin, pretended to be possessed by a Devill*, trans. Abraham Hartwell (London, 1599), 8–9.

42. This figure is based on published English possession and witchcraft-possession narratives from 1564 to 1712. Brian P. Levack reports that half of England's identifiable

demoniacs were male; my focus on published records and inclusion of a broader set of cases, including obsession, likely explains the difference (Levack, *The Devil Within*, 180–83). For an analysis of the relative dearth of adult men who acted as if they were possessed, see Sarah Ferber, "Possession and the Sexes," in *Witchcraft and Masculinities in Early Modern Europe*, ed. Rowlands, 214–25.

43. Stuart Clark, *Thinking with Demons*, 417–18.

44. Scot, *The Discoverie of Witchcraft*, 200. In this section, Scot drew upon the work of Leonardus Vairus, *De fascino libri tres* [Three books on fascination] (Paris, 1583). One of Scot's most important arguments was that spirits could not take corporeal form and therefore could not interact with humans in the ways described by European demonologists. And although he refuted Heinrich Kramer, the primary author (along with James Sprenger) of the vividly misogynist *Malleus maleficarum* (Speyer, Germany, 1487), he increased English awareness of the book by addressing it.

45. Sébastien Michaelis, *The admirable historie of the possession and conuersion of a penitent woman Seduced by a magician that made her to become a witch. . . .* , trans. W. B. (London, 1613), 76–79.

46. *Witches apprehended, examined and executed, for notable villanies by them committed both by land and water. . . .* (London, 1613).

47. Alexander Roberts, *A Treatise of Witchcraft: wherein sundry Propositions are laid downe, plainely discovering the Wickednesse of that damnable Art. . . .* (London, 1616), 40–45.

48. Thomas Cooper, *The mystery of witch-craft: Discovering, the truth, nature, occasions, growth and power thereof. . . .* (London, 1617), 180.

49. Harsnett, *A discovery*, 20.

50. Ibid., 68.

51. Ibid., 75.

52. This view is informed by Michel Foucault, *Discipline and Punish: The Birthplace of the Prison*, trans. Alan Sheridan (New York: Vintage, 1979). Foucault interestingly addressed possessed female nuns in his lecture "26 February 1975," reprinted in *Abnormal: Lectures at the Collège de France 1974–1975*, ed. Valerio Marchetti and Antonella Salonomi (London: Verso, 2003). For an analysis of the possessed nuns at Loudun in the 1630s, see Michel de Certeau, *The Writing of History*, trans. Tom Conley (New York: Columbia University Press, 1988), 244–68.

53. On attributions of possession symptoms to illnesses, see Levack, *The Devil Within*, 26–29.

54. Chrysostom, *Disclosing of a late counterfeyted possession*, sig. B3r.

55. Edward Jorden, *A briefe discourse of a disease called the suffocation of the mother. . . .* (London, 1603). For the pertinent documents and analysis, see MacDonald, ed., *Witchcraft and Hysteria*.

56. See Laqueur, *Making Sex*; Fletcher, *Gender, Sex, and Subordination in England 1500–1800*; Gail Kern Paster, *The Body Embarrassed: Drama and the Disciplines of Shame in Early Modern England* (Ithaca, NY: Cornell University Press, 1993); Gail Kern Paster, *Humoring the Body: Emotions and the Shakespearean Stage* (Chicago: University of Chicago Press, 2004); and Harvey, *Reading Sex*.

57. Fisher, *The Copy of a Letter*, sig. B3v–B4r.

58. For analysis of how early modern English concepts of fact, testimony, and witnesses affected perceptions of evidence against witches, see Barbara J. Shapiro, *A

Culture of Fact: England, 1550–1720 (Ithaca, NY: Cornell University Press, 2000), esp. 179–83.

59. On the controversies over demonic and witchcraft-possession in France, and Brossier in particular, see Jonathan L. Pearl, *The Crime of Crimes: Demonology and Politics in France, 1560–1620* (Waterloo, Ontario: Wilfrid Laurier University Press, 1999), 48–56; and Ferber, *Demonic Possession and Exorcism in Early Modern France*, esp. chap. 3.

60. [Marescot], *A True Discourse, upon the matter of Martha Brossier*, 6–7.

61. Ibid., 32.

62. Ibid, 15–16.

63. A. Ri., *The triall of Maister Dorrell*, 98.

64. More, *A true Discourse*, 26–29.

65. Ibid, 26–27, 29.

66. Ibid., 25.

67. During the reign of Elizabeth I, both the queen and her counselors were believed to have been threatened by image magic, sorcery, and witchcraft, prompting searches for conspirators. These incidents also strengthened the association writers drew between "witchcraft" and metaphorical threats to the established order (see Stuart Clark, *Thinking with Demons*, 558–59; and Thomas, *Religion and the Decline of Magic*, 513).

68. More, *A true Discourse*, 83.

69. The quotation, a paraphrase of Stephen Bradwell's manuscript "Mary Glovers Late Woeful Case, Together with her Joyfull Deliverance" (1603), fol. 26r–29v, was published in George Sinclair, *Satan's invisible world* (Edinburgh, 1685), 96; and R. B. *Kingdom of Darkness* (London, 1688), 18–19. For Bradwell, see MacDonald, ed., *Witchcraft and Hysteria*.

70. Swan, *A true and briefe report*, 27–28.

71. In this case, the suspect Mother Elizabeth Jackson was found guilty and sentenced to the maximum available sentence under the witchcraft statute of 1563: a year's imprisonment and time at the pillory (see MacDonald, *Witchcraft and Hysteria*, xv–xix).

72. Swan, *A true and briefe report*, 47–48.

73. Ibid., 51.

74. When James I became England's king in 1603, he had already published an account that decried the menace of witchcraft, namely *Daemonologie: In forme of a dialogue, divided into three bookes* (London, 1597). Soon after, however, he revealed skepticism about the demoniacs he encountered—much to the disappointment of the godly clerics who presumed he would be an ally. On this transition, see G. Maxwell-Stuart, "King James's Experience of Witches, and the 1604 English Witchcraft Act," in *Witchcraft and the Act of 1604*, ed. Newton and Bath, 31–46.

75. On these developments, see Clive Holmes, "Witchcraft and Possession at the Accession of King James I: The Publication of Samuel Harsnett's *A Declaration of Egregious Popish Impostures*," in *Witchcraft and the Act of 1604*, ed. Newton and Bath, 69–90.

Notes to Chapter 2

1. A version of this chapter appeared as "Witchcraft, Possession, and the Unmaking of Women and Men: A Late Sixteenth-Century English Case Study," in *Magic, Ritual & Witchcraft* 11, no. 2 (Winter 2016): 151–75.

2. *Warboys*, sig. A3r.

3. Ibid., sig. A3v.

4. Gibson, *Reading Witchcraft*, 120–21.

5. Barbara Rosen, ed., *Witchcraft in England, 1558–1618* (Amherst: University of Massachusetts Press, 1969), 213, 33–34.

6. For analysis of the text's fractured authorship, see Gibson, *Reading Witchcraft*, 120–25.

7. *Warboys*, sig. C2r. While D. P. Walker argued that the Warboys case contained "no propaganda at all, except perhaps in favour of witch-hunting," it did reflect the ways that godly possession cases reached for legitimacy by, in part, repudiating Catholic exorcisms (Walker, *Unclean Spirits*, 5).

8. J. A. Raftis, "Social Structures in Five East Midland Villages: A Study of Possibilities in the Use of Court Roll Data," *Economic History Review*, n.s., 18, no. 1 (1965): 84.

9. Anne Reiber DeWindt, "Redefining the Peasant Community in Medieval England: The Regional Perspective," *Journal of British Studies* 26, no. 2 (April 1987): 164–68.

10. Anne Reiber DeWindt, "Witchcraft and Conflicting Visions of the Ideal Village Community," *Journal of British Studies* 34, no. 4 (October 1995): 437. Keith Wrightson wrote about a similar case in Essex, England, in the 1590s, in which "hostile reactions" to a Puritan family there related partly to their status as "newly established manorial lords. . . . Elsewhere responses to the imperatives [of deference] . . . could exacerbate rivalries" in these communities (Wrightson, "Politics of the Parish in Early Modern England," in *The Experience of Authority in Early Modern England*, ed. Paul Griffiths, Adam Fox, and Steve Hindle [Basingstoke: Macmillan, 1996], 29–30).

11. DeWindt, "Witchcraft and Conflicting Visions," 458, 108n.

12. Keith Wrightson, *Earthly Necessities: Economic Lives in Early Modern Britain, 1470–1750* (New Haven: Yale University Press, 2000), 138, 187–88. On economic change from 1550 to 1650 and the ways people used new measures to account for their worth by the mid-seventeenth century, see Alexandra Shepard, *Accounting for Oneself: Worth, Status, and the Social Order in Early Modern England* (Oxford: Oxford University Press, 2015).

13. Shepard, *Accounting for Oneself*, esp. chap. 2.

14. Harsnett, *A discovery*, 93.

15. John Darrell, *A Detection of that sinful, shamful, lying, and ridiculous discours of Samuel Harshnet. . . .* (London, 1600), 21.

16. Ibid., 39. The Throckmortons' possession symptoms likely also influenced the young demoniac John Smith, whose witchcraft-possession case resulted in several executions (see Kittredge, "King James I and 'The Devil Is an Ass,'" 195–209).

17. C. L'Estrange Ewen noted that "The most dangerous period was the decade 1598–1607, being the last six years of the reign of Elizabeth and the first four years of James I . . . when 41 *per centum* of persons indicted were sent to the gallows" (L'Estrange Ewen, ed., *Witch Hunting and the Witch Trials*, 31). Lyndal Roper writes that there was

a "dramatic peak in the 1580s and 1590s" in the witch-hunts of Europe (Roper, *Witch Craze*, 16–17). Expanding upon the work of Barbara Rosen, Marion Gibson argues that English witchcraft pamphlets changed after 1590, when predominantly documentary sources gave way to narrative ones with more immediately apparent biases and agendas (Gibson, *Reading Witchcraft*, 113–17).

18. Moira Tatem suggests the case of Agnes Briggs and Rachel Pindar (1574) as a likely influence on the Throckmorton girls (Tatem, *The Witches of Warboys* [Cambridgeshire Libraries Publications, 1993], 72–73). Philip C. Almond posits the case of Anne Mylner (1564) as a significant precedent (Almond, *The Witches of Warboys: An Extraordinary Story of Sorcery, Sadism, and Satanic Possession* [London: Tauris, 2008], 36–37). For more about how the girls' environment, filled with sermons and Protestant views of witchcraft, provided material for their possession script, see Levack, *The Devil Within*, 151.

19. On cunning men and women, who provided villagers with services ranging from healing to finding lost goods or pinpointing thieves, see, for example, Thomas, *Religion and the Decline of Magic*, chaps. 7–9; and Sharpe, *Instruments of Darkness*, 66–70, 86–87, 158–59.

20. For additional information about the doctors Philip Barrow and William Butler, see G. L. Kittredge, *Witchcraft in Old and New England* (Cambridge: Harvard University Press, 1929), 302; and Almond, *The Witches of Warboys*, 20–24.

21. *Warboys*, sig. A3v. See Michael MacDonald, *Mystical Bedlam: Madness, Anxiety and Healing in Seventeenth-Century England* (Cambridge: Cambridge University Press, 1981), 191–92; MacDonald, *Witchcraft and Hysteria*, xxix–xxxi; Thomas, *Religion and the Decline of Magic*, 543; and Walker, *Unclean Spirits*, 10–14.

22. James Sharpe cites the Warboys case as an example of how possession symptoms sometimes crossed the line we draw between childhood and youth (see Sharpe, "Disruption in the Well-Ordered Household: Age, Authority, and Possessed Young People," in *The Experience of Authority*, ed. Griffiths, Fox, and Hindle, 191).

23. *Warboys*, sig. A4v. The author of this section states his intention to omit the details of the servants' afflictions from the narrative for the sake of brevity, as their afflictions were just like those of the daughters of the house. Throckmortons' daughters, given their social status, were a surely more reliable foundation on which to base a witchcraft-possession case. The authors also provide little information about Robert Throckmorton Jr., who was six years old at the start of the case and who apparently translated his sisters' speech to the adults at least once but did not appear to manifest possession symptoms himself (ibid., sig. H3r).

24. Cicely Burder was a suspect and subjected to an early scratching test, but—like the servants—she is rarely mentioned thereafter (*Warboys*, sig. B1v, B2v). A similarly shadowy figure is that of William Langley, whom Mother Samuel named in her confession as the source of her familiar spirits. Her further claim that he had carnal knowledge of her body was noteworthy because fewer English than European witchcraft-possession cases involved sex with the Devil or a devil figure (ibid., sig. D3r).

25. Ibid., sig. D3v.

26. Rosen, ed., *Witchcraft in England*, 253–54; Thomas, *Religion and the Decline of Magic*, 550.

27. *Warboys*, sig. D4r.

28. The law of 1563 stated that there would be a penalty of death for any witchcraft practice or conjuring if any of the victims died. Injury or damage to goods and chattel received one year's imprisonment with quarterly exposure on the pillory for the first offense, and death for the second. In 1604, when the law was changed, it added the feeding of a familiar to the list of crimes punishable by death. For more about the law's evolution, see Montague Summers's introduction to Scot, *The Discoverie of Witchcraft* (New York: Dover, 1972), xviii–xx; and Kittredge, *Witchcraft in Old and New England*, 282–84.

29. *Warboys*, sig. C2r.

30. Ibid., sig. F4v, G3r.

31. Ibid., sig. G3v–G4r.

32. Ibid., sig. H2v.

33. Ibid.

34. For more about trials using the Lord's Prayer, scratching, and touch tests, and the ability of people's preexisting suspicions to be supported through such testing, see Thomas, *Religion and the Decline of Magic*, 551–52.

35. *Warboys*, sig. M1r.

36. Ibid., sig. M3r.

37. Ibid., sig. N2v.

38. Ibid., sig. O3v.

39. Thomas, *Religion and the Decline of Magic*, 457.

40. *Warboys*, sig. D3v.

41. Carol Karlsen points out ways that girls and young women in New England who acted as if they were possessed found an acceptable outlet for their discontent in their antics and externalization of blame (Karlsen, *Devil in the Shape of a Woman*, 125–28). Lyndal Roper explains that possession allowed European demoniacs to voice emotions such as envy and anger, against which there was a deep cultural taboo (Roper, *Witch Craze*, 61–63).

42. *Warboys*, sig. C3v.

43. About the tests used to determine witchcraft, including the scratching test, see Thomas, *Religion and the Decline of Magic*, 543–44; and Barry Reay, *Popular Cultures in England 1550–1750* (London: Longman, 1998), 102, 112–13.

44. Thomas, *Religion and the Decline of Magic*, 544. Frances Dolan writes, "Since letting blood from the witch was thought to cure her victim, this practice also confirms a complex identification between the witch's body and that of her victim" (Dolan, *Dangerous Familiars: Representations of Domestic Crime in England, 1550–1700* [Ithaca, NY: Cornell University Press, 1994], 188).

45. Laura Gowing, *Common Bodies: Women, Touch and Power in Seventeenth-Century England* (New Haven: Yale University Press, 2003), 80.

46. *Warboys*, sig. B1v, sig. K4v.

47. Ibid., sig. K2v.

48. Ibid., sig. K4v.

49. James Sharpe points out that possession cases allowed children a rare opportunity to chide adults for their behavior. Possessed youths, caught in a liminal phase between childhood and adulthood, were particularly likely to vent frustrations in this way (see Sharpe, "Disruption," 200, 205).

50. *Warboys*, sig. M4r–M4v.

51. Ibid., sig. N2r.

52. Ibid., sig. O3v–O4r.

53. As Lyndal Roper explains, in baroque Germany diabolic marks were "often found around the genital area" (Roper, *Witch Craze*, 54). There were some English cases in which searches discovered marks in the genitals, such as in the case of Elizabeth Sawyer, as described in Henry Goodcole, *The wonderfull discoverie of Elizabeth Sawyer a Witch, late of Edmonton* (1621), sig. B3r–B3v, C3r–C3v.

54. It was considered acceptable, even necessary in some cases, for a husband to beat his wife when she behaved inappropriately. In skimmingtons, men were mocked for allowing wives to rule the household, and only excessive beating would have been likely to attract negative attention from neighbors (see David Underdown, "The Taming of the Scold," 116–36; Ingram, "Scolding Women Cucked or Washed," 48–80; Dolan, *Dangerous Familiars* [1994], chap. 5; Laura Gowing, *Domestic Dangers: Women, Words and Sex in Early Modern London* [Oxford: Clarendon Press, 1996], chap. 6; Elizabeth Foyster, "Male Honour, Social Control and Wife Beating in Late Stuart England," in *Transactions of the Royal Historical Society* [London: Butler and Tanner, 1996]: 215–25; and J. A. Sharpe, "Domestic Homicide in Early Modern England," *Historical Journal* 24, no. 1 [1981]: 29–48).

55. Keith Wrightson explains that there was a "*private* existence of a strong complementary and companionate ethos, side by side with, and often overshadowing, theoretical adherence to the doctrine of male authority and *public* female subordination" (see Wrightson *English Society 1580–1680* [London: Hutchinson, 1982], 92).

56. *Warboys*, sig. D4v.

57. Ibid., sig. H1r. The quote continues: "The olde Woman perceiving her husband thus fiercely comming towards her, fell downe presently in a counterfeit swoune before them all." When Mother Samuel awoke, one of her neighbors "peradventure better acquainted with her fashions than the rest" assuaged their concern by assuring them that she would fully recover. The narrator reports that she did, implying that her counterfeited swoon would not fool observers for a second, unlike the legitimate swoons and fits of the Throckmorton girls.

58. Ibid., sig. F1r.

59. Ibid, sig. D4v–E1r.

60. Ibid., sig. I4r. DeWindt lends this statement special significance, as evidence of Throckmorton's dependence upon Alice's confession to reinforce his version of the case's reality (DeWindt, "Witchcraft and Conflicting Visions," 442).

61. *Warboys*, sig. I4r–I4v.

62. Ibid., sig. H1r.

63. Agnes Samuel's performance at the gallows reinforces this sense of female internalization and policing of patriarchal values, as when one nearby inquired if she might ask to be spared because she was pregnant—something that had caused great mirth when her mother had attempted it: "Nay, sayd she, that will I not doe: it shall never be sayd, that I was both a Witch and a whore" (ibid., sig. O3r).

64. Ibid., sig. A3r.

65. John Stearne, *A Confirmation and Discovery of Witchcraft containing these severall particulars: that there are witches . . . together with the confessions of many of those executed since May 1645* (London, 1648), 11. Alternatively, at one point Richard Bernard singled him out: "So could Iohn Samuel the Witch of Warboys bewitch

and unbewitch, as his wife confessed." Because this text was widely used as a legal handbook throughout seventeenth-century England and New England, it played a considerable role in influencing emerging cases (see Bernard, *A guide to grand-jury men*, 156).

66. *Warboys*, sig. G3v, L2r.

67. Thomas, *Religion and the Decline of Magic*, 553–56; Alan Macfarlane, *Witchcraft in Tudor and Stuart England* (New York: Harper and Row, 1970), 158–59; E. J. Kent, "Masculinity and Male Witches in Old and New England, 1593–1680," *History Workshop Journal* 60 (Autumn 2005): 74–75. For a reconsideration of Macfarlane's thesis, with an emphasis on the ways that sympathies shifted toward accused witches as skepticism became more entrenched, see Malcolm Gaskill, "Witchcraft and Neighbourliness in Early Modern England," in *Remaking English Society: Social Relations and Social Change in Early Modern England*, ed. Steve Hindle, Alexandra Shepard, and John Walter, Studies in Early Modern Cultural Political and Social History, vol. 14 (Woodbridge, Suffolk, UK: Boydell Press, 2013), 211–32.

68. Both scolds and barrators were believed to cause disorder through aggressive speech or litigation. Whereas the scold was an entirely feminine image and crime, barratry was mostly applied to men. For information about both, and an example of a female barrator, see Gowing, *Domestic Dangers,* 115–16, 122–23, 207–8. For the link between gendered speech and witchcraft in New England, see Jane Kamensky, *Governing the Tongue: The Politics of Speech in Early New England* (New York: Oxford University Press, 1997), chap. 6.

69. *Warboys*, sig. E4v.

70. Elizabeth Foyster emphasizes the sexual control over wives that husbands needed to maintain as heads of households, but her argument extends as well to the large and small ways that a man maintained proper boundaries by remaining in authority (Foyster, *Manhood in Early Modern England*, 87–91).

71. *Warboys*, sig. E4v–F1r.

72. Ibid., sig. L1v–L2r.

73. Ibid., sig. L2r.

74. Ibid.

75. Alexandra Shepard draws a related conclusion about the range of men's antisocial and antipatriarchal actions, noting that "Men—and often men occupying patriarchal positions as well as those largely excluded from patriarchal dividends (on the basis of, e.g., age or marital status)—had considerably more latitude than women when it came to breaking behavioral codes, and in many instances antipatriarchal or resistant behavior by men was not deemed inherently threatening to the social order" (Shepard, "From Anxious Patriarchs to Refined Gentlemen?," 293).

76. Ibid., sig. L2v.

77. Ibid., sig. M2v.

78. Foyster, *Manhood in Early Modern England*, 91–94.

79. *Warboys*, sig. O1v.

80. Ibid.

81. The ballad was listed as "A Lamentable songe of Three Wytches of Warbos," licensed to John Danter in December 1593 Register of the Stationer's Company, cited in Almond, *The Witches of Warboys*, 6. For offhand citations, see, for example, T. I., *VVorld of VVonders A masse of murthers. . . .* (London, 1595), 20; and Henry More, *An*

antidote against atheisme or, An appeal to the natural faculties of the minde of man, whether there be not a God (London, 1653), 116–17.

82. *Warboys*, sig. O2v.

83. Ibid., sig. O3r.

Notes to Chapter 3

1. An earlier version of this chapter appeared as "Samuel Harsnett, John Darrell, and the Use of Gender as an English Possession Propaganda Strategy" in *The Devil in Society in Premodern Europe*, ed. Richard Raiswell and Peter Dendle, 257–82 (Toronto: Centre for Reformation and Renaissance Studies, University of Toronto, 2012).

2. Samuel Harsnett, *A declaration of egregious popish impostures to with-draw the harts of her Maiesties subiects from their allegeance, and from the truth of Christian religion professed in England, vnder the pretence of casting out deuils. . . .* (London, 1603), 166. According to the *Oxford English Dictionary*, a "mimp" was "a prim, or affectedly modest or demure, woman," and "mop" could mean both "fool or simpleton" and "young woman" ("mimp, n. and adj.," OED Online, www.oed.com).

3. Harsnett, *A discovery*, 3, 12.

4. Ibid., 15.

5. Darrell, *A detection*, sig. A3r.

6. Darren Oldridge, *The Devil in Early Modern England* (Stroud: Sutton, 2000), 12–15, 111–33; Johnstone, *The Devil and Demonism in Early Modern England*, 102–4; Richard Raiswell and Peter Dendle, "Demon Possession in Anglo-Saxon and Early Modern England: Continuity and Evolution in Social Context," *Journal of British Studies* 47 (October 2008): 738–67.

7. Harsnett advised King James during an investigation of a fraudulent possession that further galvanized the Church of England's unsympathetic position toward dispossessions. This attitude was formalized in the aforementioned Canon 72, which from 1604 made it illegal for a minister to organize private prayers and fasts or attempt any dispossession without the bishop's permission. On James's evolving views of witchcraft and possession, see John Newton, "Introduction: Witchcraft, Witch Codes, Witch Act," in *Witchcraft and the Act of 1604*, ed. Newton and Bath, 10–17; and Brian Levack, *Witch-Hunting in Scotland: Law, Politics and Religion* (New York: Routledge, 2008), 34–54.

8. For the development of Protestant views of the Devil in early modern England, see Johnstone, *The Devil and Demonism*, esp. 60–141.

9. See, for example, Thomas, *Religion and the Decline of Magic*, 536–45; and Thomas Freeman, "Demons, Deviance and Defiance: John Darrell and the Politics of Exorcism in Late Elizabethan England," in *Conformity and Orthodoxy in the English Church, c. 1560–1660*, ed. Peter Lake and Michael Questier (Rochester, NY: Boydell Press, 2000), 34–63. For an analysis of the political and religious intricacies of the Darrell and Harsnett controversy, see Marion Gibson, *Possession, Puritanism and Print: Darrell, Harsnett, Shakespeare and the Elizabethan Exorcism Controversy* (London: Pickering and Chatto, 2006); and Holmes, "Witchcraft and Possession at the Accession of James I," and Tom Webster, "(Re)possession of Dispossession: John Darrell and Diabolical Discourse," both in *Witchcraft and the Act of 1604*, ed. Newton and Bath, chaps. 4 and 5, respectively.

10. Gibson, *Possession*, 56–63.

11. Darrel, *A detection*, sig. B1v.

12. It was difficult for Darrell and his supporters to demonstrate their respect of law and authority while the Church of England's control of the Stationer's Register meant that they had to seek illegal publication abroad. Freeman writes that Bancroft's ability to "prevent his adversaries from having their works legally published in England" was one of his key advantages (Freeman, "Demons, Deviance and Defiance," 44).

13. On the extent to which Harsnett represented a factional rather than a uniform Anglican agenda, see Holmes, "Witchcraft and Possession at the Accession of James I," 70–71.

14. Craig Muldrew, *The Economy of Obligation: The Culture of Credit and Social Relations in Early Modern England* (New York: Palgrave, 1998), 2–3.

15. Ibid., 4–5.

16. Ibid., 148–49.

17. Shepard, *Accounting for Oneself*, esp. chap. 2.

18. Foyster, *Manhood in Early Modern England*, 5–9, 207.

19. Amussen, *An Ordered Society*, 152, 155. See also Shepard, *Meanings of Manhood*, 76, 82–84, 186–213.

20. Shepard, *Meanings of Manhood*, 187 and chap. 7.

21. Gibson, *Possession*, 27, 126–27.

22. Harsnett, *A discovery*, 86–87.

23. Ibid., 2–3.

24. Ibid., 4.

25. Ibid., 105.

26. Ibid., 107.

27. Ibid., 108.

28. Marion Gibson states that this was John Ireton, a respected minister who believed in Darrell but doubted William Somers. Harsnett cannily saw the potential for such discrepancies to divide the godly community (Gibson, *Possession*, 84, 142–50).

29. Harsnett, *A discovery*, 143.

30. Ibid., 191.

31. Ibid., 224.

32. Darrell, *A detection*, 66–67.

33. Ibid., 67. One of Darrell's anonymous defenders, A.Ri., expanded upon this point by citing the book of Timothy: "Receave no accusation against an elder but under 2 or 3 witnesses" (A. Ri., *The Triall of Maister Dorrell*, 5).

34. Darrell, *A detection*, 83.

35. Ibid., 139.

36. Ibid., sig. B1v.

37. Seventeenth-century definitions of "silly" include the following: "Helpless, defenceless; esp. of women and children; Weak, feeble, frail; insignificant, trifling; Unlearned, unsophisticated, simple, rustic, ignorant; Of humble rank or state; lowly; Lacking in judgement or common sense; foolish, senseless, empty-headed" ("silly, adj., n., and adv.," OED Online, www.oed.com).

38. Darrell, *A detection*, 5.

39. Ibid., 97, 172. On Harsnett's use of theatrical imagery to emphasize the fraudulent nature of Darrell's dispossessions, see Greenblatt, *Shakespearean Negotiations*, 94–128.

40. Darrell, *A detection*, 154.

41. Ibid., sig. A4r.

42. Ibid., 19.

43. Ibid., 44.

44. Ibid., 204.

45. Ibid., 120. Darrell condemned Gregory for "being in hart a papist, as is plain, in that for the space of eleven years before he had not received the lord's supper." But Darrell's anti-Catholicism was undercut by his acknowledgment that "the papists & their adherents (albeit the learneder sort of them do acknowledge a real possession and dispossession of Satan in and out of the bodies of men)." Harsnett reveled in pointing out such ambivalence.

46. Ibid., 144.

47. Ibid., 153.

48. On the humoral system's gendered implications, see Paster, *The Body Embarrassed*, 7–17.

49. In particular, Darrell noted the relative quiet about the high-status Starkies of Lancashire, whose dispossession had been one of Darrell's successes (Darrell, *A detection*, 11). For more about the Starkie controversy, see Webster, "(Re)possession of Dispossession," esp. 102–9.

50. Darrell, *A detection*, 65.

51. Elizabeth Foyster goes on to point out that in some contexts, the disorderly passions of young men could require as much regulation as that focused on women (Foyster, *Manhood in Early Modern England*, 7–8).

52. Amussen, *An Ordered Society*, 172.

53. Harsnett, *A discovery*, 27, 36. By claiming that the "learneder and sounder sort" did not believe that witches could send afflicting demons into their enemies, Harsnett came close to articulating a skepticism that in the early seventeenth century could still be branded atheistic, as to deny demons was considered by many to deny the possibility of the soul. Harsnett took care to ridicule the charges of "Atheism" levied against the commission but appears to be an important example (following in the footsteps of Reginald Scot) of a skepticism that cast elite, manly rationality against a lowly, feminized, credulity.

54. Ibid., 30, 35–36.

55. Ibid., 46.

56. Ibid., 54–55.

57. Ibid., 59.

58. Although trade was generally invoked negatively, the "calling" could be invoked in the defense of ministers like Darrell, as when Meric Casaubon wrote that "though some Protestants are of opinion, That it is not lawful or warrantable for any man to take upon him to Exorcise upon such occasions. . . . Yet where a Man hath a Calling, as if he be lawfully Called to the Ministry, and set over such a Parish where any happen to be possessed" it should be possible to attend to the afflicted, so long as proper means were used (Casaubon, *A True & Faithful Relation of What passed for many Yeers Between Dr. John Dee (A Mathematician of Great Fame in Q. Eliz. And King James their Reignes) and Some Spirits. . . .* [London, 1659], sig. C3r–C3v).

59. Harsnett, *A discovery*, 61. The *Oxford English Dictionary* explains that "The low repute in which [tinkers], especially the itinerant sort, were held in former times is

shown by the expressions to swear like a tinker, a tinker's curse or damn, as drunk or as quarrelsome as a tinker, etc., and the use of 'tinker' as synonymous with 'vagrant', 'gipsy'" (see "tinker, n.," OED Online, www.oed.com).

60. Harsnett, *A discovery*, 219–20.

61. Ibid., 221.

62. Ibid., 225. For an analysis of questions of social status and trade and their use as binary tropes in dispossession conflicts, see Gibson, *Possession*, 58.

63. Banks's dancing horse was something of a sensation in late sixteenth-century England and Europe, especially after an appearance at St. Paul's Cathedral in 1600. William Shakespeare referred to Banks's dancing horse in *Love's Labour's Lost* (act 1, scene 2). In their own critique of Darrell, ministers John Deacon and John Walker also wrote, "So could *Bankes his blacke horse* very sensiblie demonstrate what money some had in his purse, with sundrie other *trickes* more admirable then this by much: and yet not possessed at all with a *Diuell*" (Deacon and Walker, *A Summarie Answere*, 74).

64. As Kathleen Sands states: "The sexual implications of this episode were by no means unusual among cases of demon possession. Demoniacs frequently manifested behavior that onlookers could (and did) construe as sexual" (Sands, *Demon Possession in Elizabethan England* [Westport, CT: Praeger, 2004], 117–19). Anti-Catholic propaganda in England also drew upon sexualized images of nuns and priests and made the most of these associations when relating possession narratives. Harsnett made these charges even more explicitly when criticizing the behavior of Father William Weston with the youths in Denham in 1585–86.

65. Harsnett, *A discovery*, 300–314. For more about Protestant attitudes toward miracles in a postapostolic age, see Thomas, *Religion and the Decline of Magic*, 73–77.

66. Darrell, *A detection*, 189.

67. Ibid.

68. Harsnett was aided in this project by the widespread cultural suspicion of unruly apprentices. Paul Griffiths argues that although apprentices varied in "status, wealth, and occupational prestige," there was a broad connotation of apprentices with disorder in early modern England (Griffiths, *Youth and Authority: Formative Experiences in England, 1560–1640* [New York: Clarendon Press, 1996], 160–69). See also Ilana Krausman Ben-Amos, *Adolescence and Youth in Early Modern England* (New Haven: Yale University Press, 1994), 196–200; and Shepard, *Meanings of Manhood*, chap. 4.

69. Darrell, *A detection*, 190.

70. Ibid., 191.

71. Thomas Darling, the "Boy of Burton," was a pious youth who aspired to be a preacher. For his account, see *The most wonderfull and true storie, of a certaine witch named Alse Gooderige of Stapen hill, who was arraigned and conuicted at Darbie at the Assises there as also a true report of the strange torments of Thomas Darling, a boy of thirteene yeres of age, that was possessed by the deuill. . . .* (London, 1597).

72. Darrell, *A detection*, 180.

73. Ibid., 186.

74. Harsnett, *A discovery*, 279 [misprint of 297].

75. Ibid., 7.

76. Ibid., 57–58. For more about the timing of Darrell and More's treatment of the Starkies and their delayed publication about the case, see Gibson, *Possession, Puritanism, and Print*, 38–45.

77. "lewd, adj." (OED Online, www.oed.com).

78. "gross, adj. and n.4" (OED Online, www.oed.com).

79. Deacon and Walker, *A Summarie Answere*, and *Dialogicall Discourses of Spirits and Divels* (London, 1601). For more on these developments, see Gibson, *Possession*, 145–50.

80. Walker, *Unclean Spirits*, 53–73; Gibson, *Possession*, 154–160. For the view that Darrell conducted "pious fraud," see F. W. Brownlow, *Shakespeare, Harsnett and the Devils of Denham* (Newark: University of Delaware Press, 1993), 10, 60, 64. Brian Levack argues that "Darrell taught William Somers how to effect the illusion that a lump in his stomach travelled through his body by moving his fist under his bed sheets" (Levack, *The Devil Within*, 155).

Notes to Chapter 4

1. Godly writers decried the "Sadducism" of those who, like their scriptural forebears the Sadducees, denied the existence of the soul or afterlife. Men like Mather argued that to deny the reality of spirits, devils, and witches contradicted Scripture and was akin to atheism (Cotton Mather, *Memorable Providences Relating to Witchcrafts and Possessions. A Faithful Account of many Wonderful and Surprising Things that have befallen several Bewitched and Possessed Persons in New-England*. . . . [Boston, 1689], 3–45, http://quod.lib.umich.edu/e/evans?didno=N00392.0001.001;firstpubl 1=1470;firstpubl2=1790;rgn=full+text;size=25;sort=occur;start=1;subview=detail;typ e=simple;view=reslist;q1=memorable+providences).

2. Ibid., 2–3.

3. Ibid., 14–15.

4. Ibid., 8–9.

5. Scot's *The Discoverie of Witchcraft* was reprinted in 1651, under a title that much more overtly expressed skepticism: *Scot's Discovery of Witchcraft Proving the Common Opinions of Witches Contracting with Divels, Spirits, or Familiars; and Their Power to Kill, Torment, and Consume the Bodies of Men Women, and Children, or Other Creatures by Diseases or Otherwise; Their Flying in the Air, &C. to be but Imaginary Erronious Conceptions and Novelties*. . . . (London, 1651).

6. R. B. [Richard Baddeley], *The boy of Bilson: or, A true discovery of the late notorious impostures of certaine Romish priests in their pretended exorcisme, or expulsion of the Divell out of a young boy*. . . . (London, 1622), 51.

7. Anglican clergyman Peter Heylyn had criticized Darrell's dispossession of seven demoniacs in Lancashire in the 1590s, claiming that "when they were taught by Mr. *Darrel* to play the *Demoniacks*, [they] were also taught by him to promote the cause. As often as any of those Ministers, who were conformable to the Church . . . did come to visit them, and in their hearing read some Prayers out of the Common-prayer Book, the Devil was as quiet as any Lamb, as if he were well pleased with that Form of Service, or that there was not any thing in those Prayers, or the men that used them, to trouble him or disturb his peace" (Heylyn, *Keimelia 'ekklesiastika, The Historical and Miscellaneous Tracts of the Reverend and Learned Peter Heylyn*. . . . [London, 1681], 156). See also Harsnett, *A Discovery*, 35. For a defense of Darrell's actions in the 1590s, see More, *A true Discourse*.

8. Cotton Mather, *Memorable Providences*, 22–23.

9. Ibid., 23. On the extensive cultural and material significance of books and Bibles, see David Cressy, "Books as Totems in Seventeenth-Century England and New England," *Journal of Library History* 21, no. 1 (Winter 1986): 92–106.

10. Cotton Mather, *Memorable Providences*, 24.

11. Ibid., 40–41.

12. Ibid., 49.

13. Ibid., sig. A4v. The phrase "go then, my little book" echoes the preface to the second part of John Bunyan's *Pilgrim's Progress* (London, 1678). I thank Susan Murray for alerting me to a still earlier reference, in the epilogue of Chaucer's *Troilus and Criseyde*.

14. Two particularly important fraudulent witchcraft cases involved the twelve-year-old John Smith in 1616, whose antics resulted in the execution of nine persons as witches, and eleven-year-old Edmund Robinson, who accused several witches in Lancashire in 1633. For the former, see the letter from Alderman Thomas Heyrick, of Leicester, to his brother Sir William, July 18, 1616, reprinted in Kittredge, "King James I and 'The Devil Is an Ass,'" 197–98. King James himself rebuked the presiding authorities Justice Winch and Serjeant Crew for their credulity, and the two also appear to have been lampooned in Ben Johnson's play *The Devil Is an Ass*, first performed in 1616 and published in 1631. In the Robinson case, both the boy and the suspects were moved to London and examined, under which pressure the boy admitted to having fabricated his tale (John Harland and T. T. Wilkinson, eds., *Lancashire Folk-Lore: Illustrative of the Superstitious Beliefs and Practices, Local Customs and Usages of the People of the County Palatine* [New York: Scribner, 1867], 195–201). Robinson was also included in John Webster's *The Displaying of Supposed Witchcraft: Wherein is Affirmed that There are Many Sorts of Deceivers and Impostors and Divers Persons under a Passive Delusion of Melancholy and Fancy. . . .* (London, 1677), 276–79. The story provided the inspiration for Thomas Heywood and Richard Brome's play *The Late Lancashire Witches* (1634), so called to distinguish Robinson's case from the earlier deadly witchcraft outbreak in Lancashire in 1612 (Heywood and Brome, *The Late Lancashire Witches* [London, 1634]). For an analysis of both outbreaks, see Robert Poole, ed., *The Lancashire Witches: Histories and Stories* (Manchester: Manchester University Press), 2002.

15. There were relatively few published demonic or witchcraft-possession cases in England between 1620 and 1650, and the most influential was Richard Baddeley's aforementioned exposé of a fraudulent Catholic exorcism of William Perry. The Boy of Bilson, as Perry was called, eventually confessed that he had faked his symptoms, but not before Catholic priests labored to impress observers with their ability to exorcise the boy. The text extended Harsnett's attack on Darrell as well as Catholic priests, and this winning formula led Perry's case to be mentioned in such influential texts as Richard Bernard's *A guide to grand-jury men* (1627). The Bilson fraud was reproduced in myriad publications and explicitly resurrected in a 1698 case, discussed below. A handful of published accounts appeared in the Civil War era, many of which equivocated on the proper diagnoses in light of uncertainty about the role of natural causes. One notable demonic possession case was that of Joyce Dovey, whose struggles with her godly keeper ended without a clear conclusion (see *A Strange and true relation of a Young Woman Possest with the Devill* [London, 1646]).

16. See Sharpe, *Instruments of Darkness*, 140; and Frederick Valletta, *Witchcraft, Magic and Superstition in England, 1640–1670* (Aldershot, UK: Ashgate/Routledge, 2000).

17. Malcolm Gaskill, *Witchfinders: A Seventeenth-Century English Tragedy* (London: John Murray, 2005), 260–79, 283–85.

18. A mix of demonic and witchcraft-possession pamphlets appeared in England, in addition to cases referenced in demonological and medical tracts. There were signs of fracturing in the genre, as texts ranged from protests about the elusiveness of justice (Margaret Muschamp, 1650); accounts that blurred the boundary between the agency of devils and witches (James Barrow, 1664); familiar but controversial Puritan dispossessions (Thomas Sawdie, 1664); and several that stressed the importance of sharing such wonders to combat atheism and Sadducism. In New England there were a few unpublished instances of witchcraft-possession; the only published material before 1680 related to Elizabeth Knapp, a young woman in Groton, Massachusetts, who became possessed in 1671. Her attending minister, Samuel Willard, refused to accept her accusations of witchcraft and ultimately oversaw Knapp's confession to (nearly) capitulating to the Devil's demands. The tone that Willard set with Knapp demonstrates that there was nothing inevitable about the later outbreak at Salem (see Willard, *Useful Instructions for a Professing People* [Cambridge, MA, 1673]; Increase Mather, *Remarkable Providences*, 140–42, 196; Increase Mather, *Cases of Conscience: concerning evil spirits personating men, witchcrafts, infallible proofs of guilt in such as are accused with that crime. . . .* [Boston, 1693], 33; and Cotton Mather, *Magnalia Christi Americana* [London, 1702], 333). For an analysis of the psychology of the Knapp affair, see John Demos, *Entertaining Satan*, chap. 4.

19. On the migration, see Stephen Foster, *Their Solitary Way: The Puritan Social Ethic in the First Century of Settlement in New England* (New Haven: Yale University Press, 1971); David Cressy, *Coming Over: Migration and Communication between England and New England in the Seventeenth Century* (New York: Cambridge University Press, 1987); Virginia DeJohn Anderson, *New England's Generation: The Great Migration and the Formation of Society and Culture in the Seventeenth Century* (New York: Cambridge University Press, 1991); and Alison Games, *Migration and the Origins of the English Atlantic World* (Cambridge: Harvard University Press, 1999).

20. Perry Miller's *Errand into the Wilderness* (New York: Harper and Row, 1956) introduced the thesis of the Puritans' millennial mission. For a revision, see Theodore Dwight Bozeman, "The Puritans' 'Errand into the Wilderness' Reconsidered," *New England Quarterly* 59, no. 2 (June 1986): 231–51. For an overview of these events as context for witchcraft, see Norton, *In the Devil's Snare*, esp. 94–96. For broader analysis of the political implications, see Kenneth Silverman, *The Life and Times of Cotton Mather* (New York: Harper and Row, 1984), 62–82; and Stephen Foster, *The Long Argument: English Puritanism and the Shaping of New England Culture, 1570–1700* (Chapel Hill: University of North Carolina Press, 1991), 234–85.

21. This view of the Glorious Revolution reflects the Puritans' twinned abhorrence of Catholicism and toleration of religious diversity, though Scott Sowerby argues that James's policies were a triumph for their efforts to promote religious toleration among the English (see Sowerby, *Making Toleration: The Repealers and the Glorious Revolution* [Cambridge: Harvard University Press, 2013]).

22. For a condemnation of Hopkins's methods, if not witchcraft itself, see John Gaule, *Select Cases of Conscience Touching Witches and Witchcrafts* (London, 1646). Circumspect and skeptical tracts also followed, by Henry More, Thomas Ady (whose 1655 publication later played a pivotal role in George Burroughs's trial), and Meric Casaubon. See also Ryan J. Stark, *Rhetoric, Science and Magic in Seventeenth-Century England* (Washington, DC: Catholic University of America Press, 2009). Fraud and melancholy featured significantly in myriad seventeenth-century possession publications, especially after the broader dissemination of Robert Burton's *The Anatomy of Melancholy*, the first edition of which had appeared in 1621.

23. Of witchcraft-possession cases that appeared in published sources in the 1680s, there were examples that blurred the line with poltergeist activity (Elizabeth Burgess, 1681); that highlighted the symptoms of possession but marketed a natural cure (Margaret Gurr and a servant boy, ca. 1681); that involved a group of children who mounted a successful witchcraft-possession outbreak (in Bury St. Edmunds, 1682); and cases involving foreigners, Quakers, and ambivalent medical diagnoses. By the 1690s, more possession accounts appeared and ushered in renewed controversy over questions of religion, fraud, and natural causes. See, for example, the cases of William Legg, Nathan Crab, Thomas Spatchet, Sarah Bower, James Day, and Richard Dugdale. Dugdale's case, discussed below, blended the categories of obsession and possession with witchcraft overtones and prompted a controversial pamphlet war that pitted godly and Anglican clergy against each other just a few years after Salem.

24. For the broader context of wonders, see Peter G. Platt, ed., *Wonders, Marvels, and Monsters in Early Modern Culture* (Newark: University of Delaware Press, 1999); and Jane Shaw, *Miracles in Enlightenment England* (New Haven: Yale University Press, 2006). For New England, see David Hall, *Worlds of Wonder*, esp. chaps. 1 and 2.

25. Increase Mather, *Disquisition Concerning Angelical Apparitions*, in *Angelographia* (Boston, 1696), 19.

26. Cotton Mather, *Memorable Providences*, 64.

27. On the Neoplatonists and the ways that natural philosophy played out in printed texts, see Thomas, *Religion and the Decline of Magic*, 222–28; and Shapiro, *A Culture of Fact*. On the importance of literacy and books in New England, and the transatlantic market for godly literature, see David Hall, *Worlds of Wonder*, 43–61. For the emergence of printing and print culture in New England, see Worthington Chauncey Ford, *The Boston Book Market 1679–1700* (Boston: Merrymount Press, 1917); Charles E. Clark, *The Public Prints: The Newspaper in Anglo-American Culture, 1665–1740* (New York: Oxford University Press, 1994); Hugh Amory and David D. Hall, eds., *A History of the Book in America*, vol. 1: *The Colonial Book in the Atlantic World* (New York: Cambridge University Press for the American Antiquarian Society, 2000).

28. Richard Baxter, *The certainty of the worlds of spirits* (1691). Cotton Mather also sought to remain connected to England through his pursuit, and eventual achievement, of membership in the Royal Society. On transatlantic correspondence relating to scientific knowledge and the natural world, see Susan Scott Parrish, *American Curiosity: Cultures of Natural History in the Colonial British Atlantic World* (Chapel Hill: University of North Carolina Press, 2005).

29. Shapiro, *A Culture of Fact*, 180. The Mathers valued the defenses of the spiritual world articulated by Cambridge Platonists such as Henry More, Nathaniel Culverwell, and Ralph Cudworth but differed from them on critical points of latitudinarianism

and orthodoxy (Michael G. Hall, *The Last American Puritan: The Life of Increase Mather* [Hanover, NH: Wesleyan University Press, 1988], 285–86).

30. Opposing views—that any number of witnesses would be insufficient to prove witchcraft, and that the senses were insufficient to discern the nature of spirits—were forwarded by John Webster in *The Displaying of Supposed Witchcraft.* . . . (London, 1677) and John Wagstaffe, *The Question of Witchcraft Debated.* . . . (London, 1669). See also Shapiro, *A Culture of Fact*, 182; and Thomas, *Religion and the Decline of Magic*, 577–79.

31. Robert A. Gross, "Texts for the Times: An Introduction to Book History," in *Perspectives on American Book History: Artifacts and Commentary*, ed. Scott E. Casper, Joanne D. Chaison, and Jeffrey D. Groves (Amherst: University of Massachusetts Press, in association with the American Antiquarian Society and the Center for the Book at the Library of Congress, 2002), 11–12. See also Tessa Watt, *Cheap Print and Popular Piety, 1550–1640* (New York: Cambridge University Press, 1991).

32. For an overview of texts that support this view of literacy and Puritan authority, see Jill Lepore, "Literacy and Reading in Puritan New England," in *Perspectives on American Book History*, ed. Casper, Chaison, and Groves, 17–44.

33. For New England witchcraft outside of Massachusetts, see John M. Taylor, *The Witchcraft Delusion in Colonial Connecticut 1647–1697* (New York: Grafton Press, 1908); Richard Godbeer, *Escaping Salem: The Other Witch Hunt of 1692* (New York: Oxford University Press, 2005); and Emerson W. Baker, *The Devil of Great Island: Witchcraft and Conflict in Early New England* (New York: Palgrave Macmillan, 2007). For American witchcraft beyond New England, see Alison Games, *Witchcraft in Early North America* (Lanham, MD: Rowman and Littlefield, 2010); Owen Davies, *America Bewitched: The Story of Witchcraft after Salem* (New York: Oxford University Press, 2013); and Matthew Dennis and Elizabeth Reis, "Women as Witches, Witches as Women: Witchcraft and Patriarchy in Colonial North America," in *Women in Early America*, ed. Thomas A. Foster, 147–68 (New York: New York University Press, 2015).

34. Norton, *In the Devil's Snare*, 8–12. On the pressures spanning the period from King Philip's War (1675–76) to King William's War (1688–97), see esp. chaps. 4, 5, and 7.

35. In New England from 1680 to 1700, readers would have learned about various witchcraft-possession cases, some of which blurred the lines with poltergeists (John Stiles and the Waltons in Great Island, New Hampshire); some that involved Quakers; some ambiguous witchcraft-possession cases (Philip Smith); and some relatively straightforward witchcraft-possession cases (involving two girls in Hartford and the Goodwin children). New England readers would also have encountered references to English and European cases.

36. On gender and Native Americans, see, for example, Karen Ordahl Kupperman, *Indians and English: Facing Off in Early America* (Ithaca, NY: Cornell University Press, 2000); and Ann M. Little, *Abraham in Arms: War and Gender in Colonial New England* (Philadelphia: University of Pennsylvania Press, 2007). For a pertinent analysis of the interplay between Europeans, Indians, and Africans in Virginia, see Brown, *Good Wives, Nasty Wenches & Anxious Patriarchs*, esp. 42–74. For gender and the Quakers, see Phyllis Mack, *Visionary Women: Ecstatic Prophecy in Seventeenth-Century England* (Berkeley: University of California Press, 1992); and Judith Jennings, *Gender, Religion, and Radicalism in the Long Eighteenth Century: The "Ingenious Quaker" and Her Connections* (Burlington, VT: Ashgate, 2006).

37. On gender and manhood in English colonies, see Edmund S. Morgan, *The Puritan Family: Religion and Domestic Relations in Seventeenth-Century New England* (Boston: Trustees of the Boston Public Library, 1944); Brown, *Good Wives, Nasty Wenches, and Anxious Patriarchs*; Wilson, *Ye Heart of a Man*; Toby L. Ditz, "What's Love Got to Do with It? The History of Men, the History of Gender in the 1990s," *Reviews in American History* 28 (2000) 167–80; Ditz, "The New Men's History and the Peculiar Absence of Gendered Power"; Trevor Burnard, *Creole Gentlemen: The Maryland Elite, 1691–1776* (New York: Routledge, 2002); Anne S. Lombard, *Making Manhood*; Thomas Foster, *Sex and the Eighteenth-Century Man*; Thomas Foster, ed., *New Men*; Elaine Forman Crane, *Witches, Wife Beaters, and Whores: Common Law and Common Folk in Early America* (Ithaca, NY: Cornell University Press, 2011).

38. Kenneth Silverman describes the Puritans' sense of besiegement after a series of "invasions" by the Dominion governor Edmund Andros, royalist Edward Randolph, fire, smallpox, Quakers, Anglicans, the French, and Indians (Silverman, *The Life and Times of Cotton Mather*, 82). On the pressures that provided context for the Salem outbreak, see, for example, Karlsen, *The Devil in the Shape of a Woman*, 226–31; Godbeer, *The Devil's Dominion*, esp. chap. 6; John McWilliams, "Indian John and the Northern Tawnies," *New England Quarterly* 69, no. 4 (December 1996): 580–604; Norton, *In the Devil's Snare*; and Benjamin C. Ray, *Satan & Salem: The Witch-Hunt Crisis of 1692* (Charlottesville: University of Virginia Press, 2015), chap. 9.

39. Norton, *In the Devil's Snare*, 126–28, 142.

40. Louis J. Kern, "Eros, the Devil, and the Cunning Woman: Sexuality and the Supernatural in European Antecedents and in the Seventeenth-Century Salem Witchcraft Cases," in *Perspectives on Witchcraft: Rethinking the Seventeenth-Century New England Experience*, Essex Institute Historical Collections, vol. 129, no. 1 (January 1993): 3–38.

41. Proctor strove to resist the proceedings and suggested that he could beat some of the afflicted out of their fits, as seen in Bernard Rosenthal, gen. ed., *Records of the Salem Witch Hunt* (Cambridge: Cambridge University Press, 2009), documents 58, 501, pp. 179, 538. Proctor also wrote a petition to area ministers that decried the harsh treatment of his sons and the Carrier boys to procure their confessions, and asked that the magistrates be replaced, in document 433, p. 486. John Willard similarly strove to defend himself when examined, supposedly offering "large talk," which led the court to inform him that they had not sent for him to preach, in document 173, p. 287. As in Burroughs's case, Willard's accusers reported seeing apparitions of his victims crying out for vengeance, some of whom explicitly requested that the accuser acquaint the magistrates to Willard's crimes, in documents 178, 185, 269, pp. 293, 297, 360. For a suggestive earlier case involving a contentious and litigious man, see the analysis of John Godfrey in Demos, *Entertaining Satan*, chap. 2.

42. Norton, *In the Devil's Snare*, 124.

43. For the witchcraft-possession overtones to Anne Hutchinson and Quakers, see Karlsen, *The Devil in the Shape of a Woman*, 14–19, 120–25, 190–94; and Godbeer, *The Devil's Dominion*, esp. chap. 6. The Mathers engaged in published battles with Quakers in which they depicted the dissenters as possessed by devils. See, for example, Increase Mather, *Remarkable Providences*, 344–48; and Cotton Mather, *Memorable Providences* (Boston, 1689) to which is appended Mather's rebuttal of George Keith, who had attempted to defend Quakerism from Increase Mather's prior accusations, 1–14.

44. Susan Broomhall and Jacqueline Van Gent, *Governing Masculinities in the Early Modern Period: Regulating Selves and Others* (Burlington, VT: Ashgate, 2011), 15–17.

45. The boundaries between these groups were not always fixed, since some who acted as if they were afflicted or possessed, like Deliverance Hobbs and Mary Warren, also confessed to witchcraft. None of the small number of male afflicted accusers in Essex County accused Burroughs. Of his nonafflicted accusers, only three were women, two of whom were married to men who also lodged accusations. The exception was Hannah Harris's testimony about Burroughs's ill treatment of his wife in Casco/Falmouth, cited in Rosenthal, gen. ed., *Records of the Salem Witch Hunt*, document 492, pp. 530–31.

46. See Reis, *Damned Women*; Godbeer, *The Devil's Dominion*, 114–19; and Karlsen, *The Devil in the Shape of a Woman*, esp. chaps. 4 and 5.

47. See Karlsen *The Devil in the Shape of a Woman*; and Norton *In the Devil's Snare*, respectively.

48. For more on how possession "constituted both abdication and recognition of responsibility," see Godbeer, *The Devil's Dominion*, 113–16; and Reis, *Damned Women*, chap. 5.

49. Citing Richard Bernard's *A guide to grand-jury men*, Increase Mather agreed that an apparition generated "great suspicion" but could not be held as conclusive evidence of witchcraft (Increase Mather, *Cases of Conscience* [Boston, 1692], 31–32). On the question of spectral evidence, see Sarah Rivett, *The Science of the Soul in Colonial New England* (Chapel Hill: Omohundro Institute for the University of North Carolina Press, 2011), esp. 256–70.

50. Rosenthal, gen. ed., *Records of the Salem Witch Hunt*, document 124, pp. 244–45.

51. Ibid., document 121, pp. 242–43.

52. Ibid., document 457, pp. 505–6.

53. For the comparison of the patriarchal family to a "little commonwealth," see William Gouge, *Of Domesticall Duties* (London, 1622). The concept provided the analytical framework for John Demos, *The Little Commonwealth* (1970; New York: Oxford University Press, 2000).

54. Rosenthal, gen. ed., *Records of the Salem Witch Hunt*, document 425, p. 475.

55. Ibid., document 425, pp. 473–77.

56. I am grateful to Richard Godbeer for mentioning this when commenting on a previous version of this chapter.

57. Burroughs's failings as a father overlapped with his potential limitations as a true Puritan minister. Bernard Rosenthal has argued that the Mathers' acceptance of the charges against Burroughs may have related to suspicions that he was a Baptist, based not only on his failure to secure baptisms for his own children (beyond the eldest) but also on his refusal to take communion on a few occasions. On Burroughs's religious identity, see Bernard Rosenthal, *Salem Story: Reading the Witch Trials of 1692* (Cambridge: Cambridge University Press, 1993), chap. 7, esp. 145–46.

58. Rosenthal, gen. ed., *Records of the Salem Witch Hunt*, document 85, p. 207.

59. Ibid., documents 120, 124, 128, 129, pp. 240–41, 245, 247–48, 248.

60. Ibid., documents 85, 125, 457, pp. 207, 245–46, 505–6.

61. For Burroughs as a special case, see Norton, *In the Devil's Snare*, chap. 4; and Rosenthal, *Salem Story*, chap. 5.

62. The Reverend Samuel Parris, in whose home the afflictions began in 1692, himself complained about the same sort of logistical challenges. Salem Village struggled with and over their ministers until Joseph Green, who replaced Samuel Parris and lasted longer as minister than his predecessors (Boyer and Nissenbaum, *Salem Possessed*, esp. chaps. 2, 3, and 7).

63. Rosenthal, gen. ed., *Records of the Salem Witch Hunt*, document 126, pp. 246–47.

64. Ibid., document 125, pp. 245–46. See also Norton, *In the Devil's Snare*, 150–53, 247–48.

65. On independence and "usefulness" as central to colonial concepts of manhood, and on colonial men's imperative to find a calling and be serviceable in their household and beyond, see Wilson, *Ye Heart of a Man*, chap. 1.

66. Beyond this briefly named "negro" servant, there were the two enslaved African women, Mary Black and Candy, who were named and examined but never placed on trial. For more about their cases, see Ray, *Satan and Salem*, 201–5.

67. Rosenthal, gen. ed., *Records of the Salem Witch Hunt*, document 446, p. 497. Burroughs's second wife, Sarah, was the sister-in-law of examining judge John Hathorn, which contributed to the judge's knowledge about the minister, as explained in Norton, *In the Devil's Snare*, 125.

68. Rosenthal, gen. ed., *Records of the Salem Witch Hunt*, document 492, pp. 530–31.

69. Ibid., documents 173, 174, 485, 487, pp. 286–89, 526–27.

70. Ibid., documents 85, 120, pp. 207, 241.

71. Ibid., documents 130, 447, pp. 249, 497.

72. Ibid., documents 634–35, pp. 646–47. Bernard Rosenthal suggests that Greenslit's deposition may have resulted from an attempt by Greenslit to save his mother, Ann Pudeator, who was executed just days later.

73. Ibid., document 120, p. 241.

74. Ibid., document 493, pp. 531–32.

75. Ibid., documents 122, 457, pp. 243, 506.

76. Ibid., documents 123, 124, 129, 425, 456, 525, pp. 244, 248, 475–77, 505, 561–62.

77. For the support of Rebecca Nurse and the Proctors, see ibid., documents 254, 433, 495–96, pp. 349, 486, 533–36. In the case of Mary Bradbury, however, strong support and a petition appear to have helped her escape despite being indicted (ibid., document 431, pp. 483–84).

78. Norton, *In the Devil's Snare*, 251.

79. Thomas Ady, *A Candle in the Dark: Or, A Treatise Concerning the Nature of Witches & Witchcraft: Being Advice to Judges, Sheriffes, Justices of the Peace, and Grand-Jury-men, what to do, before they passe Sentence on such as are Arraigned for their Lives as Witches* (London, 1656). See also Ady's *A Perfect Discovery of Witches: Shewing the Divine Cause of the Distractions of this Kingdome, and also of the Christian World. . . .* (London, 1661).

80. Karlsen, *The Devil in the Shape of a Woman*, 47–52.

81. While the actual trial records have not survived, myriad pretrial examinations and testimony about the accused provide considerable detail about the nature of the proceedings. For an overview and analysis of the legal proceedings, see Richard B. Trask, "Legal Procedures Used during the Salem Witch Trials and a Brief History of the Published Version of the Records," in Rosenthal, gen. ed., *Records of the Salem Witch Trials*, 44–63. For lay people's struggle against the law's emphasis on evidence

of a demonic compact, see Richard Weisman, *Witchcraft, Magic, and Religion in Seventeenth-Century Massachusetts* (Amherst: University of Massachusetts Press, 1984), esp. chap. 7. On how the divide between lay and elite conceptions of witchcraft made it difficult for magistrates to convict, see Godbeer, *Devil's Dominion*, esp. chap. 5. On the extent to which the laity and magistrates shared a sense of the Devil's agency, broadly defined, see Reis, *Damned Women*, esp. chap. 2.

82. Deodat Lawson, *A brief and true narrative of some remarkable passages related to sundry persons afflicted by witchcraft at Salem Village Which Happened from the Nineteenth of March to the Fifty of April 1692* (Boston, 1692); Deodat Lawson, *Christ's fidelity the only shield against Satans malignity. Asserted in a sermon delivered at Salem-village, the 24th of March, 1692* (Boston, 1693).

83. Lawson, *Christ's Fidelity*, 25, emphasis added.

84. Ibid., 30–43.

85. Ibid., 55.

86. For an analysis of the ways Parris's sermons, in combination with conditions endemic to Salem Village, contributed to the climate that spurred on the witchcraft trails, see Boyer and Nissenbaum, *Salem Possessed*, chap. 7.

87. Lawson, *Christ's Fidelity*, 56, 73.

88. Lawson, *Christ's Fidelity*, 2nd ed. (London, 1704), reprinted in Charles Wentworth Upham, *Salem Witchcraft: with an Account of Salem Village and a History of Opinions on Witchcraft and Kindred Subjects*, vol. 2 (Boston: Wiggin and Lunt, 1867), 535.

89. Historians have argued for centuries about Cotton Mather's responsibility for witch-hunting, depicting him variously as fanatical, ambivalent, or much maligned. For the former, see Charles Wentworth Upham, *Lectures on Witchcraft, Comprising a History of the Delusion in Salem, in 1692* (Boston: Carter, Hendee and Babcock, 1831), 102–14; and George Bancroft, *History of the United States of America. . . .*, vol. 2 (New York, 1891), 51–69. For a more ambivalent view, see Silverman, *The Life and Times of Cotton Mather*, esp. 97–137. For a decidedly pro-Mather account, see Hansen, *Witchcraft at Salem* (New York: Braziller, 1969).

90. Cotton Mather, *Memorable Providences*, 29.

91. Cotton Mather, *Wonders of the Invisible World Being an Account of the Tryals of Several Witches Lately Executed in New-England* (Boston and London, 1693); Silverman, *The Life and Times of Cotton Mather*, 115.

92. Cotton Mather, *Wonders of the Invisible World*, 94–104. A hack copy of *Wonders of the Invisible World* was published as *A True Account of the Tryals, Examinations, Confessions, Condemnations, and Executions of Divers Witches, at Salem, in New-England* (London, 1692) and placed Burroughs as the last of the five witch case studies. The London edition, which contained a preface by Richard Baxter, reproduced the five case studies on pages 60–65. For an overview of the origins of *Wonders of the Invisible World*, see *Narratives of the New England Witchcraft Cases*, ed. G. L. Burr (New York: Scribner, 1914), 194–195, 205–8; and Mary Rhinelander McCarl, "Spreading the News of Satan's Malignity in Salem: Benjamin Harris, Printer and Publisher of the Witchcraft Narratives," *Essex Institute Historical Collections* 129, no. 1 (1993): 53–60.

93. Cotton Mather, *Wonders of the Invisible World*, 33. Kenneth Silverman argues that Mather's protestations that he wrote under command, despite having initially

asked Stoughton's permission to publish the work, appears to reveal his growing ambivalence toward Stoughton as it became increasingly difficult to defend the use of spectral evidence (Silverman, *The Life and Times of Cotton Mather*, 116). For more details of John Dunton's sensational makeover of Increase and Cotton Mather's work for their London publication, see Albert B. Cook, "Damaging the Mathers: London Receives the News from Salem," *New England Quarterly* 65, no. 2. (June 1992): 302–8.

94. Cotton Mather, *Wonders of the Invisible World*, 50, 56.

95. Ibid., 34, 36.

96. Ibid., 35.

97. Ibid., 36–37. On the "Seven of Lancashire" dispossessed by John Darrell and George More in the late 1590s, see More, *A true Discourse*.

98. Cotton Mather, *Wonders of the Invisible World*, 39.

99. This premise was also forwarded by the afflicted accusers, some of whom averred that "such as have received the Devil-Sacrament can never Confess." This likely steeled the magistrates' resolve in examining the accused but does not seem to have made them doubt the guilt of those who confessed (Lawson, *Christ's Fidelity*, 2nd ed., 534).

100. Increase Mather, *Cases of Conscience*, sig. G4r; *Diary of Cotton Mather*, 152–54.

101. Increase Mather, *Cases of Conscience,* sig. G4v. "The Return of Several Ministers Consulted" is widely attributed to Cotton Mather despite being published anonymously in June 1692, just days after Bridget Bishop's execution. The source is reprinted in David Levin, ed., *What Happened in Salem: Documents Pertaining to the Seventeenth-Century Witchcraft Trials* (New York: Harcourt and Brace, 1960), 2nd ed., 110–11, and its attribution addressed there and in Silverman, *The Life and Times of Cotton Mather*, 100–101.

102. Increase Mather, *Cases of Conscience*, sig. G2v–G3r.

103. John Hale, *A Modest Enquiry into the Nature of Witchcraft* (Boston, 1702), 27–28.

104. Ibid., 31.

105. Ibid., 31, 33.

106. Ibid., 34–35.

107. "Letter of Thomas Brattle, F.R.S., 1692," in *Narratives of the New England Witchcraft Cases*, ed. G. L. Burr, 168, 1n.

108. On the founding of the church in 1698–99 and the Mathers' resistance to its ecumenism, see Silverman, *The Life and Times of Cotton Mather*, 146–56.

109. "Letter of Thomas Brattle" in *Narratives of the New England Witchcraft Cases*, ed. Burr, 170–71. The characterization of Salem versus Boston gentlemen was also used in the dialogic publication by Samuel Willard, *Some Miscellany Observations On our present Debates respecting Witchcrafts. In a Dialogue between S. & B.* (Philadelphia: Printed by William Bradford, for Hezekiah Usher, 1692). The pamphlet falsely listed its publication information to hide the fact that it was published in Boston at a time when the governor halted publications about witchcraft in order to prevent further controversy. For an explanation of its attribution, see Chadwick Hansen, *Witchcraft at Salem*, 187–88.

110. "Letter of Thomas Brattle," in *Narratives of the New England Witchcraft Cases*, ed. Burr, 169.

111. Ibid., 174, 184.

112. Ibid., 185.

113. Ibid., 184, 188–89.

114. A sixth man, Giles Corey, died while being questioned; he was pressed with heavy stones in an attempt to force him to enter a plea.

115. "Letter of Thomas Brattle," in *Narratives of the New England Witchcraft Cases,* ed. Burr, 177.

116. Brattle's turn against the credit of these accusers and confessors was mirrored by Samuel Willard, who emphasized in *Some Miscellany Observations* that if the afflicted were not only bewitched but possessed by devils, this invalidated their testimony (see Willard, *Some Miscellany Observations,* 7–11).

117. M. Halsey Thomas, ed., *The Diary of Samuel Sewall, 1674-1729,* vol. 1 (New York: Farrar, Straus and Giroux, 1973), 284.

118. Sewall's apology came five years later, in 1697 (see Richard Francis, *Judge Sewall's Apology: The Salem Witch Trials and the Forming of an American Conscience* [New York: Fourth Estate/Harper Collins, 2005], chap. 9).

119. Robert Calef, *More Wonders of the Invisible World: Or The Wonders of the Invisible World, Display'd in Five Parts. . . .* (London, 1700), 103–4.

120. "Letter of Thomas Brattle," in *Narratives of the New England Witchcraft Cases,* ed. Burr, 172.

121. Hale, *A Modest Enquiry,* 167–68.

122. Cited in Richard Francis, *Judge Sewall's Apology,* 174. For more about Jacob Melyen, see Evan Haefeli, "Dutch New York and the Salem Witch Trials: Some New Evidence," *Proceedings of the AAS: A Journal of American History and Culture Through 1876* (October 2000): 110; pt. 2, 277–308.

Notes to Chapter 5

1. For analysis of Mercy Short and her ties to the Maine frontier, and Burroughs, see Norton, *In the Devil's Snare,* 176–82.

2. Calef, *More Wonders of the Invisible World,* 1.

3. Ibid., 2.

4. On the ways that articulations of dreams and visions could allow Indians to stake claims to spiritual parity with Europeans, see Ann Marie Plane, *Dreams and the Invisible World in Colonial New England: Indians, Colonists, and the Seventeenth Century* (Philadelphia: University of Pennsylvania Press, 2014), chaps. 2 and 6.

5. See, for example, Cotton Mather, *Ornaments for the Daughters of Zion. Or, The character and happiness of a vertuous woman: in a discourse which directs the female-sex how to express, the fear of God, in every age and state of their life. . . .* (Cambridge, 1691).

6. See Jill Lepore, *The Name of War: King Philip's War and the Origins of American Identity* (New York: Vintage, 1998); Kristina Bross, *Dry Bones and Indian Sermons: Praying Indians in Colonial America* (Ithaca, NY: Cornell University Press, 2004); Linford D. Fisher, *The Indian Great Awakening: Religion and the Shaping of Native Cultures in Early America* (Oxford: Oxford University Press, 2012); Edward E. Andrews, *Native Apostles: Black and Indian Missionaries in the British Atlantic World* (Cambridge: Harvard University Press, 2013); Kathryn N. Gray, *John Eliot and the Praying Indians of Massachusetts Bay: Communities and Connections in Puritan New*

England (Lewisburg, PA: Bucknell University Press, 2013); and Plane, *Dreams and the Invisible World*.

7. Tituba and John Indian were slaves in the Reverend Samuel Parris's house. Tituba's confession and naming of other witches, and John Indian's actions as an afflicted accuser, helped determine the direction of the outbreak. On Tituba in particular, see Elaine G. Breslaw, *Tituba, Reluctant Witch of Salem: Devilish Indians and Puritan Fantasies* (New York: New York University Press, 1996); and Bernard Rosenthal, "Tituba's Story," *New England Quarterly* 71, no. 2 (June 1998): 190–203.

8. *Diary of Cotton Mather*, 172.

9. Ibid., 173; David Levin, *Cotton Mather: The Young Life of the Lord's Remembrancer, 1663–1703* (Cambridge: Harvard University Press, 1978), 244.

10. Mather also recorded in his diary that another unnamed "young Woman being arrested, possessed, afflicted by evil Angels, her Tormentors made my Image or Picture to appear before her . . . that shee began in her Fits to complain that I threatened and molested her." Mather recorded how dangerous news of this events would have been to his reputation—rather than reflecting upon what sins of his might have brought on this apparition—but interpreted her speedy delivery as a sign of God's approbation (*Diary of Cotton Mather*, 175, 178–79).

11. Calef, *More Wonders of the Invisible World*, 4.

12. Cotton Mather, "A Brand pluck'd out of the Burning," in *Narratives of the New England Witchcraft Cases*, ed. Burr, 255–87; Cotton Mather, "Another Brand pluckt out of the Burning," in Calef, *More Wonders of the Invisible World*, 1–13, 3.

13. Marilynne K. Roach, *The Salem Witch Trials: A Day-by-Day Chronicle of a Community under Siege* (Lanham, MD: Taylor Trade, 2002), 420; Norton, *In the Devil's Snare*, 293.

14. Calef, *More Wonders of the Invisible World*, 3.

15. On the similarities between the symptoms of the afflicted in Salem and those experienced during the spiritual awakening in Northampton, Massachusetts, in 1734–35, see Boyer and Nissenbaum, *Salem Possessed*, 27–30.

16. Calef, *More Wonders of the Invisible World*, 3.

17. Ibid., 4.

18. Ibid., 5.

19. Ibid., 5–7.

20. *Diary of Cotton Mather*, 86–91. See also Levin, *Cotton Mather*, 106–8. For a corresponding view of the meaning of angels, see Increase Mather, *Angelographia* (1696).

21. The Swedish case took place in Mohra in 1670 and was included as an attachment to Joseph Glanvill's *Saducismus triumphatus* (1681).

22. Calef, *More Wonders of the Invisible World*, 8. Mather made it clear in his diary that the angelic spirit instructed Rule to "count mee her Father, and regard mee and obey mee, as her Father," in *Diary of Cotton Mather*, 175.

23. Calef, *More Wonders of the Invisible World*, 9.

24. Ibid., 10–11. Richard Baxter provided the preface for Cotton Mather's *Late Memorable Providences Relating to Witchcrafts and Possessions. . . .* (London, 1691).

25. Michael G. Hall cites some support for the contention that "the Mathers, father and son, controlled the Boston press," including the controversies in 1699–1700 over Bartholomew Green's unwillingness to print a pamphlet that blatantly contradicted Increase Mather's writing against recent liberal church reforms, and Solomon

Stoddard's *Doctrine of Instituted Churches* (London, 1700) (see Michael Hall, *The Last American Puritan*, 299–301).

26. Calef, *More Wonders of the Invisible World*, 11.

27. Ibid., 12.

28. Levin makes a similar point about Mather's investment of "an immeasurable quantity of feeling and belief in the millennial significance of both the new government and the wonders that had already entered New England from the invisible world" (Levin, *Cotton Mather*, 216).

29. Silverman, *The Life and Times of Cotton Mather*, 132.

30. *Some Few Remarks upon a Scandalous Book, against the government and Ministry of New England, Written by one Robert Calef. Detecting the Unparrallel'd Malice & Falsehood, of the said Book, and Defending the Names of several particular Gentlemen, by him therein aspersed & abused*. . . . (Boston, 1701), http://quod.lib.umich.edu/e/evans/N00812.0001.001?view=toc.

31. Chadwick Hansen sought to redeem the Mathers against these charges, such as those found in John Greenleaf Whittier's "tiresome little poem" called "Calef in Boston" (1849). On this view, and Margaret Rule, see Hansen, *Witchcraft at Salem*, 190–95, 202–3.

32. Calef, *More Wonders of the Invisible World*, 13.

33. Ibid., 15.

34. Ibid., 13–14.

35. For an analysis of the boudoir scene in literature, see Felicity Nussbaum, *The Brink of All We Hate: English Satires on Women, 1660–1750* (Lexington: University Press of Kentucky, 1984), 105–14. While this technique can be traced back to Juvenal's "Sixth Satire," it remained in popular use in the seventeenth and eighteenth centuries. Some examples include Thomas Killigrew, *Parson's Wedding* (1639); John Oldham, "A Satyr upon a Woman who by her Falsehood and Scorn was the Death of my Friend" (1678); Robert Gould, "Love Given O'er: Or, a Satyr Against the Pride, Lust, & Inconstancy, &c., of Woman" (1680); and Ned Ward, *Female Policy Detected*, (1695). This trope lasted into the eighteenth century and may be seen in two of Jonathan Swift's famous poems, "A Lady's Dressing Room" (1730) and "A Beautiful Young Nymph Going to Bed" (1734).

36. Calef, *More Wonders of the Invisible World*, 14.

37. Ibid., 5–6.

38. Ibid., 20.

39. Ibid., 21.

40. Ibid., 21–22.

41. Ibid., 6.

42. Ibid., 16.

43. Ibid., 18–19.

44. Ibid., 23–24.

45. Ibid.

46. Ibid., 24.

47. Ibid., 19.

48. Ibid., 17.

49. John Gaule, *Select cases of conscience*, (1646); William Perkins, *A Discourse of the Damned Art of Witchcraft so farre forth as it is reuealed in the Scriptures* (Cambridge, 1608); Richard Bernard, *A guide to grand-iury men*, (1627).

50. Calef, *More Wonders of the Invisible World*, 17.

51. Ibid., 23.

52. Ibid., 25.

53. Ibid., 25.

54. Ministers John Deacon and John Walker argued against John Darrell's dispossessions a century earlier by claiming that miracles had ceased, and therefore contemporary performances were tricks designed to delude (see Deacon and Walker, *Dialogicall discourses*, 327–34).

55. Richard Gildrie describes anticlericalism in colonial New England, which ranged from refusal to pay local taxes in support of a minister, failure to attend public worship, and mockery, which varied in levels of explicitness and intensity (Gildrie, *The Profane, The Civil, and the Godly*, 119–23).

56. Calef, *More Wonders of the Invisible World*, 30.

57. Ibid.

58. Seven men signed its preface, including John Goodwin, about whose possessed children Cotton Mather wrote in *Memorable Providences* (1689) (see *Some Few Remarks*, 1–4).

59. *Some Few Remarks*, 10.

60. For analysis of Increase Mather's work to secure the new charter, see Michael Hall, *The Last American Puritan*, esp. chaps. 7 and 8. See also Cotton Mather, *Pietas in Patriam: The life of His Excellency Sir William Phips, Knt. late Captain General and Governour in Chief of the province of the Massachuset-Bay, New England. . . .* (London, 1697), later included in *Magnalia Christi Americana* (1702).

61. *Some Few Remarks*, 6.

62. Ibid., 5–6.

63. Ibid., 29.

64. Ibid., 35–37.

65. Silverman, *The Life and Times of Cotton Mather*, 130, 132.

66. *Some Few Remarks*, 25, 4.

67. Ibid., 4.

68. Ibid., 32–33.

69. Ibid., 12–14.

70. Ibid., 27, 70.

71. Ibid., 21, 28.

72. Levin, *Cotton Mather*, 187–95; Michael Hall, *The Last American Puritan*, chaps. 7 and 8.

73. *Some Few Remarks*, 35–36.

74. Ibid., 11, 25, 32, 35, 39, 40, 42, 47.

75. Ibid., 9, 22.

76. Ibid., 6.

77. Ibid., 57. For the role of gendered speech in witchcraft cases, see Kamensky, *Governing the Tongue*, chap. 6.

78. *Some Few Remarks*, 7.

79. Ibid., 25.

80. Ibid., 38.

81. Ibid., 56–57.

82. Ibid., 39–40.

83. On self-fashioning, see Stephen Greenblatt, *Renaissance Self-Fashioning: From More to Shakespeare* (Chicago: University of Chicago Press, 1980).

84. *Some Few Remarks*, 57–58.

85. Ibid., 70–71.

86. Ibid., 42.

87. Ibid., 64.

88. Burr writes that Calef "was chosen an assessor, in 1710 a tithingman. It was perhaps about this time that he retired to Roxbury, where in 1707 he had bought a place and where he was a selectman of the town when, in 1719, death found him. There . . . a stone still testifies that "Here lyes buried the body of Mr. Robert Calef, aged seventy-one years, died April the Thirteenth, 1719" (Burr, ed., *Narratives of the New England Witchcraft Cases*, 295).

89. Calef, *More Wonders of the Invisible World*, 11–13.

90. Darrell, *A detection*, 189.

91. Calef took Mather to task for writing positively about Sir William Phips's failed attempt to take Quebec (see Calef, *More Wonders of the Invisible World*, 145–48). Saco, Maine, was the site of serious battles between English and Indians since King Philip's War in 1675 to the 1720s (Norton, *In the Devil's Snare*, 102–8).

92. Calef, *More Wonders of the Invisible World*, 25. Increase Mather also had invoked "Indian Powaws (i.e. Wizards)" who "having received the Gospel, and given Good Evidence of a True Conversion to God in Christ, have, with much sorrow of Heart, declared how they had, whilst in their Heathenism, by the hands of Evil Angles Murdered their Neighbours" (Increase Mather, *Angelographia*, sig. B3v).

93. For more on the meaning of a "good death," see David E. Stannard, *The Puritan Way of Death: A Study in Religion, Culture, and Social Change* (New York: Oxford University Press, 1977); and Erik R. Seeman, *Death in the New World: Cross-Cultural Encounters, 1492–1800* (Philadelphia: University of Pennsylvania Press, 2010).

94. For an explanation of the Brattle Street Manifesto (1699) that led to controversy over access to the press and the appropriateness of certain Anglican practices in New England churches, see Michael Hall, *The Last American Puritan*, 292–301.

95. Levin, *Cotton Mather*, 232.

96. Levin writes that the new charter's institution of a royal governor and "the enfranchisement of men who were not Congregationalists, became the most effective wedge that divided secular and religious affairs" (ibid., 232). Michael Hall writes that Increase Mather's intentions aside, after the new charter a "franchise based on church membership and a government elected entirely within the colony gave way to a franchise based on property and a government supervised and directed from London" (Michael Hall, *The Last American Puritan*, 252).

97. Foyster, *Manhood in Early Modern England*, 210.

Notes to the Epilogue

1. As Owen Davies points out, more suspected witches have been killed in America through popular violence since 1692 than before (Davies, *America Bewitched*, 3). For the legacy of Salem, see Gretchen A. Adams, *The Specter of Salem: Remembering the Witch Trials in Nineteenth-Century America* (Chicago: University of Chicago Press, 2008).

2. Some examples include Samuel Petto's reprint of a case from the 1660s in *A Faithful Narrative of the Wonderful and Extraordinary Fits which Mr. Tho. Spatchet was under by Witchcraft*.... (London, 1693); Richard Dirby, *Dreadful news from Wapping: being a further relation of the sad and miserable condition of Sarah Bower a young girl, of about fourteen years of age, who is unhappily, at present, posses'd with an evil spirit*.... (London, 1693); Sir Matthew Hale, *A Collection of Modern Relations of Matter of Fact, concerning Witches & Witchcraft upon the Persons of People*.... (London, 1693); and Balthasar Bekker, *The World Bewitch'd, or, An examination of the common opinions concerning spirits* (London, 1695). There were also fraudulent possessions laid at the feet of Catholics, as in *The Detection of a Popish Cheat. Or a True Account of the Invention and Discovery of the Story of a Boys Conversing with the Devil* (Dublin and London, 1696).

3. Zachary Taylor, *The devil turn'd casuist, or, The cheats of Rome laid open in the exorcism of a despairing devil*.... (London, 1696), sig. A3v.

4. Ibid., sig. A4v.

5. Ibid., sig. B1r–B1v.

6. Ibid., sig. B2r.

7. For the Dugdale controversy, see Thomas Jollie, *The Surey Demoniack, or, An account of Satans strange and dreadful actings, in and about the body of Richard Dugdale of Surey*.... (London, 1697); Zachary Taylor, *The Surey Impostor being an answer to a late fanatical pamphlet, entituled The Surey demoniack*.... (London, 1697); Zachary Taylor, *Popery, superstition, ignorance, and knavery, very unjustly by a letter in the general pretended but as far as was charg'd, very fully proved upon the dissenters that were concerned in the Surey imposture* (London, 1698); T. J. [Thomas Jollie] *A vindication of the Surey Demoniack as no impostor, or, A reply to a certain pamphlet publish'd by Mr. Zach. Taylor, called The Surey imposter*.... (London, 1698); John Carringon, *The Lancashire Levite rebuk'd, or, A farther vindication of the dissenters from popery, superstition, ignorance and knavery unjustly charged on them by Mr. Zachary Taylor in his two books about the Surey demoniack in a letter to himself* (London, 1698); and Zachary Taylor, *Popery, superstition, ignorance, and knavery, confess'd, and fully proved on the Surey dissenters from the second letter of an apostate friend to Zach. Taylor: to which is added, a refutation of Mr. T. Jollie's Vindication of the devil in Dugdale, or, The Surey demoniack* (London, 1699).

8. For Zachary Taylor's extended comparisons to Darrell and Harsnett, see Taylor, *The Surey Impostor*, sig. A3r–A4r. Historian Wallace Notestein viewed John Darrell's involvement with Somers as fraudulent, but he inferred that the clergy involved with Dugdale were "probably honest but deluded men" (Notestein, *A History of Witchcraft in England from 1558 to 1718* [New York: Crowell, 1968], 315).

9. Jollie had been in touch with the Mathers since the 1670s, when he entered into a correspondence with Increase Mather over the question of renewing church covenants in New England (Michael Hall, *The Last American Puritan*, 147–48). The Mather library in the American Antiquarian Society has a copy of Jollie's *A vindication of the Surey Demoniack as no Impostor* that is signed "I. Mather," in which Jollie quoted Increase Mather's *Remarkable Providences*, 47–48.

10. Another notable example, which produced several published pamphlets, was the case of an eleven-year-old Scottish girl named Christian Shaw whose possession symptoms led to a trial in which some of those she named as witches confessed and

seven were executed (Brian P. Levack, "Demonic Possession in Early Modern Scotland," in *Witchcraft and Belief in Early Modern Scotland*, ed. Julian Goodare, Laura Martin and Joyce Miller [New York: Palgrave Macmillan, 2008]). Regarding continuity in belief, Ian Bostridge explains: "As a body of ideas, witchcraft had a currency and a certain viability in the eighteenth century, despite the absence of widespread or legitimate persecution. By 1736, the year of the repeal of the British witchcraft legislation, witchcraft theory was isolated and much ridiculed in print and, doubtless, coffee-house. But behind closed doors, we cannot be so sure" (Bostridge, "Witchcraft Repealed," in *Witchcraft in Early Modern Europe*, ed. Jonathan Barry, Marianne Hester, and Gareth Roberts [Cambridge: Cambridge University Press, 1996], 311).

11. *Some Few Remarks*, 42–43.

12. Richard Baddeley's *The boy of Bilson* reprinted and contradicted a previous account by a "Mr. Wheeler," now missing, entitled "A faithfull relation of the proceedings of the Catholicke gentlemen with the boy of Bilson." See also Robert Howson, *The Second Part of the Boy of Bilson: Or, a True and Particular Relation of the Impostor Susanna Fowles. . . .* (London, 1698); *The Trial of Susannah Fowles of Hammersmith: That was Try'd at London for Blaspheming Jesus Christ: and Cursing the Lord's Prayer: And who also Pretended to be Possest with a Devil* (London, 1698).

13. Robert Howson, *The Second Part of the Boy of Bilson*, 10–11.

14. Baxter, *The Certainty of the World of Spirits* (1691), 3. Baxter referred to New England cases that he gleaned from publications by the Mathers and wrote the preface to the aforementioned second edition of Cotton Mather's *Memorable Providences*, published in 1691.

15. Possession cases persisted, for this reason, well into the eighteenth century, when the Methodists and others invoked wonders to prove the power of God and the Devil in the world (see, for example, the pamphlets relating to the case of George Lukins, the "Yatton Demoniac," which took place in 1788, in Joseph Easterbrook, *An appeal to the public respecting George Lukins, (called the Yatton demoniac,) containing an account of his affliction and deliverance*, [Bristol/London, 1788]).

16. On this and the eighteenth-century decline in official prosecution for witchcraft in England, see Bostridge, *Witchcraft and Its Transformations*, 233–44.

Index

Ady, Thomas, 115, 121

African Americans, 112, 205n66

agency: access to patriarchy and, 8–9; Alice Samuel and, 54; in confession narratives, 5, 9; externalization of blame and, 6; feigned possession, 21; gendered claims to victimhood, 7; self-control during possession, 20–21. *See also* feigned and fraudulent possession; performance

alchemy, 8

Almond, Philip C., 190n18

Amussen, Susan, 73, 83

angelic possession, 7, 94, 136–37, 141–42

Anglican Church. *See* Church of England

astrology, 8

atheism: Cotton Mather "remarkable providences" and, 97–98, 102, 198n1; gendered attacks against, 71; as Harsnett-Darrell accusation, 81, 84, 196n53; as transatlantic concern, 10, 102, 171

Bancroft, Richard, 67–68, 79, 82, 88, 100

Baptists, 102, 204n57

Barker, William, 124

Baxter, Richard, 98–99, 102–3, 143, 161, 173

Bernard, William, 152

body: bodily evidence of guilt, 27, 52; characteristics of sexed bodies, 27; diabolical body marks, 52–53, 192n53;

gendered body as possession vessel, 6, 24–25, 174; humoral model of bodies, 82, 196n49; power of women's bodies, 56–57; woman's touch in patriarchal regulation, 50–51. *See also* medicine; symptoms; treatment and tests

Bostridge, Ian, 213–14n10

Boy of Bilson (William Perry), 95–96, 173, 199n15

Boy of Burton (Thomas Darling), 1, 18, 69, 89–91, 197n71

Boy of Tocutt, 102

Brattle, Thomas, 116, 125–30, 172

Brattle Street Church, 125, 167

Brigges, Agnes, 21, 27, 190n18

Brome, Richard, 199n14

Brossier, Martha, 22, 28–29

Burgess, Elizabeth, 201n23

Burroughs, George: arrest and conviction of, 105–16, 205n62; Calef reference to, 165–66; comparison with John Samuel, 100, 133; deficiencies and excesses of manhood, 11, 106–16, 118, 120–21, 128, 132, 175, 204n57; as disgraced minister, 106–10, 114–18, 129–32; execution, 100, 123, 127–29, 144; restoration of patriarchy and, 106, 123, 129–30; spectral evidence and, 119–25, 207n99; support for, 125–30

Burroughs, Sarah, 111–14

Busse, John, 124

Butler, Judith, 178n10

Calef, Robert, 11, 116, 128–29, 212n88. *See also* Calef-Mather debates
Calef-Mather debates: Burroughs gallows speech, 128–29; Burroughs Indian-witch reference, 165–66; Calef gendered failings, 158–61; Calef rationalist approach, 144–45; comparison with Harsnett-Darrell dispute, 133, 143–45, 153, 156–57, 165, 167; comprehensive scope of, 163–65; Cotton Mather gendered failings, 145, 148–51, 158–59, 204n45; defense of patriarchal authority and, 11, 142–43, 155–57, 162–64; Dugdale case references to, 172; "eight specters" of Margaret Rule, 139–42; libel suit again Calef, 167; Massachusetts charter of 1692 and, 159, 167–68, 212n96; Mather premonition and, 136–37, 141–42; Rule sexual shaming, 145–48; sanctioned scriptural methods and, 145, 151–55; sequence of manuscripts and publications, 135–36; trade-based strategies, 157
Calvin, John, 95–96
Calvinism, 31, 180n18
Carrier, Martha, 120, 124, 127
Carrington, John, 171
Casaubon, Meric, 103
Catholicism: Calef critique and, 153–55, 165–66; Catholic vs. Protestant witchcraft texts, 24; discernment faculty, 180n20; feigned possession and, 95–96, 173–74, 199n15; gendered attacks against, 71, 73; Harsnett "popery" critique and, 26, 67–68, 70, 84–86, 169–71, 196n45; Massachusetts witchcraft and, 95; New England religious disputes, 103; possession accounts and, 29, 95–96; possession symptoms and, 18; reign of James II, 101, 200n21. *See also* exorcism
Charles I (King of England), 101
Charles II (King of England), 101
Cheever, Samuel, 128
Church of England: Anglo-Atlantic tolerance for Anglicans, 166; colonist critiques of, 126; critiques of exorcism, 25–26, 67–68; critiques of Puritan dispossession, 27, 28–29, 67–68, 74–76, 194n7; Crook boy exorcism, 169–71;

English Reformation and, 2–3; Harsnett-Darrell dispute and, 25–26, 68–70, 74–75, 79–81, 92–93; New England religious disputes, 103
Clark, Stuart, 15, 16–17
community: manly credit in rhetorical disputes, 26, 72–79, 137; possession as communal/performative and, 3, 16, 31, 57; societal crisis as possession influence, 2, 12
confession (of witchcraft): Boy of Bilson fraud, 199n15; Boy of Tocutt, 102; Burroughs accusers, 107, 109–10, 118, 121, 124–28; Burroughs gallows speech, 127–29; Burroughs spectral confession, 111, 115, 116, 121; Essex (England) confessions, 101; medical corroboration and, 95; overview, 5; Salem and Essex County confessions, 100, 172, 204n45; Samuel confessions, 44–48, 52–56, 59, 61–63, 65, 190n24, 192–93n65; satanic influences and, 207n99; Thomas Darling accusee, 1
conversion: conversion accounts, 14; exorcism as tool for, 5; possession as tool for, 93, 167; as trigger for possession, 139; validity of possession accounts and, 135
Cooke, Elisha, 159
Cooper, Margaret, 9, 13
Cooper, Stephen, 13
Cooper, Thomas, 25
Cotton, John, 96
Cromwell, Henry (Williams), 39, 43, 51
Cromwell, Lady (Susan Weeks), 43, 46, 63, 65
Crook boy, 169–71

Darling, Thomas ("Boy of Burton"), 1, 18, 69, 89–91, 197n71
Darrell, John: Catholicism and, 96, 196n45; comparison with Cotton Mather, 133, 143–44; notable dispossessions, 28–30, 40; Starkie dispossession, 196n49. *See also* Harsnett-Darrell dispute; Seven of Lancashire; Somers, William
devil/devils: as agent of false guilt, 122, 154–55; as agent of false innocence, 129, 138–39, 142, 180n18, 207n99; angelic tests and, 141–42; Burroughs accusations and, 107–14, 116–17, 129, 207n99; Calef alleged affliction by, 158, 161–62; Cotton Mather on, 94, 98–99, 129, 141–42, 167–68;

diabolical body marks, 52–53, 192n53; external vs. internal attacks, 6; Harsnett-Darrell dispute and, 78–79; Margaret Cooper account of, 13, 15; New England Indians and, 99, 135; political furor attributed to, 80–81, 164–65; possession as struggle with, 15–16, 18–19, 137, 142–44, 167–68, 175–76; religious preferences and, 95–96; sexual encounters with, 190n24; skeptics affliction with, 160–61, 172; societal beliefs about, 16; temptation as possession theme, 1–2. *See also* dispossession; exorcism

DeWindt, Anne Reiber, 39, 189n10

dispossession: Darrell success with, 69–70; development of, 3; godly community role in, 14, 31; Harsnett critique of, 67–68; patriarchal order as goal, 30–31, 33–35; prayer role in, 14; as propaganda war issue, 27; sexual imposition in, 87–88, 91–92

Dovey, Joyce, 199n15

Dugdale, Richard, 171–73, 201n23, 213n9

Dunton, John, 103, 119–20

Elizabeth I (Queen of England), 2, 188n67

English Civil War (1642–51), 101

Essex (England) outbreak of 1645–47, 101

Ewen, C. L'Estrange, 189–90n17

executions: Brattle opposition to, 127; English witchcraft law, 2, 35–36, 191n28, 192–93n65; eradication of witches, 56–57; Essex (England) outbreak of 1645–47, 101; George Burroughs, 11, 100, 123, 127–28, 144; George Jacobs, 127; John Proctor, 127; John Willard, 113, 127; Martha Carrier, 127; Mary Glover (Massachusetts), 53–54; methods of execution, 177n3; proportion of women victims, 174; Salem and Essex County outbreak, 116, 127–28; Samuel family, 41, 43–44, 52–54, 56, 60, 65–66, 191n28, 192n63; of witches vs. demoniacs, 27

exorcism: Harsnett "trade" critique, 67–68, 84, 92; post-Salem exorcism/ dispossession, 169–71; Protestant dispossession and, 3, 69–70; Protestant repudiation of, 3, 5; sexual imposition in, 87–88, 197n64; technique for alternatives, 14

feigned and fraudulent possession: Agnes Briggs possession, 21; Anglican opposition to dispossession and, 194n7, 195n12; authentic performance and, 26; Brattle self-deceit argument, 126–27, 130; Catholic "discernment" and, 180n20; Cotton Mather on, 94, 103, 138–39; demonic religious preferences and, 95–96; Edmund Robinson dispossession, 199n14; gender as interpretive frame, 173–74; Grace Sowerbutts confession, 19; Harsnett-Darrell dispute and, 77–78, 92–93, 153, 198n7; John Smith dispossession, 199n14; melancholy as condition for, 101; overconvincing performances, 5, 170–71; performance of innocence, 31–33, 138–39; Seven of Lancashire dispossession and, 198n7; Susanna Fowles case, 173; tests of authenticity, 28–30; validity of apparitions and, 108; William Perry ("Boy of Bilson"), 95–96, 173, 199n15. *See also* agency; performance; treatment and tests

Fisher, John, 28

Foster, Ann, 124

Fowles, Susanna, 173

Fox, John, 95–96

Foyster, Elizabeth, 73, 83, 168, 193n70, 196n51

Galis, Richard, 19

Gaskill, Malcolm, 184n33

Gaule, John, 152

gender: angelic vs. demonic possession and, 7; Burroughs accusers and, 107; characteristics of sexed bodies, 27; dispossession as restoration of norms, 30–31; in early modern European writing, 7–8; enduring demonic relationship with, 11–12; family and partner sexual relations, 192n55, 193n70; gendering of credulity, 174–75; gender of demoniacs, 23, 25, 174; Harsnett-Darrell feminized targets, 67–68, 70–72, 73–74; humoral model of bodies, 82, 196n49; as possession mechanism, 4, 174; sexual shaming, 87–91, 145–48, 197n68; skepticism and, 25–27; social order reliance on, 175–76; witchcraft-possession and, 46–48, 49–51. *See also* body; manhood; womanhood

Gibson, Marion, 38, 73, 189–90n17
Glanvill, Joseph, 6, 99, 103
Glover, Mary, 18, 27, 31, 33–36
Glover, Mary (Massachusetts), 95
Goodwin family possession account, 94–98, 119, 165
Gowing, Laura, 50
Green, Joseph, 205n62
Greenslit, Thomas, 113
Gunter, Anne, 21

Hale, John, 116, 122, 123–25, 128, 130–31
Hall, Michael G., 209–10n25, 212n96
Harley, David, 179n12
Harris, Hannah, 112–13, 204n45
Harrison, Thomas, 17–18, 20
Harsnett, Samuel, 25–26, 32–33, 40, 67–68, 194n7. *See also* Harsnett-Darrell dispute
Harsnett-Darrell dispute (1599–1603): atheism charges in, 196n53; comparison with Calef-Mather debates, 133, 143–45, 153, 156–57, 165, 167; effect on English witchcraft cases, 100–101, 171–72; Harsnett Anglicanism and, 25–26, 67–70, 74–75, 79–81, 84–86, 92–93, 96, 153–54, 196n45; Harsnett sexual shaming, 87–91, 197n68; Katherine Wright dispossession and, 69, 74, 153; manly credit strategy, 72–79; New England disputes compared with, 104; overview, 10, 67–68, 70–72, 87–88, 92–93; Somers dispossession and, 40, 69–70, 73–80, 86, 153, 172; trade-based strategies, 83–87, 157, 196n58, 197n63; unmanly excess strategy, 79–83, 165, 195n37, 196n49, 196n51
Hartley, Edmund, 69
Hartwell, Abraham, 22, 28–29
Henry VIII (King of England), 2
Heylyn, Peter, 198n7
Heywood, Thomas, 199n14
Hobbs, Abigail, 110
Hopkins, Matthew, 101
Howson, Robert, 173
Hubbard, Elizabeth, 114
Hurdman, Margaret, 31–32
Hutchinson, Anne, 106
Hutchinson, Benjamin, 113
hysteria, 27

Indian, Tituba and John, 135, 209n7

Jacobs, George, 127
James I (King of England), 68, 101, 194n7, 199n14
James II (King of England), 101
Jollie, Thomas, 171–72, 213n9
Jorden, Edward, 27
Jorden, Joan, 30

Karlsen, Carol F., 178n8
Kent, E. J., 58
Keysar, Elizar, 114
King, Daniel, 115
Knapp, Elizabeth, 119, 180n15

Lancashire outbreak, 19, 21, 31, 92–93, 198n7
Lawson, Deodat, 106–7, 116–18, 121, 124
Levack, Brian P., 6, 186–87n42, 210n28
Levin, David, 167–68, 212n96
Lewis, Mercy, 108
Luther, Martin, 95–96

Macfarlane, Alan, 58
manhood: access to patriarchy and, 8–9, 53–55; Burroughs conviction and, 11, 106–16, 118, 120–21, 128, 132, 175, 205n65; Cotton Mather gendered failings, 145, 148–51, 158–59; in demonic possession, 3–4, 7; Harsnett-Darrell dispute overview, 70–72; John Samuel gendered failings, 41, 49–50, 56–57, 58–66, 175; male antipatriarchal behavior, 193n75; male barrator character type, 58–59, 193n68; male domestic violence, 53–55, 58, 111–14, 118, 120–21, 128, 192n54–55, 192n57; male witchcraft, 8, 24–25, 57, 115–16, 184n33, 186–87n42; manly credit in rhetorical disputes, 26, 72–79, 137; Robert Calef gendered failings, 158–61; sexual shaming in Harsnett, 89–90, 197n68; transatlantic patterns in, 4. *See also* body; gender; patriarchy
Marescot, Michel, 28–29
Marprelate controversy (1588–90), 81
Marsden, Thomas, 169–71
Martin, Susanna, 120
Mather, Cotton: as attendant at executions, 127–28; Boy of Tocutt account, 102; comparison with John Darrell, 133, 143–44; on George Burroughs, 116–20, 124–29, 206–7n93; Goodwin family possession account, 94–98, 119, 165; on

Mercy Short, 133–34, 165; millennial worldview, 137, 142–44, 167–68; patriarchal authority and, 10–11, 94–95, 142–44; possession accusations against, 209n10; publishing trade and, 209–10n25; on religious tests, 95–98, 119; on Richard Dugdale, 172–73; on Sadducism, 198n1; on skepticism, 98–99; on spectral evidence, 139–42, 164, 206–7n93; transatlantic correspondence, 102–3; on witchcraft, 119–20, 122, 133–44, 147–48, 152–55. *See also* Calef-Mather debates

Mather, Increase: Burroughs conviction and, 106–7, 116, 122–23; on discernment, 7; Margaret Rule possession and, 146; Martha Goodwin possession and, 96; Massachusetts charter of 1692 and, 159, 167–68, 212n96; patriarchal authority and, 10–11, 159; on possession symptoms, 102, 180n17; publishing trade and, 209–10n25; on spectral evidence, 122–23, 141–42

Mather, Richard, 102

medicine: doctors as possession corroborators, 27, 42, 95, 201n23; illness as possession cause, 20, 26–27, 149, 170–71. *See also* body; skepticism

Melyen, Jacob, 131

Methodists, 214n15

More, George: accusations of fraud, 32; Calvinist environments and, 31; Cotton Mather on, 99; Hurdman account, 31–32; Seven of Lancashire (Starkie family) dispossession and, 17, 19–21, 69, 92–93; Somers dispossession and, 69

More, Henry, 103

Muldrew, Craig, 72

Mylner, Anne, 20–21, 28, 29–30, 190n18

Nashe, Thomas, 81

Native Americans: Cotton Mather pious Indian account, 134–35, 165–66; devil association with, 99, 135; feminine susceptibility to possession and, 135; Indian war refugees, 105, 107–8, 138; Puritans' gendered understanding of, 104; Robert Calef pious Indian account, 165–66; transatlantic connections and, 4

Norrington, Mildred, 17–18

Norton, Mary Beth, 104, 135

Noyes, Nicholas, 128

Nurse, Rebecca, 115

Nyndge, Alexander, 17–18

obsession, 5–6, 14, 18, 107–8, 179n12–13, 180n18

Parris, Samuel, 105, 107, 117, 205n62, 209n7

patriarchy: Burroughs conviction and, 106, 123, 129–30; Calef-Mather debates and, 11, 142–43, 155–57, 162–64; Cotton Mather articulation of, 10–11, 94–95, 142–44; decline of possession and, 4; differential access to, 8–9, 53–55; everyday gender practice and, 168; failed manhood as threat to, 57, 59, 66; goals of dispossession and, 30–31, 33–35; Harsnett-Darrell dispute and, 71, 73, 87, 93; male antipatriarchal behavior, 193n75; sense of entitlement/authority in, 52; skepticism as threat to, 130; social order reliance on, 175–76, 178n10; suppression of published possession narratives, 5; transatlantic connections in, 168, 176; witchcraft convictions as restoration of, 63–66, 106; witchcraft victims role in, 56; woman's touch in patriarchal regulation, 50–51. *See also* manhood; womanhood

performance: community in dispossession and, 3, 16, 31, 57; overconvincing performances, 5, 170–71; performance of innocence, 31–33, 33–35; possession as childhood self-assertion, 51, 191n49; possession as feminine self-assertion, 31–32, 48–49, 191n41; possession-obsession distinction and, 5–6, 179n12–13, 180n18; possession symptoms as, 3, 16; scripted performance as severe obligation, 28; subversive possession, 5; symptoms and narrative as mutually constituted, 9. *See also* agency; feigned and fraudulent possession

Perkins, William, 25, 152

Perry, William ("Boy of Bilson"), 95–96, 173, 199n15

Phips, William, 119, 133, 151, 165–66, 168

Pindar, Rachel, 22, 27, 190n18

poltergeists, 201n23, 202n35

possession accounts: contest for power in, 15–16, 137, 142–44, 167–68, 175–76; demonic possession, 2–4; as discursive template, 1–2, 7; gendered language in, 176; gender of demoniacs, 23, 25; narrative vs. documentary sources, 189–90n17; political and religious implications in, 5, 16; possession vs. bewitchment in, 5–6, 107, 180n15, 180n17, 200n18; post-Salem possession accounts, 11–12, 169; preternatural vs. supernatural realm in, 16, 177n2; reliability of sources in, 7; as "remarkable providences," 10, 97–99, 164; as sermons or religious tracts, 102; social status of claimants, 39, 40, 53, 56–57, 189n10; societal crisis and, 12; socioeconomic value of, 72–73; strange-and-familiar quality, 22–23; theological basis for, 68–69; *Witches of Warboys* as paradigmatic narrative, 38–39. *See also* feigned and fraudulent possession; symptoms; treatment and tests

possession chronology: Anne Mylner (1564), 3, 20–21, 28, 29–30, 190n18; Alexander Nyndge (1573), 17–18; Agnes Brigges (1574), 21, 27, 190n18; Mildred Norrington (1574), 17–18; Rachel Pindar (1574), 22, 27, 190n18; Richard Galis (1579), 19; Margaret Cooper (1584), 9, 13–14; Catholic exorcisms (1586), 67–68; Katherine Wright (1586), 69, 74, 87–91; Warboys accounts (1589–93) — *see main heading*; Seven of Lancashire (1590s), 19, 21, 92–93, 198n7; Starkie children (1590s), 17, 19, 21, 32–33, 69, 92–93, 196n49, 198n7; Margaret Hurdman (1590s), 31–32; Thomas Darling (1596), 1, 18, 69; William Somers (1597), 28–29, 40, 69–70, 73–80, 86, 87, 89–91, 171–72; Joan Jorden (1599), 30; Martha Brossier (translated 1599), 22, 28–29; propaganda war (1599–1603) — *see main heading*; Lancashire outbreak (1600), 31; Thomas Harrison (1601), 17–18, 20; Mary Glover (1603), 18, 27, 31, 33–36; Anne Gunter (1604), 21; Grace Sowerbutts (1612), 19; Margaret Cooper second account (1614), 9, 14; John Smith (1616), 17, 199n14; William Perry (1622), 95–96, 173, 199n15; period of wane in

possession cases (1630–42), 101, 199n15; Edmund Robinson (1633), 199n14; Margaret Hooper (Cooper) third account (1641), 9, 14–15; Essex outbreak (1645–47), 101; Joyce Dovey (published 1647), 199n15; Boy of Tocutt (1659), 102; Elizabeth Knapp (1673), 119, 180n15; witchcraft-possession cases (1680–1700), 201n23, 202n35; Increase Mather report (1682), 102; Goodwin children (1688), 94, 119, 165; George Burroughs (1692) — *see main heading*; Mercy Short (1692–93), 133–34, 165; Salem and Essex County outbreak (1692) — *see main heading*; Margaret Rule (1693) — *see main heading*; Crook boy exorcism (1696), 169–71; Richard Dugdale (1689; published 1697), 171–73, 201n23, 213n9; Susanna Fowles (1698), 173

postapostolic culture, 24, 68, 77, 142, 154

Presbyterian Church, 171

Proctor, John and Elizabeth, 105–6, 115, 127, 203n41

propaganda war (1599–1603): legitimacy in possession and, 10; religious dispute over dispossession, 27; skepticism and, 25–27; Warboys references in, 40; witchcraft statutes as response, 35–36. *See also* Harsnett-Darrell dispute

Protestantism: Catholic vs. Protestant witchcraft texts, 24; early witchcraft statutes and, 2, 35–36; Harsnett-Darrell dispute and, 78–79; impossibility of miracles and, 24, 142, 154–55; New England religious disputes, 103; possession conversion, 14; possession in Calvinist environments, 180n18; possession symptoms and, 16–18; repudiation of exorcism, 3, 5; treatment of demoniacs, 5

publishing trade: absence of dissenting voices, 125; English possession pamphlets, 200n18; Mather family influence in, 209–10n25; Mercy Short privately-circulated tract and, 133–34; New England development of, 102–3, 125; pamphlets as discursive device, 14; preternatural realm as theme, 16; proscription of witchcraft tracts, 207n109; saleability (sensationalism), 15; sermons and religious tracts, 102; transatlantic publication, 102–3, 119–20,

136, 141, 169, 195n12; transcripts of examinations, 116; *Witches of Warboys* as possession manual, 38–39

Puritans: Burroughs as disgraced minister, 106–10, 114–18, 129–32; Calef-Mather debates and, 11; Harsnett-Darrell dispute and, 67–68, 74–76, 81; legitimacy in possession and, 10, 28–29, 34–35; New England religious diversity, 103, 183–84n32; as Warboys influence, 38. *See also* propaganda war

Putnam, Ann, Jr., 109

Putnam, John and Rebecca, 105, 110–11, 113

Quakers, 102, 104, 106, 201n23

Roberts, Alexander, 24–25

Robinson, Edmund, 199n14

Roper, Lyndal, 189–90n17, 192n53

Rosen, Barbara, 38, 189–90n17

Rosenthal, Bernard, 204n57

Ruck, Thomas, 114

Rule, Margaret: Calef account of possession of, 145–48; comparison with Mercy Short and pious Indian man, 134–35; comparison with Warboys accounts, 137; Cotton Mather relationship with, 100, 137–39, 143–44; "eight specters" evidence of, 139–42; overview, 11; Puritan patriarchy and, 142–43; scholarship on, 136. *See also* Calef-Mather debates

Sadducism, 94, 97–98, 102, 150, 171, 198n1

Salem and Essex County outbreak of 1692: historical exceptionalism of, 103–4; judicial reform as end of, 133, 168, 169, 212n96; Margaret Rule account as reprise of, 141–42; Native American influence in, 135; as paradigmatic case, 10–11; possession-obsession distinction and, 6; skeptical reaction to, 122–31; spectral evidence and, 107–12, 117–25, 139–40. *See also* Burroughs, George

Samuel family. *See* Warboys possession accounts

Sands, Kathleen, 197n64

Satan. *See* devil/devils

Scot, Reginald, 24, 95

Seven of Lancashire (Starkie family), 17, 19, 21, 32–33, 69, 92–93, 196n49, 198n7

Sewall, Samuel, 128, 131

Shapiro, Barbara, 103

Sharpe, James, 178n8, 190n22, 191n49

Shaw, Christian, 213–14n10

Shepard, Alexandra, 8–9, 72, 193n75

Short, Mercy, 133–34, 137–38, 141, 154, 165

Silverman, Kenneth, 157, 206–7n93

skepticism: Brattle self-deceit argument, 126–27, 130; Calef-Mather debates and, 11, 128–29, 144–45; Calef scriptural tests and, 152–55; Cotton Mather on, 98–99, 103, 140; doctors as corroborators, 27, 42, 95; Dugdale case as boost for, 172–73; feigned possession and, 173–74; gender as tool for, 25–27; gendering of credulity, 174–75; interpretation of accounts and, 22, 140; John Hale treatise on, 123–25, 128, 130–31; physical tests administered and, 27–28; political change and, 10; satanic motives attributed to, 160–61, 172; Scot treatise on, 24, 95; as threat to patriarchy, 130; of witchcraft, 24. *See also* atheism; medicine

Smith, John, 17, 199n14

Somers, William, 28–29, 40, 69–70, 73–80, 86, 87, 89–91, 153, 171–72

Sowerbutts, Grace, 19

spectral evidence: bedside apparitions, 140; in Cotton Mather, 139–42, 164, 206–7n93; credible testimony and, 119–24, 207n99; criticism of, 141; "eight specters" of Margaret Rule, 139–40; pious Indian apparition, 134–35, 165–66; Salem and Essex County spectral appearances, 107–12, 114, 117–23; spectral corroboration of accusers, 18–19, 38–39; Throckmorton spirits, 42–43, 46–47

Starkie family (Seven of Lancashire), 17, 19, 21, 32–33, 69, 92–93, 196n49, 198n7

Stearne, John, 57–58, 101

Stoughton, William, 133

Swan, John, 31, 33–35

Symms, Zachariah, 128

symptoms (general): as external assaults, 14; possession accounts as documentation of, 2, 9; possession as communal/performative and, 3, 16, 31, 57; possession without symptoms, 180n17; transatlantic connections with, 104–5. *See also* body; possession accounts; treatment and tests symptoms (particular symptoms): absence of pain, 17; aversion to authority, 49–50; aversion to Scripture, 19–20, 49; clairvoyance, 21, 42–43, 140; convulsive fits, 17–18, 37, 94, 107; foreign language facility, 21–22; healing of wounds, 140; inability to eat or vomiting of objects, 20–21; levitation, 94–95, 140; madness, 42; remarkable strength, 17–18; severe pain, 27–28, 94; spoken fantasy narratives, 31–32; strange voices from within, 18. See also spectral evidence

Tatem, Moira, 190n18
Taylor, Zachary, 169–73
Thomas, Keith, 58, 180n15
Throckmorton family. See Warboys possession accounts
Tituba, 135
transatlantic connections: Anglo-Atlantic tolerance for Anglicans, 166; Cotton Mather transatlantic connections, 135–36, 143, 213n9; Dugdale and transatlantic accounts, 171–72, 213–14nn9–10; historical overview, 100–101; Native Americans and, 4; in New England possession narrative, 10; pious Indians and English women, 135; possession symptoms and, 104–5; post-Salem possession accounts, 11–12, 169; prevalence of female accused witches, 3; seventeenth-century patriarchy and, 168; shared beliefs, 4; transatlantic nonconformists, 102–3; transatlantic patriarchal order, 176; transatlantic publication, 102–3, 119–20, 136, 141, 169, 195n12
treatment and tests: coerced eating and drinking, 30, 140; coerced oaths, 45–48, 50, 52, 61–64; confinement, 44–45; countermagical practices, 43; fasting, 95; feigned possession and, 26, 28–30; injury and infliction of pain, 30, 33–35; language tests, 21–22; noxious and stinking fumes, 28; overview of physical consequences, 27–28; prayer, 95; religious tests, 95–98, 119; sanctioned scriptural methods, 5, 145, 151–55; scratching experiment, 45, 49–52, 56, 61, 190n24; sense of entitlement/authority in, 52; theological implications of results, 27, 28–29. See also body; symptoms

Walcott, Mary, 114
Walker, D. P., 180n15
Warboys possession accounts (Throckmorton and Samuel families, 1589–1593): account of Jane, 37; childhood role in, 190n22; claims to authority in, 9–10, 53–55; comparison with George Burroughs, 100, 105–6, 133; comparison with Margaret Rule, 137; comparison with the Goodwin family, 95; confession, 44–48, 55–56; earlier possession influences on, 190n18; economic and political context, 40–41; gender role in, 46–48, 49–51; judicial convictions, 62–63, 65; legacy of, 64–66; possession performances, 19–20, 41; propaganda role in, 189n7; Samuel family executions, 43–44, 53–54, 56, 60, 65–66, 191n28, 192n63; scratching experiment, 45, 49–52, 56, 61, 190n24; social class role in, 190n23; Throckmorton deal offer, 59; Throckmorton-Samuel family relationship, 39–40, 43–44, 53, 56, 57; witchcraft accusations, 41–48; Witches of Warboys as possession manual, 38–39
Webber, Mary, 112–13
Webber, Samuel, 113
Whitgift, John, 68, 81
Willard, John, 105–6, 113, 127, 203n41
Willard, Samuel, 96, 180n15
Willard, Simon, 113
William and Mary (King and Queen of England), 101
Williams, Abigail, 110, 113
Wilson, Hugh, 75
Winthrop, John, 102
witchcraft: afflicted vs. nonafflicted accusers, 11, 107–16, 129, 204n45; Burroughs minister-to-witch unmaking, 106–10, 114–18, 129–32; Calef scriptural tests and, 152–55; confession of, 5, 44–48, 55–56; Cotton Mather stance on, 119–20, 122, 133–44, 147–48, 152–55; countermagical practices, 43; English royalty and, 68, 188n67, 188n74, 189–90n17, 194n7; English witchcraft law, 2, 35–36, 191n28, 192–93n65, 194n7,

213–14n10; male witchcraft, 8, 24–25, 57, 115–16, 184n33, 186–87n42; possession visions of, 18–19, 37–38; Quakers as accusation targets, 106; witch trial scholarship, 8, 182–83n26; women-as-witches association, 3, 23–25, 57–58, 115–16, 174, 178n8, 186–87n42

witchcraft-possession: as challenge to religious hierarchy, 130; conversion as trigger for, 139; Cotton Mather on, 94; defined, 1; early modern England acceptance of, 3; English literary corpus on, 99–100; externalization of blame and, 6; feminine empowerment and, 49–50, 107; Harsnett critique of, 84; as moral contest, 15–16, 137, 142–44, 167–68, 175–76; physical/mental afflictions and, 27

womanhood: female scold character type, 58, 193n68; hysteria as fraudulent possession, 27; possession as self-assertion, 31–32, 48–49, 191n41; Salem female accusers, 104; sexual shaming in Calef, 145–48; sexual shaming in Harsnett, 87–91; susceptibility to possession, 24–25, 49, 56–57, 79, 107–8, 135; woman's touch in patriarchal regulation, 50–51; women-as-witches association, 3, 23–25, 57–58, 115–16, 174, 178n8, 186–87n42. *See also* body; gender; patriarchy

Wormall, William, 113

Wright, Katherine, 69, 74, 87–91, 153

Wrightson, Keith, 39, 192n55

ABOUT THE AUTHOR

Erika Gasser is assistant professor of history at the University of Cincinnati.

EARLY AMERICAN PLACES

Colonization and Its Discontents: Emancipation,
Emigration, and Antislavery in Antebellum Pennsylvania
Beverly C. Tomek

Empire at the Periphery: British Colonists, Anglo-Dutch Trade,
and the Development of the British Atlantic, 1621—1713
Christian J. Koot

Slavery before Race: Europeans, Africans, and Indians
at Long Island's Sylvester Manor Plantation, 1651–1884
Katherine Howlett Hayes

Faithful Bodies: Performing Religion and Race
in the Puritan Atlantic
Heather Miyano Kopelson

Against Wind and Tide: The African American Struggle
against the Colonization Movement
Ousmane K. Power-Greene

Four Steeples over the City Streets: The Social Worlds of
New York's Early Republic Congregations
Kyle T. Bulthuis

Caribbean Crossing: African Americans and the Haitian
Emigration Movement
Sara Fanning

Insatiable Appetites: Imperial Encounters with Cannibals in the
North Atlantic World
Kelly L. Watson

Unfreedom: Slavery and Dependence in
Eighteenth-Century Boston
Jared Ross Hardesty

Dark Work: The Business of Slavery in Rhode Island
Christy Clark-Pujara

*Vexed with Devils: Manhood and Witchcraft in
Old and New England*
Erika Gasser

Printed in the United States
By Bookmasters